THE
FIRST
STRANGE
PLACE

THE
FIRST
STRANGE
PLACE

Race and Sex
in World War II Hawaii

Beth Bailey
David Farber

THE JOHNS HOPKINS UNIVERSITY PRESS

Baltimore and London

Hardcover edition, *The First Strange Place: The Alchemy of Race and Sex in World War II Hawaii,* published in 1992 by the Free Press
This edition is reprinted by arrangement with the Free Press,
a division of Macmillan, Inc.
Johns Hopkins Paperbacks edition, 1994
4 6 8 9 7 5 3

The Johns Hopkins University Press
2715 North Charles Street
Baltimore, Maryland 21218-4363
The Johns Hopkins Press Ltd., London
www.press.jhu.edu

Library of Congress Cataloging-in-Publication Data

Bailey, Beth L., 1957–
The first strange place : race and sex in World War II Hawaii /
Beth Bailey and David Farber.
p.   cm.
Originally published: New York : Free Press, © 1992.
Includes bibliographical references and index.
ISBN 0-8018-4867-9 (pbk. : acid-free paper)
1. World War, 1939–1945—Social aspects—Hawaii.   2. Hawaii—Race
relations.   3. World War, 1939–1945—Women—Hawaii.   4. Hawaii—Social
conditions.   I. Farber, David.   II. Title.
[D744.7.H3B35 1994]
940.53´969—dc20
93–43661
CIP

A catalog record for this book is available from the British Library.

For Max

"This is a strange land and they keep telling me I am in the US, but from the time I walked off the ship I have doubted it."

"History is being made, and although our part will never be mentioned, at least we have had a hand in it."

—Military Censors' Files
Hawaii, 1941–45

Contents

Prologue:
December 7, 1941

8:00 a.m., St. Augustine's Church, Honolulu. Ten-year-old Eloise Ornelles was the first of those attending early mass that Sunday morning to hear the bombs falling. Or rather, she heard a funny rumbling sound that made her curious. Using an excuse familiar to any ten-year-old who ever sat restlessly through a church service on a sunny day, she told her father she needed to get a drink of water. Once outside, she ran across the street to Waikiki Beach and stood there in the sand, enjoying the sight of planes swooping and diving in the sky overhead. It was the best war game she'd ever seen: so many planes, such realistic sound effects. She stayed there, staring at the sky, for much longer than even the most tolerant parent would have let her get away with, but when her father found her he was upset for another reason. He pushed her into the car, shouting, "We're being attacked by the Japanese."[1]

It's no surprise that a little girl would not recognize war when she saw it, but even seasoned military men rejected the evidence of their own eyes. Colonel William Farthing, watching the planes diving on Pearl from the control tower of nearby Hickam Field, commented to his companion, "Very realistic maneuvers. I wonder what the Marines are doing to the Navy so early Sunday." A group of soldiers on Hickam's Parade Ground drew the same conclusion,

1

attributing the splashes in the harbor to Navy "water bombs." When an oil tank blew, sending flames shooting into the air, the men agreed with wisdom born of experience that some poor Navy flier was going to catch hell for that mistake. Seconds later, one of the planes dived toward Hickam Field, a rising sun emblazoned on its fuselage. "Look," said one of the men, "there goes one of the red team." Then the plane dropped a bomb.[2]

Island residents were used to war games and drills and simulated dogfights, and many who did not live near the military installations and weren't listening to the radio didn't know about the enemy attack until late in the day. The first announcements on the radio came within minutes of the attack: at 8:04 a.m., KGMB interrupted its musical program to broadcast an order for all military personnel to report to duty. The station repeated the order at 8:15 and 8:30, but did not announce news of the Japanese attack until 8:40. Between announcements, the station returned to its scheduled programming, and island residents who tuned in only to hear the light-hearted popular song, "Three Little Fishes" (swimming in the "iddy biddy pool"), turned off the radio, reassured that nothing serious could be happening.[3]

But gradually the announcements became more urgent. Frustrated that listeners did not seem to understand that the islands were really under attack, the manager of KGMB shouted into the microphone: "This is no maneuver. This is the real McCoy!" He was to repeat these words over and over on that long day.[4]

Soon, the radio stations were broadcasting orders to the citizenry: ". . . stay off the streets. Do not use your telephone. The island is under enemy attack. Do not use your telephone. Stay off the streets. Keep calm. . . . In the event of an air raid, stay under cover." Governor Poindexter came on the radio to proclaim a state of emergency, and then, at 11:41 a.m., the Army ordered all commercial radio stations off the air, fearing that Japanese planes could use the signals to navigate by. Later that day, the stations returned to the air to broadcast an announcement that Hawaii was now under martial law. The statement was broadcast three times: twice in English and once in Japanese.[5]

Eloise's family—she and three of her four brothers and her

sister, her parents, one set of grandparents, and an aunt—huddled by the radio like everyone else, turning the dial to try to pick up the police band, worrying, praying. But in some ways life went on as usual for the children. Late that afternoon an old Japanese man came by on his daily rounds, selling manapua from two buckets he carried on a wooden pole balanced across the back of his neck. The younger Ornelles children ran out to buy the treats; the attack had not destroyed their appetites, nor had it made them suspicious of this Japanese man who was a regular part of their lives. The Ornelles family had Japanese friends, patronized Japanese tradespeople. They didn't confuse them with the enemy.

Many island residents made the distinction between Japan and the people of Japanese descent in Hawaii quite easily—perhaps too easily. Daniel Inouye, then a seventeen-year-old senior at McKinley High School and an instructor for a volunteer Red Cross station, headed for his post at Lunalilo School as soon as he heard the news. Fires had broken out throughout the city, including one at the Lunalilo School first aid station itself. A building next to the school caught fire and some of the residents had died, trapped behind a wall of flames. Fifty-seven civilians died on Oahu that day, and another 280 were injured.[6] Dan worked for almost twenty-four hours without rest, treating the wounded and the maimed, carrying dead bodies to a makeshift morgue. Exhausted and filled with rage, he yelled out toward the vanished planes: "You dirty Japs!" Later he would hear those same words directed at him, and only then would he come to understand the look on his father's face, "the special horror," as they listened, together, to the first radio report of the Japanese attack on the United States.[7]

The sort of violent outburst against the Japanese and Japanese Americans that happened on the mainland did not come on Hawaii, though rumors of sabotage ran rampant. Elizabeth Beach Brown, a young haole wife and mother living in the town of Hilo on the Big Island, recorded the rumors in the diary she began on December 8th, but she also expressed sympathy for the plight of the Japanese. "There are so many nice Japanese here in the Islands who are feeling it all very keenly," she wrote on December 9th. "They look very glum on the streets." The next day's entry notes: "Today I picked up a Japanese girl and took her downtown. She said she was carrying the whole responsibility for this awful affair. She was so sure that this could never happen, and has been preaching that it couldn't. She had just recently come back from Japan and is decidedly pro-American."[8]

Others took the rumors more seriously. Another haole woman wrote in her diary:

> Well we were still in one piece, so went to Lihue R[ed] C[ross] station and made Ser. [surgical] dressings all morning—came home and worked at Koloa RC making Hospital gowns till 4 P.M. Came home exhausted with all the rumors and chit chat of the women & my Jap cook met me & asked if I'd go up to the store & get her some ant poison! Ordinarily that was a simple enough request but you see we had had stories as far back as 1940 & all through 1941 that the Japs on the Is. were all set to kill or poison every haole on the Islands the moment War struck. So I was stunned—but I didn't let on—Only that—Oh! Oh! its come—I didn't know what to do—If I didn't get the ant poison she would know I was scared of her—& I was—but we could not lose face we all pretended to our citizen servants that we trusted them to be loyal Americans, She had been with the family 18 yrs. knowing very well they all weren't—. . . .

The writer, Helen Knudsen, did go to the store, and was greatly relieved to find there was no ant poison available. Her peace of mind evaporated the next day when her maid reported triumphantly that she'd found the poison at another store. "When I went to bed," she wrote of that evening, "I laid myself out in my best nitie [sic]—I'd be beautiful in death! I kept waiting for the agonizing death of poison but finally went to sleep. . . ."[9]

Of course, rumors flew among the Japanese and Japanese-American population as well. Col. V. S. Burton noted in his war diary, "Rumors of mass deportation to the island of Kahoolawe [sic], where they would be left to starve, were rife,"[10] and fears of deportation or internment had much more truth than any of the rumors of sabotage. In the end, though, Hawaii's nisei and issei population would not suffer the fate of their counterparts on the mainland. Despite strong pressure from the Secretary of the Navy, Frank Knox, Military Governor General Emmons refused to allow mass internment. In a radio broadcast on December 21st, he attempted to set the rumor mill to rest. He stated emphatically:

> There is no intention or desire on the part of the federal authorities to operate mass concentration camps. No person, be he citizen or alien, need worry, provided he is not connected to subversive elements. . . . While we have been subjected to a serious attack by a ruthless and treacherous enemy, we must remember that this is America and we must do things the American Way. We must distinguish between loyalty and disloyalty among our people.[11]

Emmons' power as military governor came from the federal government, and here he was playing a complicated hand, trying to circumvent federal intentions. He stalled, he dragged his feet, he made practical arguments and created bureaucratic complications. In the end, he won a limited victory. Only 1,444 people of Japanese ancestry from the islands were interned—not, as the Secretary of War had requested, "all of the Japs."[12]

Emmons' actions were possible in large part because the people of Hawaii opposed mass internment. One reason was certainly economic: resettling 37 percent of the islands' population would wreak havoc on the economy. While a few extremists in the business community saw the war as an opportunity to prevent "the sure political and economic domination by the Japanese" in the future, most of the powerful kamaaina (old-timer) haoles agreed with the head of the Honolulu Chamber of Commerce, who wrote: "There are 160,000 of these people who want to live here because they like the country and like the American way of life. . . . The citizens of Japanese blood would fight as loyally for America as any other citizen."[13]

The crucial difference between Hawaii and the mainland did not lie in the actions of the most powerful, either Emmons or the haole elite, but in the place the Japanese had made for themselves in the complicated ethnic and racial community of the islands. In California, people of Japanese ancestry made up only one percent of the population; in Hawaii, the Japanese were the largest ethnic group and Asians made up the majority of the islands' population. The Japanese were not competing for work with a white working class—there was no such thing in Hawaii. Having largely passed out of the plantation system, they were not isolated in one sector of the economy, nor were they completely segregated into ethnic enclaves. They had become an integral part of Hawaii's culture. Writing on the history of Asian Americans, historian Ronald Takaki explains: "While the Japanese in the islands had become 'locals,' members of the community in Hawaii, their brethren on the mainland had been forced to remain 'strangers.' Different histories were coming home to roost in Hawaii and in California."[14]

Of course, the actions of Americans of Japanese ancestry or AJAs, as they were called, did much to convince Hawaii's citizens of their loyalty. In the tense hours following the attack, Hawaii's Japanese, nisei and issei alike, worked to shore up Hawaii's defense. Like the rest of Hawaii's people, men and women of Japanese ancestry stood in the long lines to donate blood for the wounded and volunteered in Red Cross stations or as truck drivers for the Citizen's Defense Committee. Two thousand nisei young men, members of the Hawaii Territorial Guard, stood guard that frightening first night when everyone expected the enemy to return. The Japanese contributed heavily to war-bond drives and, in a clearly intended declaration of loyalty, presented the U.S. government with a check to be used for "bombs on Tokyo."

Furthermore, Japanese leaders urged their community to downplay any signs of loyalty—even cultural loyalty—to Japan. They closed the Japanese language schools and launched a "Speak English" campaign. Traditional Japanese dress became rare on the streets of Honolulu, the Japanese language signs were taken down. People dismantled household shrines, burned Japanese-language magazines and books, even personal records and photographs. Immigrant Japanese stopped celebrating Girl's Day and Boy's Day; religious ceremonies such as *bon* dances ceased. Japanese bakeries even substituted Army Counter-Intelligence mottoes for the traditional Japanese sayings baked inside rice cakes. One new motto read: "The sun rises but always sets," a pointed reference to Japan's rising sun.[15]

December 7, 1941

When a call was issued for nisei volunteers, Governor Emmons asked for 1,500; 9,507 men came forward. Many of Hawaii's AJA volunteers served in the 100th Battalion, which eventually was merged with the "Fighting 442nd" Regimental Combat Team. These nisei soldiers fought some of the bloodiest battles of the war. In 1943, one of Hawaii's Japanese wrote to an AJA soldier in training at Camp Shelby: "The tension of the Hawaiian people has been relaxed and life in Honolulu is coming back to normal . . . With you and the rest doing a good job there [Camp Shelby] we in Hawaii are receiving the same treatment as pre-war days."[16] Of course, while war raged with Japan, the lives of Hawaii's people of Japanese descent could never completely return to normal.[17]

Most of Hawaii's residents accepted the loyalty of AJAs and behaved more or less as before. This does not mean that there was no anti-Japanese sentiment. Such feelings were of long standing in the islands, and had grown stronger as the nisei began to increase their economic and political power. A man could write, "I presently plan to move [upon retirement] to California and let the damned Japs have the place. They will be in full control of things here by then . . . they are getting so blamed cocky, especially the 2nd generation, that I feel as though I am living on top of a boiling seething kettle, the poor white people are taking it on the chin," and still not question the *loyalty* of Hawaii's AJAs.[18]

It is also important that racial/ethnic tensions in Hawaii were never simply bipolar. There were existing tensions among Hawaii's many ethnic groups, and the war exacerbated them. For example, island residents complained bitterly about the Chinese and Chinese Americans who, according to wartime stereotypes, were only interested in "stay[ing] out of the Services, bond booths, & blood banks & to purchase real estate as fast as their incomes allow."[19]

The progress of the war in the Pacific certainly made tensions worse between the Japanese Americans and Korean Americans or Filipinos. Elizabeth Beach Brown wrote in her diary on April 12, 1942:

Bataan fell today, which made us all sick at heart. The men have surely fought gallantly. The Filipinos in the Hawaiian Islands are restless over the turn of affairs in the Philippines. Most have mothers, fathers, sisters, brothers, uncles and aunts, and some even wives over there. Most of them here do not like the Japanese, and it was feared at first that they would get out their cane knives and sharpen them for a new business. Because of the large Filipino population, many have said that if the Japanese here ever started any trouble, the Filipinos would take care of the situation in no time.[20]

Hawaii's people of Japanese ancestry also had to contend with a constant influx of people from the mainland—people who looked in Japanese faces (or Chinese or Filipino, for that matter; many could not tell the difference) and saw "the enemy." "When we wanted some meat or fish," recalls one man, "we had to go to the market disguised as Chinese or another nationality." What particularly disturbed him, somehow, was having to dress his one-year-old daughter in a Chinese dress.[21] And the larger problem was that too many people from the mainland could not tell the Japanese from the Chinese anyway. One old Chinese man put a sign in the back window of his car that read: "I am not Japanese." His granddaughter, who was a little girl at the time, explains: "He was afraid of bein' attacked or lock up cause mebbe some haole don't know that he's Chinese. I tink you gotta be pretty lolo (stupid) fo mix em up ya? We don't look anyt'ing like da Japanese."[22]

An apocryphal story circulated among the kamaaina in the early days of the war: a soldier disembarking from his transport sees a nisei member of the Home Guard in his uniform, guarding the port, and gasps, "My God, we're too late."[23] The story was funny in this version, but the consequences of such misunderstandings usually were not at all funny. There was a fair amount of anger directed at Hawaii's Japanese, and violence occasionally broke out. One event showed the full horror of the Pacific war: Marines who had survived Tarawa were shipped back to Hawaii to "recover"; many lost control at the sight of Japanese faces. "We civilians especially the Japanese, are afraid to go to town," wrote one resident of the Big Island in a private letter. "They think they have to take this island over too. There has been street fights, stabbings and killings." One AJA wrote: "Back home is terrible. Plenty of rape and assault cases . . .

December 7, 1941

The Marines & soldiers are doing many trouble for the Japanese. They even kill them on sight. Nobody bothers about it." It seems that no one was killed in fact, but there was a great deal of violence and people believed murders had taken place. One man wrote: "I saw a sailor on the street the other day with the scalp of a Jap, he was waving it around in the face of a Japanese girl on the street." Both verbal attacks and physical beatings happened with alarming frequency.[24]

Despite the attacks, many AJAs tried to understand what the Marines had been through, and even—in private letters—refused to condemn them for their actions. One AJA wrote of recent attacks, moving rapidly from fear to gratitude: ". . . the marines who have returned from battle areas are rough and we are afraid of them. After all they are the powerful men who had seen action and we can't blame them, and probably we should be thankful to them."[25] Another struggled more directly with the issue that tormented all Americans of Japanese descent:

> They are a desperate bunch of whom all the civilians fear them. We find them very rough and nasty. But then, I guess they are not to be blamed after all the life of going through the hardship at Tarawa and the south seas. . . . They certainly hate the Japs which is the right attitude to all us Americans but many times they have the wrong impression of us.[26]

Yet another set aside the question of Japanese identity, focusing on the tragedy of war: "Their actions, upon hitting shore on civilized land, was something terrible. It seemed that many had lost their standards of morals, manners and good judgment. . . . War did terrible things to these boys. I hope that our boys in Italy will keep their good standards."[27] Following the violence of the survivors of Tarawa, the military command tried not to let men who had seen the worst of the fighting near Hawaii's AJAs.

Hawaii's Americans of Japanese ancestry endured a "special horror" in what one called a "war with our ancestors."[28] But though their experiences in Hawaii were difficult, their experience was not that of the Japanese on the mainland. One AJA wrote in a private letter in 1944: "I am happy to be living in Hawaii and not in Calif.

Here I am proud to be an American & more than willing to do my share . . . I would have turned bitter if I were living in Calif. . . . A place where many people are trying to desecrate the very principles for which we are fighting. . . ." Another wrote: "In Hawaii we have lived through this test—a beautiful reality that some mainlanders will never believe."[29]

But on the night of December 7th, 1941, all those struggles lay in the future. The people of Hawaii, divided by so much, were joined in fear, waiting for the Japanese planes to return. Commercial radio stations returned to the air in the late afternoon, announcing:

> Please turn out your lights . . . Hawaii is observing a complete blackout. Turn out your lights. This means the whole Territory. Turn out your lights and do not turn them on for any purpose whatsoever. Turn off your lights and keep them off.[30]

That night the people of Hawaii sat in darkness. Around seven o'clock Elizabeth Brown heard "a squadron of planes going quite fast and traveling quite high" pass over Hilo headed in the direction of Honolulu.[31] At 7:14 p.m., the police radio in Honolulu announced that Pearl Harbor was being bombed again. All over Honolulu, people looked out into darkness broken by tracer bullets and the flames of falling planes. Very few people went to bed that night. It was much later that they learned that the Japanese had not returned, but that the planes shot down had been American planes from the *Enterprise*, which had been searching the seas for Japanese aircraft carriers.[32] This tragic accident might have seemed yet another omen of the horrible loss of life to come, but those who sought omens found a more encouraging sign. "Shortly before midnight," wrote one who sat in the darkness that night, "the moon began to rise, and a vivid lunar rainbow, the old Hawaiian omen of victory, arched over the dark city."[33]

Fearing the return of the Japanese, people did what they could. Eloise Ornelles' family followed the directions published in the newspaper and built a bomb shelter in their yard. They struck water long before the shelter was deep enough, but they rounded the top

December 7, 1941

off "like a giant mushroom that had just grown there" and stocked it with food and blankets and first-aid supplies. The air raid alarms went off with regularity in the early days of war, and the Ornelles family piled into the shelter. For the younger children, it was an adventure. Eloise's twin brothers would begin to eat as soon as the shelter door was secured. "If I'm going to go, at least I'm going to go with a full stomach!" one or the other would say. It wasn't an adventure to Eloise's mother, who knew that each alarm might be real. She was grateful as each alarm proved false, and restocked the food without complaint.

Gas masks were distributed to everyone on the islands, and Eloise's father assembled his family for a timed drill. Lined up in the back yard, masks in hand, the children thought it a game. "At the word 'go' we all flipped open the snap and got our masks out and on our faces in just a few seconds," Eloise recalled. "But poor Grandpa became confused. Instead of whipping his mask out of the case and onto his face, he started to unwind the cording on the case. My brother, Axel, teased him. 'Grandpa, you'd be dead and buried before you got your mask on!' Suddenly it wasn't funny anymore."[34]

It never was funny to most of the adults, though many tried to keep their fear from the children. Far from the carnage on Oahu, Elizabeth Brown worried about her infant daughter and tried to make plans for her family's safety. "We have been boiling water although at every intake to the city water supply there are guards with drawn bayonets so that no one could poison it," she wrote in the first days of war. "Bombing is an awful thing to think of here as most roofs are just tin which wouldn't even slow down a bomb, and the ground is solid lava rock which would explode any bomb and send the fragments flying in all directions." Four months later she wrote:

> We have so much practice firing of big guns around here, that if and when the real thing occurs I think we won't be so panicky. Round metal disks painted yellow have been put up in each block to be struck in case of a gas attack. We have been told that some of the gases smell like flowers. The other morning I was in the yard and smelled a perfectly gorgeous odor, took several deep

breaths of it, and then suddenly felt that it might be poison gas. It made me sick and weak all over. It took several seconds before I figured out that gases could not be distributed unless there were planes overhead.[35]

Elizabeth looked to the sky in fear; others had more vivid images of invasion. Americans knew what had happened in Shanghai and elsewhere. Some Army Nurses, thinking of stories they had heard about the "rape of Burma," made the doctors promise to kill them if the islands were overrun by the Japanese.[36]

Some decided to evacuate. The first ship with evacuees from Hawaii reached San Francisco on Christmas Day. It had been a grim and frightening crossing; the ship was carrying badly wounded survivors of the Pearl Harbor attack, and the civilian passengers spent many hours of those tense days rolling bandages for the wounded. Those offered the option of evacuation faced a difficult decision. The trip itself might be more dangerous than remaining in Hawaii. Leaving behind husbands, parents, and friends could not be easy. Agonizing over her decision, another kamaaina woman wrote in April 1942:

Some days are so serene—happy children, normal busyness. Others are punctuated by unexplained noises, lights, and the recurring wondering whether the things might happen here which have happened in Hong Kong, Singapore, Mandalay. God only can guide us as to what to do and whether to go to California or stay.[37]

In the end, about 20,000 military dependents and 10,000 women and children from the islands—mostly haole—evacuated to the mainland. The Ornelles family was Portuguese; the childrens' greatgrandparents had come to work in the cane. Eloise Ornelles, with a child's certainty, believed those who left were cowards.

But the people who were afraid had reason to be. Hawaii was not secure. The Japanese planes did not return, but Japanese submarines shelled outer islands several times during December. Several ships were torpedoed and sunk near the Hawaiian Islands. Air-raid sirens screamed in the dark stillness of the blackout, or emptied busy daytime streets. The air-raid alarms began to come more frequently in March of 1942. Hospital ships unloaded wounded men. The war news was grim: Guam, the Philippines, Wake Island, Burma, Bataan. People made plans, devised codes for communication. They watched the movements of the fleet, trying to see patterns and judge danger. For the first six months of war, Hawaii was at risk.

On June 4, 1942, Elizabeth Brown wrote in her diary: "We are again on a special alert. The rumor is that Midway is having an attack." Her husband convinced her to take their baby daughter away from Hilo and wait at their cottage near the volcano until it was safe to return. The cottage was remote, in a way, but not remote from war. Just seventy-five yards from the cottage was a machine-gun nest, manned twenty-four hours a day. Waiting at the cottage, she wrote on June 6th: "The news began to come over the radio of the tremendous battle taking place at Midway. We listened to every broadcast we could get, as we knew that the failure of our fleet to stop them would mean trouble for Hawaii."[38] The Battle of Midway was a major turning point in the Pacific war. It was especially significant for Hawaii, for it signaled that the islands were no longer in immediate danger. Nonetheless, the islands were officially designated as a combat zone until April 1944.[39]

In the weeks and months that followed Pearl Harbor, new patterns emerged day by day. People who had lain awake all night waiting for the bombs to fall eventually began to sleep. People grew used to the nightly blackout, which left them in a darkness that extended for a 2,100-mile radius. Gas masks and ID tags, martial law, lines, and rationing were simply facts of life in wartime Hawaii.[40]

The war was a constant and threatening presence in Hawaii more than in any other part of the United States. Civilians in Hawaii felt the burdens of war and saw its horrors more intimately than most Americans. But there was a certain irony in their experience. The citizens of Hawaii feared an enemy invasion. That never happened. What would actually change their lives and their world was a friendly invasion.

Introduction:
Wartime Hawaii and
American Identity

It's hard not to begin with Pearl Harbor—the Japanese planes streaming across the island early that Sunday morning, a little girl dressed for church, her eyes raised suddenly to the sky, the plumes of smoke and screams of men in pain, rumbling thunder that bespoke torpedoed ships and grounded planes. Confusion and death. War had come to Hawaii.

War came to the mainland differently. War came to the mainland as news, the breaking story of the Japanese attack conveyed to a transfixed nation in the shocked tones of radio announcers. It was already afternoon in most of the rest of America, the six-hour time difference to the east coast only underscoring how far away Hawaii was. A hundred years earlier it would have taken weeks for news of such a distant place to reach the President and the public, but World War II was being fought in a world increasingly connected and torn apart by the miracles of technology.

All over the mainland, people stopped, still. To say that war came to the mainland with less immediacy does not mean that it came with less weight. The news fused Americans into a people joined, in those first hours, by the understanding that their world had changed.

15

Wartime Hawaii and American Identity

Not everyone who heard the earliest broadcasts knew where Pearl Harbor was, or even that it was part of the United States. Hawaii was a distant territory of the U.S., the fruit of one of the nation's relatively few successful imperial ventures in the late nineteenth century. But it was the Japanese attack on American soil that justified—even demanded—war, and President Roosevelt drew the connection firmly in his address to the joint houses of Congress on December 8th. He offered no fine distinctions of distance or territorial status, but began: "Yesterday, December 7, 1941—a date which will live in infamy—the United States of America was suddenly and deliberately attacked by naval and air forces of the Empire of Japan." The attack on the Territory of Hawaii propelled the United States into war; it also served to define Hawaii, in newly emphatic terms, as part of America.

In neither history nor memory does President Roosevelt's summoning of the nation displace Pearl Harbor itself. The attack on Pearl Harbor—which was also an attack on the air bases at Hickam, Wheeler, Kaneohe, and Ewa and on Schofield Barracks—maintained its symbolic centrality as the moment of genesis, the act that established the "perfidy," "treachery," and "savagery" of the Japanese. In the sunken tomb that had been the *Arizona*, alone, 1,177 men lay dead.

But Hawaii would play much more than a symbolic role in America's war effort. The islands were already home to America's Pacific Fleet; Japan was not just trying to hit something identifiably "American," but a crucial military target. The U.S. military presence in Hawaii had already begun to grow in the preceding decade as the situation in Asia and the Pacific had worsened. Following the attack on Pearl Harbor, the islands were overwhelmed by a flood of servicemen and war workers, for Hawaii served as staging ground for a war that had to be waged across vast expanses of ocean.

President Roosevelt's declaration of war, ratified by Congress in less than an hour, only one vote short of unanimity, launched Americans into motion. Men went into the service, whether by choice or by draft, and were sent around the nation and around the world. Over 12 million Americans served in the military during the war years. Some of the moves Americans made were insignificant geo-graphically but important socially, as in the case of women who took previously undreamed-of positions as war workers in defense facto-ries. Other moves covered great distances, as people flocked to well-paid defense jobs in other parts of the country or followed loved ones to their military postings. More than 15 million civilians moved across county lines. The farm population dropped by 17 percent, but 2.5 million Americans moved *to* farms. Southerners moved north, northerners moved south, and 1.5 million people moved to Califor-nia.[1] Of these Americans on the move, a huge number of men and a much smaller number of women spent time in Hawaii during the war.

This book is about those men and women, and also about the people of Hawaii, on whom the war placed great demands.[2] It is about their heroism and struggle, their ambition, pettiness, garden-variety decency, racism, meanness, generosity, anger, cynicism, sorrow, pain, love. It is about people living through a difficult time as best they could.

But even more fundamentally, it is about cultural contact—not only between the people from the mainland and the people of Ha-waii, though that encounter is of central importance, but between all the men and women whose lives were disrupted by war. The phrase "cultural contact" may sound strange, for we are talking about contact between Americans, in America. Shared identities, however, do not necessarily mean identical cultures. Americans, while joined by common nationality, were divided by other identi-ties—those of region, religion, gender, class, of race and ethnicity. These other identities mediated the claims of nation, but the special wartime truth of the statement, "we are all Americans," made the contacts we trace extraordinarily complex.

As for being "in America"—Hawaii was more properly a terri-tory of the United States, a colonial possession.[3] Metaphorically, Hawaii was our border of war, an ultimate frontier, the edge of our world. Hawaii, where Americans came together in the common national cause of waging war, was therefore a liminal place. That liminality, combined with Hawaii's specific society and culture and the ever-present fact of war, created a highly charged arena in which the individual dramas of cultural contact were played out. In Hawaii during World War II, people of different backgrounds were brought together in a common cause. This contact—collision, even—of cultures led to struggle and contestation, and sometimes to negotiation, improved understanding, or change.

In these stories of cultural contact, we are attempting a kind of multicultural history. We are not looking at groups in isolation, nor do we presume the overriding importance of one category of definition. Instead we are looking at people who, by choice or otherwise, were thrust into uncertain and ill-defined contact with others who were different in important ways. We are writing about the ways people meet, act, interact, and thereby form the warp and woof of American history. We are trying to understand how Americans, within a given set of structural constraints and power relations, understood themselves and interpreted their experiences.

In recent decades Americans have come to focus, almost obsessively, on the differences that divide us, especially those of gender and race. This focus has helped us to see the inequality and oppression that have compromised America's promise for millions of its citizens. But this concern about difference has also, all too often, led us to view our social constructs of gender and race as timeless, transhistorical facts. This is not simply historically inaccurate, it is dangerous. It denies the complexity of individual and group identities, and in a fundamental way, it denies the possibility of change.

This book offers, in its focus on World War II Hawaii, a piece of the prehistory of our understanding of difference. World War II initiated a series of changes that had crucial consequences for American society. The demands of war upset existing patterns. The war forced people into motion and created openings for an increasingly powerful and active federal government. The war fostered nationalism and encouraged the emergence of a national culture. It laid bare social problems. America's wartime experience demonstrated both the possibilities and the limits of a unifying national identity, and it forged the conditions for struggle and for change.

In the years following World War II, Americans struggled with the meaning of American identity—not just in intellectual debates about "the American character," but also in the everyday actions of millions of Americans. In the postwar mass migration to the suburbs and the celebration of a booming middle class, Americans were recasting the meaning of difference. The suburbs (and the middle-class ethos they often stood for) offered a meeting place for people of rural and urban backgrounds, for people of different class origins newly re-classed into the expanding middle (often boosted by a VA loan or a GI Bill education), for people of different ethnic origins newly recast as "white." (The fact that large-scale immigration to the U.S. had been halted in the 1920s and would not resume until the Immigration Act of 1965 is crucial to this story.)

Because the ugliness of racial segregation is so clear to us, we underestimate the ways old identities were being reshaped or discarded, old categories of definition redefined. People in the 1950s who called on notions of a virtually universal middle class and moved to the suburbs were not simply fleeing those unlike themselves, nor were they rejecting the importance of categories of difference. They were *recasting* difference; perhaps they were calibrating it more carefully according to the new demands of postwar American society and economy.

But just as the focus on a singular "American culture" and "American character" in the 1950s helped strip away some of the definitions that had divided the American people, it left others in stark relief. As claims of class and ethnicity and region were attenuated, the always crucial categories of race and gender seemed more fundamental than ever.

In some ways, World War II Hawaii is an odd focus for this set of concerns and questions about American identity. Hawaii was a strange place—strange to the newcomers, made strange to its residents by the facts of war. Hawaii is about as far from "representative" as one can get in 1940s America. Hawaii was at the margin of American life as well as of the war. But sometimes it is at the margins that the messy definitions and complicated interactions are pushed to extremes and made visible; far-reaching changes sometimes germinate in marginal places.

This book explores the significance of cultural contact among Americans in a series of five fairly discrete essays, unified by intertwining questions and concerns. First, we consider what categories of identity mattered during the war years, and how those categories structured both individual interactions and large-scale social change. Second, we analyze the role of the wartime state in managing the contacts and confrontations brought about by the war. The federal government took on immense power in its effort to win the war, often riding roughshod over local authorities, local customs, individual rights, and traditional ways of life. In both its civilian and military forms, the federal government used wartime powers to force Americans to put their common interest above the differences that otherwise divided them.

Finally, we try never to lose sight of Hawaii itself—not only its social organization or even its weather and landscape, but also its image as inscribed in popular culture and mainland myth. We pay careful attention to the complexity of individual actions, decisions, and emotions, for we are trying to explore the connections between large-scale historical events and individual lives. Individuals do not act in a vacuum. Their choices are constrained by both structural imperatives and cultural ideas of what is normal or acceptable. Within those limits, however, difference does exist—among groups, among individuals. From an awareness of the complexity of these differences, as in Hawaii during the war, change may be born.

How did Americans define themselves and one another in the war years? First, to 1940s Americans, region was crucial. It is hard to appreciate the degree of hatred many southerners still felt at that time toward "damn yankees," or how impossibly alien a Brooklyn kid was then to a farm boy from Iowa. There was no bicoastal culture. Harlem was a vast distance from rural Georgia; Texas was a world away from Minnesota; California, equally remote from both. Many of the people set into motion by the war had never traveled to another part of the country; this was particularly true of the people who lived in the Hawaiian Islands.

Even though radio and mass-circulation magazines and the increasing ease of train and automobile travel had done much to vitiate regional boundaries, for most Americans local origin was still an essential part of one's identity. Most looked at people from other regions with suspicion, if not hostility. The ways of signaling class status or "respectability" differed from region to region. Ways of expressing friendliness, deference, anger—all differed. The outward signs—of speech and accent, of dress, of manners—that seemed so natural at home did not always translate. People from different regions often could not read each other's backgrounds or even their intentional signals.

Gender differences were crucial as well. The human sciences in the first half of the twentieth century stressed the differences between the sexes, and most people "knew" that men and women were fundamentally different creatures. The ideal spheres of male and female activity were certainly separate in 1941, though the Depression and then the war did much to disturb the casual equation of women with home and men with work. But gender difference was more than an ideological stance during World War II. The war brought the differences between men's lives and women's lives into sharp contrast. Men fought. Women didn't.

Of course, nowhere near half of American men of draftable age saw actual combat in World War II, and many American women served their country, whether in the armed forces or in defense jobs. But women were not drafted, nor were they expected to serve. The experience of war created a very specific gulf between men and women. These different experiences would have important consequences after the war.

The importance of race—and to a lesser extent, ethnicity—in 1940s America cannot be overstated. For those not classified as "Caucasian," race was the fundamental fact of life. Legal Jim Crow flourished in the South and discriminatory conditions existed throughout the country. While discrimination against blacks was most institutionalized, Hispanics, Asian Americans, and Native Americans were profoundly affected by the meanings attached to the color of their skin. Race is undeniably still important, but its role in today's society comes nowhere near the blatant and inescapable force of racialism and racism in the 1940s.

Most white Americans, on the other hand, gave little thought to race. Whiteness was the "natural" condition, not something of which one had to be aware. Beyond that unvoiced assumption about their own normality, many white Americans gave little thought to the issue of race as it had to do with others. Many Americans of European ancestry had never even spoken to an African American, a Hispanic, or to someone of Asian ancestry. They rarely encountered nonwhites in their daily lives and almost never on the public stage of national events. And many of those who did regularly encounter black people or Asian Americans did not think about race as an issue, for they interacted within structures of hierarchy and deference. All of this, of course, was experienced and understood in different ways in different regions. White southerners, by and large, were more accustomed to being around black people, but were also the quickest to take offense at any mixing of the races on grounds of implied equality.

Though one might well imagine this society in terms of a simple division between "whites" and "nonwhites," that bipolar model is too simple. There were enormous differences between blacks from the urban north and the rural south. Asian Americans were not a single, unified group by any means, and few people of Asian ancestry saw themselves as somehow the same as African Americans or Hispanics. And though white men and women (with the exception of Jews) did not encounter the sorts of institutional and personal racism that characterized the experience of Asian and African Americans during the war, "white" was not a coherent category either. Just as they were divided by region, whites were also split by ethnic origin and by what was often its most central expression, religion. The all-white worlds of much of the military and some defense workplaces during the war were therefore not homogeneous. There was the lone Jew in a company of Italian Catholics; Scandinavian Lutherans mixed with Scotch-Irish Baptists; Irish mixed with Poles and WASPs. People readily defined themselves as Polish or Irish or Italian. Ethnicity was a basic part of who one was, and served as often to bind strangers together as it did to divide them.

What made the already crucial categories of race and ethnicity doubly important was Hawaii itself. Hawaii's population was a mixture of racial and ethnic groups unlike anywhere else in the United States. In Hawaii, white Americans were not in the majority, and though racial and ethnic hierarchies undeniably existed, they differed from those on the mainland. In Hawaii, "whiteness" was not the natural condition. Here, white men were suddenly made to feel that *they* were the ones who were different. Such a reversal of "normality" was all the more disconcerting because it took place in what was, after all, America. Few of the white mainlanders really understood the complexities of Hawaii's racial system. Some praised what they saw as unprecedented racial equality; others were upset by it; still others, just confused. But no one could come to Hawaii and fail to notice race. The issue suffused wartime Hawaii. It could not be avoided.

Region, gender, race/ethnicity—these, of course, are not the only sources of identity. Class is undeniably important, as are age and education.[4] So is marital status and sexual preference. Occupation or profession also matters—though many of the people we describe were too young to have embarked upon careers before the war. In time of war, the distinction between military and civilian may be the central distinction for men. For women, then as now, it mattered quite a lot what they looked like.

None of these categories can be considered absolute. Within certain very important limits, people juggled the categories, constructing shifting and complex identities for themselves in the specific historical and social circumstances of wartime Hawaii. And in Hawaii, as people from a wide variety of backgrounds came together, they operated by different sets of rules, and they often misunderstood the rules of others. Thus, for virtually everyone who came from the mainland, Hawaii was a strange place. And for the people of Hawaii, the "malihini," or newcomers, were quite literally strangers. But the difference was never a simple bipolar one. All the categories entered in, often unpredictably, making Hawaii an exceedingly strange place for all concerned.

———

Hawaii is not a neutral environment. Its landscapes are striking, vivid, extreme: the blues and greens of sky and sea and mountain foliage, the red dirt, the white sand, the sometimes overwhelming fragrance of flowers, the awe-inspiring vistas. Hawaii is one of the most beautiful places in the world. Some of the men and women who came to the islands saw it that way. But the vista from the pali (cliff) trail is not necessarily beautiful to men on a forced march with forty-pound packs. Hawaii is not "paradise" to a man on his way to war who longs to be back home in North Dakota.

Furthermore, Hawaii is not uniform. On the leeward side of Oahu, men choked on the dry red dust. Up in the mountainous jungle training camp, men shivered through the torrential winter rains. Rainfall in Honolulu, where most of the servicemen and war workers were based, hit a low of 10.3 inches and a high of 27.4 inches during the war years. In Hilo, on the Big Island, it rained 143.42 inches in 1942 alone. While the temperate climate (Honolulu's temperature ranged from 62 to 85 degrees in 1944) might seem a blessing, for many of the malihini the lack of perceptible seasons increased the strangeness of Hawaii.[5]

Part of our task, in portraying Hawaii, is to restore its historicity—to banish the image of Waikiki tourist hotels and streets crowded with Japanese and American tourists in aloha wear. Hawaii in 1940 was a vastly different place. War dawned on the Hawaii of *From Here to Eternity*—a small world of rough men and prostitutes, of drinking, gambling, sex, violence, and despair. War dawned on the "Paradise of the Pacific," on Waikiki's three major hotels, the Royal Hawaiian, the Moana, and the Halekulani, exclusive establishments for the glamorous and wealthy people who were Hawaii's tourists in the 1930s. War dawned on a plantation society—sugar cane, pineapple, coffee. Close to one-quarter of the islands' population lived on plantations in 1940.[6] And war dawned on what was still, in many ways, a colonial society.

Hawaii's economy and politics were controlled in 1940 by a white elite, led by a group known locally as the "Big Five." Hawaiians had called the first white foreigners who came to the islands "haoles," which literally means "stranger," and the term came to be used by all island residents, including the white population. Many of the haole elite were the descendants of (primarily American) missionaries, merchants, and sea captains who had come to Hawaii in the early nineteenth century and gradually gained political power over the Hawaiian people and control of approximately three-fourths of Hawaii's land. The Big Five—the corporations of Castle & Cooke,

Ltd.; Theo. H. Davies, Ltd.; H. Hackfeld & Co. (later, American Factors); C. Brewer & Co.; and Alexander and Baldwin, Ltd.—had consolidated power by the end of the century, culminating in their ouster in 1893 of Queen Liliuokalani, who had attempted to break their control.[7]

The white revolutionaries tried to have Hawaii annexed by the United States. American public opinion was in favor: "Liliuokalani give us your little brown hannie!" was the rallying cry in the forty-four states. But the newly elected President Cleveland was anti-imperialist. He sent an agent to investigate and, based on his delegate's report that the majority of Hawaiians opposed the measure, killed the treaty of annexation that had been negotiated by the prior administration of President Harrison. Cleveland attempted to restore Liliuokalani to the throne, but the former queen insisted that if returned to power she would, "as the law directs," behead the revolutionaries; and in any case, the Big Five would not budge. Hawaii thus existed as an independent republic until 1898, when it was annexed by the American government under President McKinley.[8]

The oligarchy of haole families that had built an empire dominated Hawaii for the next forty years. Yet their economic expansion and extension of political control changed Hawaii's social structure, sometimes in unintended ways. Having dispossessed the Hawaiian people, they initiated a decline in the economic status, power, and even population of people of Hawaiian ancestry. By the 1880s, Hawaiians were no longer the majority in their own islands. By 1900, Hawaiians were no longer the largest ethnic group in Hawaii, as the haole owners brought successive waves of immigrants to Hawaii's shores to work on the growing plantations. While Hawaiians had worked on plantations in substantial numbers in the nineteenth century (one in four in 1887), as a group they disliked this work; and, by 1932, Hawaiians made up only 1 percent of plantation laborers. Most Europeans brought over as laborers didn't like the work, either; few stuck it out, and most of those who did were given preferential treatment and promoted very quickly.

Workers came or were brought in large numbers from Portugal,

China, Japan, Puerto Rico, and the Philippines. Decade by decade, statistics show the changes clearly, as when the Japanese population jumped from 116 to 12,610 in six years (1884–1890) or the Filipino population increased from a little more than 2,000 to over 21,000 in the ten years between 1910 and 1920.[9] As new immigrant groups moved into plantation work, other groups moved on, finding other sorts of work, often moving up in status as a new group took the bottom rung.

In 1940, no ethnic group claimed a majority in Hawaii. The largest group were those of Japanese ancestry, who made up more than one-third of the islands' population. The next largest group, according to census data, were Caucasians, at 24.5 percent.[10] That number, however, meant little to residents of the islands. The categories established by the U.S. census office did not correspond to Hawaii's racial/social designations. The more important category in Hawaii was haole, a term which did not apply to all "Caucasians," but only to those ethnic groups who had not originally come to the islands as plantation laborers.[11] This designation ruled out the Caucasian Portuguese and Puerto Ricans. Less than 15 percent of the islands' population was haole; and here, race and class were closely linked. Other than the enlisted men in the armed forces, who were not considered part of the islands' real population, there was no haole working class on the islands. The term "local" covered the rest of the islands' people, the majority of whom were, in today's language, people of color.

Though the haole elite still controlled the islands' politics and economy in 1940, their power increasingly rested on a very delicate balance. Sheer numbers conferred electoral power. And the social structure was changing as well. Even though the plantation system still flourished, Hawaii was becoming less and less divided into owners/managers and plantation workers. Several groups, particularly people of Chinese and Japanese ancestry, had left the work in the cane fields. In and around Honolulu, a middle class of Asian business and professional people was emerging. More haoles were coming from the mainland, and not all of them fit into the traditional elite. From the 1920s on, the haole elite itself had become increasingly divided on political and social issues, especially those concerning education.[12] Those who came from the mainland did not usually understand the complexity of Hawaii's social and racial hierarchy. But by entering this world—all the more so without understanding it—they further upset the delicate balance that had favored the haole elite.

———

Hawaii was a war front for only a few hours, but it was not ever quite the home front either. Hawaii was too intimately connected to the war, both from its brief experience as a war zone and because it was so clearly a military zone throughout the war. Hawaii—Honolulu in particular—was overcrowded and tense. While their difficulties were insignificant compared to the disruptions, dangers, and deprivations faced by the civilian populations of countries like Great Britain and the Soviet Union, Hawaii's people felt the effects of war more directly than any other American community. They lived with what they, at the time, called "war nerves."

The civilian men and women who came as war workers (82,000 were present in Hawaii at one point) often did not find what they expected. Lured by the promise of high wages and important war work, many discovered that recruiters had embroidered the facts. Those who came early found chaotic conditions, crowded and substandard housing, few recreational facilities, and a populace that eyed them with suspicion. Hawaii's war workers, many of whom saw their labor as a form of patriotic service, were crucial in winning the war. The excellence of Hawaii's war workers was recognized with the Army and Navy "E," which was awarded to defense plants (including the Pearl Harbor Naval Yard) seventeen times during the war. Still, the life of a defense worker was often not a happy one.

The rawest emotions, perhaps, were those of the men who actually fought in the Pacific war. Paul Fussell, in *Wartime,* makes us confront the horror and obscenity of this war. In a voice of outrage, he shows us the bodies of the dead—bodies that have been blown to bits, dismembered, eviscerated. He tells of the madness induced by the sights and sounds of combat, of a coxswain at the helm of a landing vessel in the assault on Tarawa who "went quite mad, perhaps at the shock of steering through all the severed heads and limbs near the shore." He also tells of madness induced by unrelenting fear, by the "slowly dawning and dreadful realization that there was no way out, that . . . it was only a matter of time before they got killed or maimed or broke down completely."[13] Hawaii was the place where men waited to be shipped into this terrible combat; it was also where, having experienced the unspeakable, they were sent to rest and regroup before being sent back.

Compared to the words of those who fought—Fussell included—words of hope, love, patriotism, and idealism sound hopelessly compromised. That does not mean they are not also true in some important way. In giving voice to these emotions, we are not trying to draw a moral equivalency. Granting the primacy of Fussell's emotional landscape, we write about the other side of war, the world outside the combat zone. Men who had survived the slaughter on Tarawa did come face to face with young volunteers mouthing what seemed so clearly to be platitudes about honor and sacrifice. Men who could not talk about the horrors they had lived did have to talk, somehow, to young women who wanted to call them "heroes." They had to communicate to their families and loved ones, to all the people far behind the lines who survived their war of waiting by cultivating feelings of love, hope, pride, patriotism. Emotion ran high in wartime Hawaii, and as much as anything else, it shaped the experience of cultural contact and conflict.

———

Though we emphasize the many ways in which people are pulled apart by conflicting claims of gender, race, region, occupation, status, and myriad individual differences, these individual lives were all fundamentally shaped by the war. To a great extent, therefore, the people we describe were united by a common cause. That doesn't mean that all were enveloped in a patriotic fervor, but that the large-scale imperatives of waging a war strongly influenced their daily lives. This is especially true for military personnel and war workers, but it is also true of the people of Hawaii.

For most of the war, Hawaii was under martial law. Military rule was declared at 4:25 p.m. on December 7th, and lasted until

October 24th, 1944—well after any immediate danger had passed.[14]
The military was prepared for martial law; the plan had been developed in advance, beginning in August 1941. The major in charge
of it kept his developing plan in what he called the "God Forbid"
file.[15]

Martial law affected the civilian population of Hawaii in matters
ranging from blackout regulations and wide-scale censorship to labor laws and judicial changes that abridged Hawaii residents' fundamental civil rights. Martial law would also involve important
changes in the role of the state, signaling the increased and continuing willingness of the federal government to impose its
nationally-minded agenda over local priorities.

The Big Five supported military rule, and members of the elite
played significant roles in the military government. But what they
would eventually learn was that the priorities of the federal government were not necessarily those of the local elite, in matters ranging
from the rights of prostitutes to the treatment of African-American
servicemen.

The intervention of the state in a form more direct and powerful
than in any other American community during the war provided a
sort of free space for social contestation. Even if not fully by intention, agents of the federal government—albeit in the form of the
military and martial law—*sometimes* emerged as limited guarantors
of equality during the war years. In asserting its own interests, the
government thus created inadvertent openings which different
groups would use in their struggles for equality or autonomy.[16]

———

Hawaii was "the first strange place" for almost a million of the
soldiers, sailors, and marines who fought in World War II and for
tens of thousands of war workers who answered the call for volunteers. Hawaii was a place of extremes, and those extremes reveal the
tensions of the time and the possibilities it promised for the future.
The ways in which the peoples of Hawaii and the men and women
from the mainland made sense of one another, became friends,
became lovers, speaks to the possibilities realized and unrealized in
the new America that was born in World War II.

1

Into the War Zone

The Men Who Died Down Under

We sent them down to land that God forgot
  Islands pestilential, girt with fear
Cursed with sun, soil of lush green rot,
  More than a world away from their heart's desire.

We cannot give them now the breath of Maine,
  The tang of Iowa when fall begins;
For now they lie the prey of distant rain,
  Silent beneath strange stars and alien winds.

Pfc. Martin S. Day
Paradise of the Pacific
July 1944

The war in the Pacific was a war of unspeakable horror, and Hawaii was the midpoint on the way to that war. For many of the men who journeyed into the Pacific, Hawaii never became more than a midpoint, a limbo between the two places that had meaning. Hawaii was not home and it was not war. It was only a place of waiting.

Hawaii, though, was a complicated place, and the servicemen and war workers made an uneasy entrance into the island world. Hundreds of thousands of them spent some considerable length of

31

time in Hawaii; millions passed through. The men could not help but have some impact on the islands; the islands could not help but have some impact on the men. The common emotions of men in war were given shape by the specifics of Hawaii, as the men attempted to negotiate the complex boundaries of a multiracial society and to square the gritty tedium of wartime Honolulu with the romantic myths they'd learned about it. "Believe me if Paradise is anything like this I'll take my chances in Hell," a war worker wrote home. "Honolulu in itself is about the dirtiest town I've ever been in and I've been in quite a few . . . Japs, Chinks, Hawaiians all run about barefoot, dirty & unkempt. The morals out here are disgusting."[1]

This war worker's metaphor was not original; countless men and women from the mainland took the stock image of Hawaii as "Paradise" and made the obvious leap to its opposite, "Hell." They were reacting, however, not only to the mythic representations of Hawaii that played well on the mainland (especially in February), but to the insistent claims of the haole elite who controlled Hawaii's newspapers, magazines, and radio stations.

"The Paradise of the Pacific," they called "their" island, sounding for all the world like the prewar tourist brochures that had lured a very different group of people to its shores. And all too often they said it without the grace note of irony, without the raised eyebrow and implied quotation marks that would have allowed for the barbed wire on the beaches, the sweating crowds on the bus to Waikiki, the shortages of meat, of liquor, of women.

The phrase was a talisman of sorts. It expressed faith, during those long months between the bombing of Pearl Harbor and the Battle of Midway, that there would be a future. And it claimed some continuity with the past. Life had been good for those middling- to upper-class haoles in the years before the war. To be fair, one had to give them credit: it took nerve to move to that speck of land in the middle of the Pacific in the days before commercial air travel drew Hawaii closer to the mainland.[2] No matter how gracious the living or how beautiful the scenery—no matter that, by 1940, one could see Hollywood films there and buy New York fashions—the Territory of Hawaii was an isolated outpost of American life, and the middle-class whites were a decided minority.

Into the War Zone

The war put a great strain on Honolulu, and much of the pressure came from the drastic—and largely unanticipated—increase in its population. By its overwhelming numbers, the military made the difference. But the civilian population of Oahu also jumped—from 258,000 in 1940 to 348,000 in 1945. Mainland defense workers accounted for a large part of that increase. Most of the war workers were young white men, between twenty and forty years old without families.[3] The presence of these men was unsettling, partly because of who they were, and partly because of how they fit into Honolulu's complicated class and racial hierarchy.

The tactful references in Hawaii's local publications described the war workers as "rough-hewn." One sociologist referred sarcastically to the "smart set of defense worker . . . who wear the multicolored aloha shirts with tails flapping in the breeze [and] . . . have the reputation for pitching endless numbers of wild parties."[4] The territorial Health Department reported that "groups of war workers in this community apparently contain a rather notable number of unstable, alcoholic, psychoneurotic or psychopathic individuals."[5]

In actuality, the workers varied greatly in character and behavior. Some of the men sought adventure: they were either young men who had never traveled or men who were used to moving around, working in rough, temporary jobs as loggers or longshoremen. Others were men who had been buffeted by the Depression. The high wages and unlimited overtime they were promised seemed a way to work themselves and their families back into stability or even prosperity. More than a few were men who had been classified 4-F and who wanted to go to Hawaii because it was as close as they could get to the war. Going to Pearl Harbor seemed a patriotic duty. "While I am sorry I left my family," wrote one worker in a letter to the mainland, "I can truthfully say I do not begrudge the good job I left behind me to come here. I know I am sacrificing something for my country like all should do. I bitch like all normal Americans do but just the same here I am at least trying to do a job and give something to my country." Another explained: "Whenever a bunch of ships come in . . . we work all the hrs. we can stand. We don't mind . . . it makes up somewhat for not being able to get into the service."[6]

While many were hard workers, inspired by patriotic ideals or family obligations, others were alienated men with little stake in society. Many were rough, hard-drinking, prone to fighting. But at the same time, military contractors learned quickly that the quiet family man was often a worse bet than men who had knocked around some or young men who had not yet settled down. Family men got homesick and were often less able to adjust to the hardships and isolation of war work in Hawaii.[7] Clearly homesick and tired, one of these tried to explain to his wife why he felt he could not come home. "I really hate to be a quitter Honey," he wrote,

> ". . . there's so darn many fellows that hasn't got the guts to stick it out, I hate to be one of them. I do realize that there's a hell of a slaughter going on, and when I think of those precious boys that are facing sure and sudden death, that hurts worse than my personal feelings."[8]

Some of the men were troublemakers and some were adventurous youths and some were rock steady, but the citizens of Honolulu cast a suspicious eye on all alike. Few distinctions were made, as one young office worker at Hickam found to his chagrin. He thought of himself as cultured, or at the very least respectable; he was taking courses at the university and had been an Arthur Murray dance instructor in Detroit. But when he answered an ad about a room, the lady of the house said straight out, "We want no defense workers here," and slammed down the phone.[9]

Part of Honolulu's suspicion was based on experience. The "professional hell raisers" were often most visible—not only were they the noisiest, they were more likely to be living in town than in the workers' housing at Hickam or the Navy's CH-3 (a community of single men with a population larger than Las Vegas). Housing administrators had little control over those men who spent themselves in "nightly orgies" of drinking and gambling in the overcrowded rooms. Their best option was to evict the men, leaving them to find their own housing in Honolulu proper—where they contributed to the stereotype of the drunken mainland defense worker.[10]

The stereotypes were based on more than experience, however.

When Cory Wilson, a University of Hawaii sociologist, described the defense workers he'd studied, he kept circling back to the issues of race and class. When the defense worker isn't in "dirty work clothes," Wilson wrote, he likely is wearing a "purple spangled aloha shirt. . . . Defense workers have almost taken these shirts away from the natives and Filipinos [those groups at the bottom of Honolulu's race-class hierarchy] . . . Though he looks at other racial groups with a condescending air, we suspect that his social status at home was somewhere in the lower brackets." And then the heart of the critique: "There is no doubt he is making a wheelbarrow load of money which he doesn't know how to handle properly. It doesn't seem right that these men, a majority having less than a high school education, should make more money than our college graduates."[11]

Clearly, boundaries were being upset. This was the first large group of Caucasians to do manual labor on Oahu.[12] Hawaii was not used to white men of the working classes—not unless they were in uniform. The invasion was unsettling for the white middle-class and elite, many of whom believed both in racial tolerance and in a natural social hierarchy closely tied to race.

The influx was no less unsettling for local people. Many of the mainland war workers were self-consciously and blatantly racist. Military censors found constant angry statements about the local population in letters home. One censorship report included the following "typical unfavorable comment": "Here is where the Black, Brown and Yellow man is 'Lord of all he sees' the 'Paradise of the Oriental.' Here he struts and the 'Powers that Be,' bend over backwards to please him." While prewar Hawaii had not offered full racial equality to all its citizens, there had been little of such blatant, ugly racism. These sentiments were not confined to private letters, but charged the air in Hawaii's newly crowded streets.[13] Most local people simply tried to keep their distance from the war workers.

If the civilian influx changed the feel of Honolulu, the military influx changed the way it looked. Honolulu was jammed with men in uniform—men standing in long lines waiting to enter a movie theater, or a bar, or a brothel, or a laundry. Although troop strength and movements were closely guarded secrets, it was apparent to all that Honolulu had become a sort of crossroads of the Pacific—men going out to war, men coming back. There was also a large population of servicemen who spent the war on Oahu. Some were there to guard the island (almost 4,000 men were in Hawaii's Coast Guard); others were awaiting orders that never came; still others were manning the bureaucratic machine of war. Servicewomen—a few thousand WACs and SPARS and WAVES and Marines—began to appear in 1944, but were never a large presence.

After Midway, as the war became more distant, Hawaii was increasingly the point of assembly for Pacific campaigns. Marine-Corps strength fluctuated: up to 60,000 in the spring of 1944 and then sharply down as 40,000 shipped out to the Marianas; up to 79,000 in January 1945 and down again to 22,000 in February. Counting the sailors was more complicated. Though naval strength on Oahu peaked in December of 1944 with 137,200 men, that number doesn't include the "men afloat." Hundreds of thousands of men were on ships in the Central Pacific—550,000 in the spring of 1945, just before the invasion of Okinawa. Almost all came ashore at least once, perhaps as many as 35,000 at a time. But the soldiers were by far the largest stationary group. Late in the war, troops were being assembled to invade the Japanese mainland. By June of 1945, 253,000 soldiers were massed on Oahu. It seems that there were often more servicemen than civilians on Oahu.[14]

None of this was completely new. Pearl Harbor had long been a naval port and the "pineapple army" had maintained a peacetime presence.[15] The army men of prewar days were known to be rough—often men with no place back home. Many had spent some hard years during the Depression and had joined the regular army simply for a steady three meals a day. Soldiers and sailors were thus a familiar presence in Honolulu, and a district of bars and brothels had grown up to serve them. Enlisted men made only $21 a month (paid monthly), but their money was important to the local economy. Through the money they spent, they had contact with some of the local people. "Shackjobs" were common with local women, especially those of Hawaiian or Filipino descent.[16]

But to a great extent, these men were out of sight of the island's haole middle class and elite. The men were secluded at Schofield and Hickam and Pearl Harbor, well away from the downtown business and shopping districts, much less the residential areas of Pacific Heights and Kahala. Cab fare to town was expensive, and a soldier had to budget carefully to afford one good night in town and still have money for liquor and cigarettes (or even cold drinks and ice cream) for the rest of the month.

Some tried to build their capital in the gambling sheds and some played a dangerous pickup game in Waikiki bars. Men who frequented certain bars could be relied on for drinks and dinner, and sometimes for cash. Playing this game—even to the point of having sex—did not make the soldier a homosexual in the eyes of most of his comrades. But it was dangerous for both parties: servicemen could be court-martialed for sodomy; gay men risked physical violence. While most of the men involved, civilian and military, tried to keep out of sight of authorities, sometimes troubled relations became public. When one soldier, "embarrassed and angry" at himself for having "gone with a queer" stole his companion's wallet, the man went to the police, and the soldier found himself court-martialed. [17]

Despite the sometimes rowdy groups of sailors, and the regular payday excesses, the military presence was not overwhelming before 1941. The soldiers and sailors were effectively segregated from the haole community by the seemingly insurmountable barriers of money, geography, and class. They had been simply ignored. The war changed all that. Not that servicemen were welcomed with open arms; barriers remained. (Even those people, haole or local, who opened their homes and stretched their hospitality to the limits could make hardly a dent in the population of lonely, homesick men and boys.) But now there were too many men to ignore. And while one could at least *try* to ignore the war workers, the servicemen were no longer simply servicemen. They were "our boys," who were going to fight—and perhaps die—in a very brutal war.

People in Hawaii felt a profound ambivalence toward the hordes of men, many still adolescents, who overran the island. The servicemen were a more diverse group than the volunteer army had been—between the draft and the wave of volunteer enlistments following Pearl Harbor, the military enrolled a broad spectrum of American men. But the soldiers and sailors and marines were still men in uniform, and the uniform bestowed a kind of anonymity on its wearer. The soldiers and sailors observed the conventions of a society of men, of young men who may soon be dead. They spoke in obscenities. They drank too much. They chased women—without proper regard for Honolulu's careful boundaries of class and race. Many people viewed this behavior with pity and horror and the kind of resolve one develops from carrying gas masks to weddings. But looking at the groups of drunken sailors and the aloha-shirted war workers with three days' growth of beard who seemed to have taken over the town, they sometimes thought (and they knew it was irrational) that it was these men, and not the Japanese enemy, who were responsible for spoiling their paradise.[18]

The men in uniform called Oahu "The Rock." They called them all rocks, the bits of land scattered in the vast ocean over which so many Americans and Japanese men and boys fought and died. But it was for Oahu that they reserved the capital "R" and the anger that was born not of suffering, but of disillusion and frustration. Part of the problem was that many of the men had believed the myth of Paradise. They'd seen the movies and they expected, as the Morale Services Section of the Central Pacific Base Command discovered, "a hula girl under every palm tree."[19] Hawaii Hollywood-style was such a staple of 1930s filmmaking that the *New York Times* reviewer of the 1939 film, *Honolulu*, refers sarcastically to "the well-known Hollywood suburb of Wacky-ki."[20] The most unlikely people turned up in grass skirts. Clara Bow, back in 1927, had starred as Hula Calhoun, "a persistent and frank girl who worries Honolulu either by riding her horse into a sitting room or taking her Sealyham terrier to the dinner table." The "vivacious and charming" Miss Bow, the *New York Times* reviewer notes, "is first perceived swimming in a mountain lake and then is seen in a native dance."[21]

The 1930s audiences saw such movies as *Hawaii Calls* and *Hawaiian Nights* at the Palace in New York. *Honolulu*, a Metro-Goldwyn-Mayer effort, featured Eleanor Powell hula-dancing, and

Dorothy Lamour sashayed through a whole range of tropical locales in the briefest of sarongs.[22]

Probably the most popular of the "tropical pictures" was Paramount's 1937 musical comedy, *Waikiki Wedding*. Bing Crosby, as the public relations agent for Imperial Pineapple, has to convince the Pineapple Girl contest winner (played by Shirley Ross) that Hawaii is a terribly romantic place so that she won't complain in letters home. Crosby persuades her through a combination of tropic sunsets and romantic maneuvers, pausing to sing such songs as "Sweet Leilani" and "Blue Hawaii" (which Elvis Presley would sing over the credits to *his* 1961 Paramount film).[23] *Waikiki Wedding* featured a whole troupe of dancers under the direction of LeRoy Prinz, Hollywood's most prolific choreographer. They hula'd in grass skirts on the beach, undulated around "tribal campfires," and sang "In a Little Hula Heaven."[24] This image was pure Hollywood, but the safely exotic screen version of Hawaii sold well.

Millions of Americans saw these films and others like them. In the Depression years, despite hard times, between 60 and 75 million people—roughly half of the U.S. population—went to the movies every week. The war didn't change that: movie attendance hit its height in 1946.[25] In a country that was still amazingly provincial, with vast differences between regional cultures and between urban and rural peoples, the movies provided a common language for America. "Any chicken has to be a Lana Turner or a Hedy Lamarr to rate more than . . . two bucks for a usual date," a Philadelphia teenager wrote to a national magazine, and everyone knew what he meant.[26] "You're no Clark Gable yourself," was the correct—and expected—retort. The movies provided a frame for experience, a shorthand for communication. By December 7, 1941, millions of Americans knew what Hawaii looked like and what it stood for in the iconic universe of the movies. Judging from the response of the wartime arrivals, a great many of them had taken the films at face value. "I expected . . . hula girls running around," said one soldier. "And I expected to find grass huts here," said another.[27]

Servicemen, by and large, had no choice about where they went. Though the Hollywood version may have fostered disillusion, it did not affect troop movements. War workers, on the other hand, could choose. Workers were desperately needed in Hawaii—for machine shops and maintenance crews and assembly lines, for filing and typing in the bureaucratic jungle ("Washington, D.C. with palm trees") that Honolulu had become.[28] Much of the work was dirty and unpleasant (early on, workers from the mainland had been assigned to salvage bodies from Pearl Harbor), and recruiters found that the mythic romance of the islands was their best recruiting aid.[29] Mainland war workers, in overwhelming numbers, told the University of Hawaii sociologist Cory Wilson that they'd been drawn by the myth—or as rendered in 1940s' academese, by "the romantic lure of the islands caused by years of successful advertising."[30]

On recruiting posters for defense work in Hawaii, Diamond Head loomed over a pristine beach lined with palm trees. It was a picture straight from a prewar travel brochure. Now different advertisers were targeting a different audience, but the image worked just as well. Gene Simonson, a nineteen-year-old Arkansas farm boy kept out of the war by the scars that an undiagnosed case of tuberculosis had left on his lungs, saw the poster and applied on the spot. He traded his job making steel control cables for B-24 Liberator bombers in Texas for work in Hawaii, purely on the strength of that picture.[31]

Diamond Head was a welcome sight to the men who crossed to Hawaii, if only because it marked the end of the ocean trip. Gene Simonson made his crossing from Seattle. He'd already traveled cross country, assigned with thirty-five or forty other newly trained mechanics to a Pullman car. It was a long trip, and they never once left that car. In Seattle, they settled down to wait; the passage schedule was never certain. Only two days later the call came, and they were taken aboard the ship. More than one of the men was too drunk to walk and had to be "poured aboard."

The ship was the *John W. Weeks*, a Liberty ship outfitted as a troop carrier. The workers shared the vessel with a battalion of GIs headed for the Philippines. The GIs were on duty: they stood guard, cleaned the ship (including the war workers' quarters), trained and drilled. The civilians had nothing to do but kill time, and there was some tension between the two groups. Time died hard aboard ship, and conditions were such that the war workers never imagined they were on a cruise to the islands. The men's hold was "strictly GI," even though they were all civilians. Canvas bunks were laced to steel frames and stacked five high; the mess halls had waist-high tables but no chairs; the food was monotonous and they ate only two meals a day.

Many of the men on the Pacific passage didn't spend much time in the mess hall. Few had been on the open seas before and the pitching and rolling of the ship was too much for them. The *Weeks'* propeller kept breaking the surface, intensifying the vibrations in the hold. Just outside of Puget Sound, they were already getting a taste of the vastness of the ocean. But even there, just off the coast, the war made its presence felt. It took two or three minutes for a submarine to sight and fire a torpedo with any degree of accuracy, so the ships zigzagged, changing course every two or three minutes throughout the entire trip, rocking in the rough seas. The trip was long, and rumor had it that the ship went north almost to Alaska before heading south to Hawaii—another precaution against submarines. Gene Simonson lost his breakfast as soon as the ship left Puget Sound, the oatmeal pouring out in a solid, warm stream. For the next five days he lay in his bunk, too seasick to do more than stagger to the latrine as the ship turned and pitched. Even so far from the grim islands of the South Pacific, nature and war seemed to conspire against men.

The approach to Hawaii confirmed the fact of war. Patrol planes circled overhead while tugs pulled open the antisubmarine nets. But the first sight of Diamond Head made the malihini, or newcomers, forget the war—if only for a moment.[32]

"The approach to Honolulu is incredibly beautiful, even from a transport," wrote a man who was "stationed in Paradise." "At the first wonderful appearance of the islands across the jade distance, one knows at once that no matter what disillusionments may lie ahead he has found romance for a moment. . . . That first impression can never be wholly eradicated."[33]

One young Navy flier, bound for the South Pacific, watched the approach to Honolulu from the deck of the Liberty ship, *Lavaca*. The sea meant little to him. He was at home in the air, knowing the loneliness of the void, the "shapelessness and endlessness of space," seduced by the sense of "dominion a pilot feels when his plane reaches a commanding altitude and he looks down on the world that stretches out beneath him." He was a middle-class boy from Minneapolis who had recently married a southern girl he scarcely knew. He was straining for adulthood and afraid that too many doors were slamming shut behind him. Stretching to recover the man he was at nineteen—still immortal, still awaiting the big test—Samuel Hynes recalled the mythic power of Hawaii. "Hawaii would be the first strange place," he recalls,

> the edge of a world that was not like anything back home. No one I knew had ever been there, except maybe a few Marines, and it existed in my imagination as a mixture of myths. The beach at Waikiki was a part of the romantic mythology of Minneapolis, a place taken out of a song, like Paris in the spring—it was all leis and hula girls and ukuleles. But Pearl Harbor was a part of that mythology, too; it was the stab in the back, the day that would live in infamy, columns of black smoke and diving planes. I couldn't put the two together into one place. [34]

The tensions between these powerful myths, both clearly articulated in the national consciousness, might have been reconciled in the image of Diamond Head, its pristine beaches laced with barbed wire. Hawaii offered many images of violated purity in those years. But what could not be reconciled with either myth was Honolulu, itself.

With one day of liberty in Honolulu, Hynes and his friend, Rock, decided to chase the romance. They went to Waikiki, had a drink at the Royal Hawaiian, wandered through the disappointingly small town that was Honolulu. The buildings were low; the streets were narrow and crowded with sailors. It looked, Hynes thought, like a set for a war movie. It looked like any other Navy town. Like so many of the men who passed through Honolulu, they couldn't think of anything to do. " 'Nothin' but Amarillo with a beach," Rock said. [35]

Into the War Zone

The myth of Paradise was exploded—or at least complicated—by the reality of life on an island on the fringes of the war zone. Longtime residents of the islands reported "looks of startled horror" when they told men in uniform, "I have lived in Hawaii for many years."[36] Men responded to Honolulu with a bewilderment that was sometimes poignant. "It's strange to see so many servicemen walking around town, but I guess I'll get used to it . . .," ventured Private Samuel Schwartz, recently of St. Louis. "As far as I'm concerned Hawaii has been a disappointment," Sgt. Ellsworth Bellows commented tentatively. "I guess it's because they give it such a buildup back home."[37]

Elizabeth Beach Brown wrote in her war diary about the disillusion of soldiers who were arriving in Hilo by the boatload. It had been raining for days on end (not unusual in Hilo), and one of the newly arrived soldiers had asked a friend of hers, "Do you live here because you *have* to or because you *want* to?" Another asked, "What do we want to defend this place for? Why don't we give it away?" Elizabeth mused: "When it rains for days and one is in a strange country and forced to be out doors in the rain and mud, I guess it is rather dismal."[38]

Between the ruptured expectations and the wartime inconveniences, life in Hawaii was frustrating, and men complained. They complained about the petty annoyances of daily life. They complained about their boredom. They even complained about the climate in sunny Honolulu. Most of all, they complained about the women—or the shortage of women. The number of men on the island at any given time was a closely guarded military secret, and a Japanese spy could have been driven mad trying to derive accurate figures from all the published speculations on the sex ratio. Estimates began as low as 150 to 1. When Miss Fixit, the *Honolulu Advertiser* columnist who'd won the hearts of the men stationed on the island, reported that figure, she received a scathing letter from an army officer. "How can you be so inaccurate," he demanded, "when every man knows there's at least a thousand men to every woman?" The compromise figure was "500 Men to a Girl."[39] Odds were high. Dates were scarce. The soldiers put it this way (with apologies to Winston Churchill): "Never have so many pursued so few, with so much, and obtained so little."[40] Pushing for a triple entendre, men complained about the "meet shortage."[41] (There was a meat short-age in Honolulu, and spam sandwiches were no substitute for steak. But most men in Honolulu—malihini and kamaaina, haole and lo-cal—knew that the brothels offered a choice of "meat": white or dark.)

In terms of petty annoyances, the problems of transportation narrowly edged out the problem of laundry. "I know there are seats on Honolulu buses, because I see people sitting on them," passed for humor in wartime Honolulu. (Another popular joke was about nightlife: "A friend of mine complains because there is no nightlife in Honolulu. Guess there are no mosquitoes in his neighbor-hood.")[42] Buses were so crowded that sailors hoping to make con-nections from the Waikiki train to the Pearl Harbor bus started jumping out the windows as soon as the train slowed down to pull into the station. The more daring sometimes got seats. The cautious ones waited for another bus. Being out after curfew brought a stiff fine, and taxis charged up to 50 cents a mile—when the driver would stop for you—with the result that people jammed themselves on the bus, hanging out doors and windows, pressed into a sweating mass of humanity.[43] Here many servicemen and war workers had their most intimate contact with the people they called "natives," and the contact wasn't always pleasant. The motion of the buses down Honolulu's crowded streets threw people into each other, and an innocent step to regain one's balance could easily erupt into a fight.[44]

The local bus company made heroic efforts to handle the traffic, which could run to 340,000 passengers a day. They managed to add 102 buses to the original fleet of 215 over the course of the war—quite a feat, since war production took precedence over civilian needs. A factory had "diverted" the buses to Honolulu, and many made the 110-mile circuit of the island proclaiming their route as "42nd Street—Crosstown." In the face of a drastic labor shortage, the bus companies recruited servicemen as part-time drivers.[45] Still, everyone told the stock story about the bus driver who'd pulled over at a hot-dog stand, leaving his passengers to swelter while he ate his lunch, smoked a cigarette, and traded a few stories with the pro-prietor, only to "climb back aboard his overstuffed vehicle with no other explanation than a lusty belch."[46] That, they said, could never happen in the States.

They were probably right. The culture of Hawaii was very different, and complaints about the islands often hinged on comparisons with home. "Home" was almost always a specific place— South Carolina, Harlem, Colorado. No matter where they were, when men who went to war recorded the names of their fellows, they also recorded their hometowns. It was important. Place mattered. It gave you an identity beyond "GI." And in the days before the interstate highway system and network television, regional identities—and regional differences—were very strong. Many of the men, especially the young ones, had never been away from home before.

The war threw men together without much attention to background. If the man from Virginia eyed the Minnesotan with distrust, if the man from Iowa couldn't penetrate the Brooklyn accent of his bunkmate, it was small wonder that the local culture of Hawaii was mysterious.[47] And one should not forget the overlay of race. In the story above, the bus driver was always identified as a "Kanaka bus driver." While "kanaka" simply means "man," or more generally, "people," it is used here to show that the driver was a "native."

For a time, the "Letters from Readers on Timely Topics" column in the *Honolulu Star-Bulletin* was dominated by servicemen vying in their condemnation of Hawaii and promotion of their own home states. "Before we left 'heaven's shore,' meaning New York City," a letter from five Coast Artillery men began, "we had some very mistaken ideas of this so-called Paradise of the Pacific. But after a year and a half on this rock we can only say that in all our wanderings this is about the worst spot we've ever been in." After running through the traditional catalog of complaints, they conclude: "We, the undersigned, from Westchester, the scenic wonderland of New York, are prepared to discuss this matter more fully with anyone holding the opposing viewpoint." (Evidently they weren't willing to chance using real names: the letter was signed "Red Ireland, Rocky Bernarducci, Lefty D'Alessandro, Jock Jackson and Hoagy Carmichael.")[48]

A great many did agree with their assessment of Hawaii (one

man from South Carolina wrote to propose a new nickname for Hawaii: "The Land of Fruits and Nuts"). Everyone, however, was promoting his home state. The comparisons are sometimes funny, but still poignant, bespeaking homesickness more than anything else. A man from Texas, a college graduate, told an interviewer: "This is the hell-hole of the world, I volunteered to come out—why, I don't know. If I ever come back, it won't be of my own accord; it will be in a box. It's too confining—no New York—no night clubs. In Texas you might go 100 miles in an evening." (He seemed to be confused about the precise location of New York.) Another man, a southerner, said simply: "I was disappointed in Waikiki Beach. Have you ever been to Virginia Beach?"[49]

Some men did like Hawaii (between three and seven thousand would choose to settle on Oahu after the war[50]), and a few were even willing to defend it in print. But they were clearly bucking the trend. The convention was to despise the place. In a *New Army and Navy Review* profile of "A Gob on Leave," a seaman from the midwest confided that he "had begun to like Hawaiian music" and that "the climate was wonderful." But the author of the piece, perhaps concerned about his own credibility, hedged: "He was a little ashamed of himself. It is customary to dislike Honolulu and the island with fervor."[51]

The morale problem was obvious. Men stationed on the island for any length of time described themselves as "rock happy" or suffering from "pineapple head." The prewar "pineapple army" had complained of "The Rock" with great bitterness. James Jones' novel *From Here to Eternity* is one long testament to the despair Hawaii could inspire. But now the scale was larger, and because of the war, much more was at stake.

Morale was always an issue, and a practical one.[52] Just as the military campaigns to control prostitution were motivated more by practical concerns about the VD rate and the consequent lost man-hours than by abstract morality, concern about morale was not only a question of easing the burden on the fighting men and cheering their lonely hours. It was a question of keeping them ready and able to fight. The United States had learned hard lessons from World War I. Even though America had been in that war a relatively short time and American soldiers had been spared some of the horrific years of trench warfare, psychological casualties were high. The U.S. had spent a billion dollars to care for those disabled by "battle fatigue" in that war. Poor morale undermined the will to fight, and psychological stress was as debilitating as any physical disease. On these grounds—prodded by psychiatrists interested both in being of help and in promoting their expertise—the Selective Service Agency was already employing extensive psychiatric screening by the time America entered World War II. While the screening was sometimes perfunctory or inept (and based on psychiatric models we would not accept today), the widespread use of psychiatric examinations shows a concern about casualties of the mind as well as of the body. [53]

It was all too apparent that the morale of the men in Hawaii was not high. Even those who liked the islands could find their time there difficult. There was the strain of disillusion, countless petty frustrations, and always the shadow of war. The waiting was hard, and everyone handled it differently. [54]

When the men who survived the war look back, they talk about the waiting and war nerves. Though most agree that the time in Hawaii was difficult, they don't all tell their stories the same way. Some speak with voices of quiet pride, some are boisterous, some nostalgic. Some are still angry; others, matter of fact. A few, though they remember the loneliness and boredom and fear, say they loved the islands. Their voices soften when they describe Hawaii. The war was hard for these men, too, but they at least could see the beauty, and that helped to make it more bearable.

Frank Branigan loved Hawaii. He saw it with an artist's eye and a gentleness of spirit that were perhaps not the best qualifications for life in the infantry. Branigan had been drafted out of college. By rights, he shouldn't even have been in college. He came from one of the dispossessed families who'd lost out during the Depression. The family's Kansas farm was hit hard by the drought, and in 1936 Branigan's father moved his wife and six kids to Indiana and began again as a common laborer. By the end of the decade he'd worked his way up to sharecropping, but there was no money for something like college. [55]

But Frank took a war job in the summer of '42 and made enough money to begin his freshman year at the University of Indiana. He was the diamond in the rough that professors hope for—the kind of boy who memorizes the speeches in *Hamlet* for the sheer beauty of the language. One semester and a fraction of another, and he was drafted: a GI in the infantry. By Easter, he was on his way to Hawaii.

He was excited. He had never traveled much. (He didn't count his family's six or seven moves during the Depression. That was different.) The trip wasn't easy; he was more seasick than most and wanted nothing more than to curl up and die. But the approach to Honolulu stayed with him for the rest of his life. "The water became the most beautiful ultramarine, almost turquoise color," he remembers, "and after that we saw the white breakers on the shore and beautiful ecru sand which led inland to the palm trees that lined the shore. . . ."

Branigan found himself alone a lot. He had friends, but most of the men in his outfit were New Yorkers and slightly suspicious of the midwesterner who spent much of his free time at the university, listening to Beethoven on the Farnsworth hi-fi system and watercoloring. He'd won some respect as the company's official lifesaver and swim coach (you had to swim 100 yards in full gear to qualify for combat duty and a lot of the tough guys couldn't swim), but his "rather severe Christian upbringing" kept him apart from the men's often ribald amusements.

Branigan found beauty in the islands, from the orchids he sketched while "running problems" in the mountains to the extravagant Art Deco movie theater in Waikiki to the Hawaiian people themselves, "an extremely beautiful race; big, strong, massive people" who didn't look anything like the hula dancers in the movies he had seen. The day-to-day frustrations of the islands didn't bother him that much, but in a way, the waiting took its toll.

Like so many of the men sent out to Hawaii, Branigan never knew when he would be shipped out. He and the men in his company were always waiting to be taken to the South Pacific. They knew men who had been in combat, and not just through casual contact in the omnipresent waiting lines. Their combat instructors were often men returned from war. One lieutenant was "a wonderful soldier," but Branigan always had a fear of him, "almost as if he were a psycho . . . he had a wild view on life and a terribly sadistic attitude toward himself and his own safety." The lieutenant had been shot in the mouth and lost all his teeth. They'd been replaced with false ones, but he was left an "extremely bitter and vengeful man" who would "let men come at him with a bare bayonet and dare them to kill him." He taught the men "how to get the enemy, how not to play fair, how to gouge and injure them in the most destructive way possible." Branigan found the instruction "interesting, but also horrifying," and the presence of this man and others like him, together with tales from the South Pacific, shadowed the waiting.

Three times they told the men to get ready. Three times they took them as far as the boats. Each time, the orders were canceled, and the men went back to wait some more. The tension mounted. When a call came for volunteers for a special combat group to go down in advance of the regiment, Branigan was surprised to find himself signing up: "I just wanted to do something to get rid of the boredom of just sitting and waiting, get rid of the tension and the apprehension. . . ." All the men went down at the same time and volunteered. "It's curious what waiting will do to you," he says.

> I was always artistic and I had a fear that I would ruin my hands
> so I was a very poor sportsman in baseball. But after I volunteered
> to go down to the Pacific I found myself on a softball team one day
> catching with ease because I just no longer *cared* about my hands.

For Frank Branigan the experience had a quality of revelation, but the symbolic moment on the sunny ballfield had its dark element. One is reminded of the lieutenant and others returning from combat, who didn't care anymore either.[56] The darkness overwhelmed some men: there were two suicides in Branigan's company. They couldn't stand "the suspense of being built up and then let down and being built up and then let down," and they took their carbines and shot themselves.

The war overlaid the waiting and added an element of unpredictability to days that were otherwise mundane and often tedious. While most men just took it, putting up with what they so eloquently termed "chickenshit" and speculating on the future (depending on how optimistic you were, it was "Home Alive in '45," "Out of the Sticks in '46," "Hell to Heaven in '47," or "Golden Gate in '48"), some of the men were strung too tight. Robert Cowan, sergeant of the MPs, reported one man wandering up and down the line at the PX, alternately sobbing and ranting. "I'm going to die anyway," he kept saying. "I might as well just kill myself." He was giving all his money away, thrusting it into the hands of embarrassed strangers. The money made his threat convincing, though Sgt. Cowan, veteran of nameless island campaigns, was somewhat cynical about the whole matter. The man didn't kill himself, but he got a Section 8.[57]

Because there wasn't much anyone could do about the horror of combat or the uncertainty of waiting, those in authority attacked the symptoms of the disease. They waged their own war on boredom and alienation and tried to alleviate the frustration. The U.S.O., the various branches of the military, the "welfare departments" charged with the well-being of the war workers, and many volunteers from the island population valiantly tried to improve the lives of the wartime population, going on the theory that wholesome recreation could make the difference.

The Hawaii branch of the U.S.O. operated fifty-one clubs in the islands, the largest of which was the Army-Navy Y in downtown Honolulu. Prominent members of island society, including some members of the Hawaiian royal family, turned over estates to the military for use as officers' clubs and R&R centers. The Navy took over the Royal Hawaiian Hotel, where movie stars had stayed in prewar days. Expensive rooms went to officers for a dollar a night. Enlisted men slept free, though cots were crowded into the once-luxurious suites. The Breakers, the Navy recreation center on Waikiki, opened in December 1942. It drew up to 4,400 men a day, and Artie Shaw's Navy Band made it famous. The Army's Maluhia Club, at the other end of Waikiki, had the best dance floor on the island. Sometimes 10,000 men would pass through its doors on a single day.[58]

The heart and soul of the Maluhia was its hostess, Mabel Thomas. She oversaw an empire. The Maluhia was open seven days a week, and she was there every day. In its first eight months of business, 285,245 people came to dance, drink, see a show, or just relax. When Bob Hope appeared there, Thomas counted 24,700 men in "Maluhia's beautiful backyard," each man "comfortably seated on a blade of grass." Thomas lined up the entertainment, arranged the dances, dealt with the brass, and tried to keep things running smoothly.[59]

The first dance at the Maluhia brought forth only "four brave girls." Within a week, Thomas had managed a 1500 percent increase: sixty university girls with their dean as "chaperone." That night, she recorded Maluhia's first slap. Mabel Thomas worked magic in wartime Honolulu: within a year, she would count 250 women at Maluhia dances. Still, a ratio of 8571 men to 248 women (May 7, 1944) was rough odds. In the interest of order, she instituted the "whistle dance." No cutting-in was allowed except when the whistle blew; a lucky man with a partner was guaranteed two-and-a-half uninterrupted minutes to jitterbug or to hold a woman in his arms.[60]

Handling the crowds required, in Thomas's own words, "an iron hand, and a very quick tongue with a look that employed (sic) respect from each man attending." She was tough and strict, but the men who sought refuge there loved her. Bing Crosby paid tribute to her in his radio show, offering a "tip [of his] cocoa hat to Mrs. Mabel Thomas. . . . Mabel—or 'Mom' as the thousands of gee eyes who have hit this service center call her—is quite a gal and the good cheer, help and encouragement she gives the guys is something to shout about."[61] The real tribute, however, Mabel recorded in her diary on March 10, 1944:

> Heard frightful tales of the end of [ ] Bay 323 lads sent their last tho[ugh]ts and messages to me. Medals also. Erickerson. Willi Wilson. Gunner Goon. Duff. Hurley. God it hurts, hearing such.

She concluded the entry as always, with a tally of the day's attendance: "3547 No Fights."[62]

Thomas' days were full of heartache and hard work, but as she wrote, ". . . nothing was too much trouble when I looked at some of [the boys'] battered and weary bodies." She sought "every type of entertainment conceivable for the pleasure of the boys," and in the fall of 1943 decided to push the limits and hold a formal dance.[63]

"Maluhia did it properly," Thomas wrote with pride. They printed and sent out 10,000 invitations. They draped the ballroom's balconies with the flags of the twenty-one allied nations. "I asked the girls to really dress up, and bless their hearts, they did it proudly," she wrote. ". . . I am not exaggerating when I say, the girls were breath-taking in their gorgeous formals."

Thomas had a secret plan for the evening. She wanted the dance to culminate in a grand march, though she'd said nothing to any of the 4,000 people attending, "knowing too well, hundreds of them had never seen or been in one." She chose four women and paired them, "one with the Army, one with the Navy, one with the Coast Guard, and one with the Marines." Once she was sure that General Richardson and the "top ranking staffs of Army and Navy" were there, she divided "the girls and the boys." The band started playing—a "collegiate" march, not a military one:

> The band started playing, Col. Patrick at my side, not knowing what was going to happen with our four ladies. I brought the girls on from the left; Col. Patrick brought the boys from the right, and almost instantly they sensed the procedure, and the spirit was magnificently displayed in smiles and joyous expressions. The Colonel and I, backing away from them, brought them down the hall four abreast, and kept directing them around and around until we brought them down in the final phase of thirty-two abreast. The applause could easily have been heard blocks away, with General Richardson, perhaps, cheering the loudest.

Thomas had given "the boys" a moment to remember. She had also shown the top brass that Maluhia was a success. General Richardson sent for her to offer his congratulations; he said that the ball was nicer than anything they had ever had at West Point. Mabel agreed, from a different frame of reference. "With pride I state," she wrote, "that the Royal Hawaiian Hotel, in its balmiest days, could not boast of anything as fine as Maluhia was bringing to the enlisted personnel this evening."

General Richardson was curious about the "nationalities" of the women, and Thomas identified them for him: "Hawaiians, Japanese, Chinese, Filipino, Portuguese, Puerto Ricans, Spanish, Javanese, Malayans, French, Danish, Germans, Jewish, and Hungarians . . . the Chinese-Hawaiians and half Whites." She thought he was "emotionally affected" by their "dignified elegance," but she also realized he hadn't noticed something that showed how far Maluhia was from West Point. "Watch," she said.

> As the next dancing couples passed me I caught the eye of several of the girls and smiled proudly, then I pulled my dress up. They caught what I had referred to. They in turn pulled their dresses up. Then the General saw to his utter amazement, and opening his mouth said, "They haven't any shoes on."[64]

Mabel Thomas was proud of her successes and cared desperately about "the boys," but she had no romantic notions about what she was doing. The Maluhia, like every other place in Honolulu, was overcrowded and emotionally charged, filled with men who had been pushed, one way or another, close to the breaking point.

In her diary she notes the opening day's "lovely success," and ends the entry: "no battles." Six days later she concludes: "Fingers XX No Fights yet." But the possibility of violence was always there. "We certainly got all the rift/raft today," she wrote on Friday, June 4th, 1943. "Scum and lice—But—No Fights. The *nastiest filthiest* crowd of men Maluhia has had. Miracle No Fights." Some days they weren't so lucky. "Navy men beyond understanding tonight," reads her diary entry for August 30, 1944. "Climbed outside building very very abusive to girls and guards—all looking for fights. This was a hellish night thanks to the Navy. Not drunk but all so nasty to some of the girls. Wonder if I can take it much longer."[65]

Mabel Thomas coped with many fights, including some in which "girls" got hurt. But her nightmare, which never happened, was a full scale brawl. Monday, January 8th, 1945, she wrote:

> Terrible battle at [Kapiolani Park] tonight. Marines and Navy. One Marine killed; another not expected to recover, general free for all. . . . My constant prayer—Violence never breaks out en

masse—at Maluhia. If it does—I order all fire hoses turned on at 80 pounds pressure. That should cool them off.[66]

Mabel Thomas was a practical woman. She got the job done and she made a difference. Still, she could not change the fact of war.

It was not only servicemen who needed diversion and entertainment. Mainland war workers were often miserable and demoralized. Many, especially the ones who came early in the war, were angry and frustrated. They came with high expectations—lured by visions of Paradise and also by the extravagant promises of recruiters with a quota to meet. What they found were chaotic conditions, isolation, substandard housing, and limits on overtime (and thus on earnings) alternating with extremely long hours or no work at all. They complained that they were treated as "Okies, interlopers, and draft dodgers" by Hawaii's people. (Echoes of the Depression had not yet grown faint.) As far as recreation and morale went, government resources and local volunteer efforts centered on the men in uniform. Most war workers understood that priority, but they wanted some respect for their efforts and sacrifices as well. They didn't compare themselves to the men out in the Pacific, but they knew their lives were at least as hard as those of the servicemen stuck on "The Rock." Things got so bad that a high-ranking civil service official was brought out from the mainland to mediate.[67]

In this context, the War Worker's Committee of the U.S.O. had a difficult job. The U.S. had to win the war on the "production front" as well; the morale of these men mattered. During the course of the war, the U.S.O. entertained 151,433 workers on the production front, with everything from fishing trips to hula shows. Pearl Harbor Navy Yard instituted a "one day off in eight" program to combat absenteeism, and attempted to improve morale by offering workers full-day tours of Oahu, including lunch and entertainment, for $3 a person.[68] Workers who arrived in Hawaii late in the war remember the entertainments and tours very well. They did make a difference.

But despite the efforts of the U.S.O. and island volunteers, and despite the undeniable improvements over the situation at the beginning of the war, psychological stress was high and morale continued low.[69] In a sort of second front, the authorities decided to attack the problem of disillusion at the root. The Army and Navy began warning prospective war workers that "the Paradise of the Pacific is closed for the duration."[70] And in early 1945—rather late in the war—the Army began distributing a "wittily illustrated" booklet to all soldiers on transports en route to Hawaii. It was no more than had been done for soldiers headed for the war in Europe, but at first it hadn't seemed that such a book would be necessary for Hawaii.[71]

Much of the information—provided in somewhat self-conscious, shoot-from-the-hip democratic language—was useful preparation for wartime Honolulu. On the subject of "Girls," it straightforwardly declared:

> Girls are scarce in Hawaii. When you've been off the boat for as long as 23 minutes, you'll find that telephone numbers here carry the same classification as war plans. They're marked "Secret" and kept in money belts. If, by hook or by crook, you latch on to a few numbers besides the laundryman's (and his isn't as easy to get as you might think), you may wind up with a date. If this miracle occurs, the two of you can go swimming, take in a movie, or dance. If you're still numberless you can still go swimming, or take in a movie. Which is to say that a uniform here is about as novel as a light bulb in a prewar sign on Times Square. And there simply aren't enough wahines (gals) to go around.

This booklet contained information on everything from the history of the hula to the locations of drugstores. It also took what was, for the time, a very progressive stand on racial issues. But its main mission was to improve morale by scaling down—or changing—expectations. "The city of Honolulu is full of drug stores, department stores, soda fountains, movies, offices and even Americans," the guide declared. ". . . you're not as far away from home as you think." Recognizing that servicemen had been "bitterly disappointed" by the contrast between wartime Honolulu and "the Hawaii about which they learned through technicolor movies and tourist bureau releases," the pocket guide was a modest official attempt to stem disillusion by a timely debunking of the Hawaii myth.

Many of the kamaaina also saw that the roots of the newcomers' discontent lay not so much in Hawaii as in the war itself. But like the military authorities, they also looked to the symptoms. An editor of the Honolulu *Advertiser* (the "establishment" newspaper) wrote:

American troops sent overseas by the thousands to the world's far flung fronts are receiving mass doses of disillusion, and getting rid of notions built up in American minds by the movies. Here in the Pacific they have learned that the sun is very hot, the rain very wet, the natives as often dark and ugly as brown and beautiful. . . . Maybe that's the reason there is so much bickering and honking among the boys sent to Hawaii. They'd seen the movies. . . . Hawaii can't help the way Hollywood has pictured these islands. Hawaii just goes on being itself.[72]

Illusion and disillusion. He'd definitely got the point. But his version was a bit self-serving. If Hollywood was a dream factory, Hawaii was one of its most successful products. The "Paradise of the Pacific," the tourist mecca that Hawaii was steadily becoming, depended on those movie images. Hawaii increasingly lived off its own myth, and therefore collaborated to a great extent in creating and perpetuating it. And the myths *did* have an awkward kernel of truth. The beauty of the islands was real, and the Hollywood myth and its offspring, the tourist brochure, were attached—very securely—to scenes that actually existed.

As a result, it was hard to shake the myth, even in the face of wartime Honolulu. Each shipload of men carried fresh waves of myth to the islands: Hawaii in the mythology of New York, of Georgia, of Kansas. Honolulu was full of newly disillusioned men, of bored men feeding on their sense of betrayal. With a steady stream of newcomers, neither myth nor disillusion ever grew stale.

Samuel Hynes had pursued the myth in Honolulu and had decided that Hawaii was overvalued in the mythology of Minneapolis. But he was to confront the romantic myth of the tropics again. After his one day leave in Honolulu, he began the island-hopping flights across the Pacific to the Ulithi atoll in the Western Carolines, where he would be stationed. The first night out was spent on the coral atoll of Majuro, and they landed by moonlight. Taking a can of beer from the officers' club, Hynes went out to the beach. The moon was rising, palm trees rustled. "It was a scene that demanded sentiment," he wrote, "and I knew I should have feelings about it, sad romantic yearnings for the far off beloved, something like that. But how could I have any real response to a tropical island in the moonlight? It was too damn much, too like a movie with Dorothy Lamour; and I could only feel the way I did in movies like that— charmed, but disbelieving."[73]

Hynes, of course, was on another island. Yet his reaction recapitulates the slightly awkward sense of embarrassment so many felt about Hawaii's beauty. "Paradise" was screened by layers of mediating Hollywood myth, and therefore hard to experience authentically and immediately. For men like Hynes, intelligent and acutely self-conscious, the mediating myths could yield an ironic—and uncomfortable—distance from their immediate experiences. For those of less reflective temperament, myth might validate experience, even shape reality. Hawaii was a strange place, but one which few mainlanders encountered fresh. Furthermore, the ambivalence and anger many servicemen and war workers felt about Hawaii lay not only in the difficulty of authentic response—not only in the rub of myth and "reality"—but in the elements of myth imperfectly realized. The elements of the myth were there—but could not be had. The beauty and romance of Hawaii, just like so much else in wartime Honolulu, seemed just beyond the grasp of the men.[74]

In the spring of 1945, Naval Reserve Lieutenant Robert Ruark took on all of Honolulu. The piece he published in *Liberty* caused a furor among the old-timers, the kamaaina, some thinking ahead to statehood, some concerned about the postwar tourist trade, and some who simply loved the islands.[75] The writing must have been a highly cathartic experience for Lt. Ruark, as the reading probably was for those of the same disposition. A large part of the article is devoted to a litany of complaint. The kamaaina get theirs, and without the plaintive note of so many GI laments about the "unfriendly" civilian population. "The kamaainas resent the swarming newcomers," he wrote, "and the swarming newcomers would like to take the kamaainas, tie them in a sack, and drop them over the Pali."

[The kamaaina] glory in speaking Hawaiian instead of English, which is very fine when one is addressing Hawaiians (except that most of the Hawaiians I know can't speak their own language), but it is entirely useless as a means of communicating with somebody born and raised in Montana or Mississippi. . . . About the only time they knock off the painfully acquired Hawaiian is when they are telling some hemmed-in dogface what a wonderful place Oahu was before the Army, Navy, and Marines came out and loused it up. . . . I have a sneaking suspicion that they feel that the Jap raid on the Harbor was engineered personally by me, as an excuse to wangle free transportation to the Pearl of the Pacific.

The complaints grow to a crescendo of frustration. Girls: "Such is the numerical superiority of male to female in Hawaii that the plainest of wahines becomes obsessed with the delusion that she is a composite Grable and Lamarr." Laundry: "Eventually one is apt to acquire the nervous apprehension that a ground crew feels for the flying personnel of a bomber which is taking off on a particularly hazardous strike: only the ultimate in luck, you feel, will bring your baby back to you." Housing: "Two thousand bucks worth of wood and plaster is listed for sale as a house worth $27,000." Kamaaina, again: ". . . the civilians have a more highly developed sense of civic superiority than a Florida chamber of commerce press agent;" and finally the "much publicized Waikiki Beach," a "bathmat-sized strip of dirty sand resembling Coney Island on a hot Sunday, and the blue Pacific a snare which is full of coral to cut you, fungus to get in your ears, and seagoing slabs made up of orange peel, newspapers, and scraps of box lunches."

But the articulate lieutenant was not just venting spleen. He had an argument to make, and it was a fairly tough one that gave some meaning to all the griping. The daily frustrations were there, and he'd run through them all for good measure. He saw the pull of myth, the disillusion, the impossibility of escaping the Hollywood backdrop in a place where "a big fat Hollywoodish rainbow curve(s) down out of the Technicolor sky . . . [like] something from a cheap calendar."

His larger argument, however, relied upon a metaphor: Oahu as "rock." The rock he had in mind was the bearer of another highly specific set of American myths: Alcatraz. Like a "lifer" on the prison island, physically comfortable but "tormented by the lights of San Francisco," the serviceman and war worker in Honolulu hung in limbo, "dumped into a gorgeous tropic vacation land whose tantalizing enticements he may look at but may not touch."

Caught between home and war, in a place that was neither, the men were reminded of what they had lost when they put on their uniforms. All around them they could see the normal life that was denied them. They had the illusion they could touch it, and they were almost always disappointed. With neither "the excitement of combat or the comparative simplicity of an advanced [sic] base," Ruark argued, men could not really give up their illusions of normalcy. They were doomed to frustration and anger.

Moving quickly back to humor, Ruark insists:

> After a few months of Hawaii, the meekest Milquetoast of them all is apt to stow away on an LST bound for the nearest Jap-held isle, and after three trips on a Honolulu bus, a ninety-seven-pound yeoman second class, armed with nothing weightier than a rolled copy of the Honolulu Advertiser, would joyously leap into a Jap pillbox.

The reference to pillboxes and "Jap-held" islands was not a careless one. Ruark had begun the article with a reference to the "several million wet, insect chewed, hungry, muddy and ragged front-line military men" who could be expected to "howl profanely" at his argument. If Hawaii was "Purgatory" (as the blurb in *Liberty* announced), then Pacific combat was Hell. The islands were fought over until they were burned-out shells, and the Japanese fought to the last man.

Ruark hadn't been there. He was one of the men stationed for the duration, and he felt like an impotent bureaucrat. He wasn't alone. "Panama Joe" wrote to the Star Bulletin in 1943 that he'd gladly trade places with "those lucky guys" on Guadalcanal or New Guinea. "I used to 'sweat' the transports in and out down Panama way," he wrote. "I could always recognize one which had just come in from Oahu. The average enlisted passenger usually had a faraway look in his eyes—it was a black one—down there we called it the 'Wahoo look.' I wondered how they got it—now I know."[76]

"Lucky" was probably not the word the men on Guadalcanal

would have chosen. Sometimes, though, men who'd been at the advance bases said a version of the same thing. One man who had just come in from the South Pacific told an interviewer in 1945: "I was in the Ellice Islands before, I hate it here. Oh, it's terrible. There is just enough freedom and everything for you to think you might have something, but the restrictions and the crowds are too much. I would much rather be down on Ellice. Down there you know what you've got."[77] What they had was pretty awful, and the men who had come back from Iwo Jima and Tarawa and Okinawa had earned the right to say whatever they wanted. Ruark hadn't been there.

It took some nerve to complain about Hawaii in the face of the Pacific war. Griping was different. Everybody griped. Griping was a way to pass the time. But to insist, even in humor, that Hawaiian duty was a taste of "the horrors of war" pushes at the boundaries of credibility.

At the same time, Ruark understands that war is not only combat. In his undeniably funny attack on Hawaii, he begins to show the difficulties the men experienced—difficulties that have little to do with laundry or buses and everything to do with their sense of themselves as individuals. GI Joe: the servicemen took their name from the label "Government Issue," finding that their identity, like the clothes they wore, came from Uncle Sam.[78] The uniform didn't allow much individuality—that was the point. But it was a shock to be treated as a uniform, as a generic GI, when you still felt like Frank, Gene, Sam, or Bob. The people they passed on the street or tried to make conversation with on buses, they felt, never saw them as individuals, but only as GIs—and so treated them impersonally, and with some distrust.

The men felt it. Some understood the problems the residents of Honolulu faced. How could they give to so many? How could they distinguish among the multitudes? How could they open themselves emotionally to men whose lives were elsewhere, or to men who were likely to be shipped out with no warning and who might not come back?

Some of the GI's also understood the uglier and sadder side of it. They understood about the barriers of class and the haole fears about social hierarchy. The war complicated things, but it didn't entirely change them. The uniform was still a badge of class. That distance was harder to forgive.

Whether with understanding or with bewilderment, the men felt their exclusion, and used it to explain their feelings toward Hawaii. "I don't feel a closeness because I don't feel a part of it," said one veteran of eighteen months on the rock. "I am one of a mass which is a necessary evil. . . ." The chorus was plaintive: "I am branded, whatever I do"; "The people who are anything on the Islands want nothing to do with servicemen. I think the uniform makes the difference"; "The fact that I am wearing a uniform works against me." A contemporary sociologist concluded that the servicemen were "keenly aware of their loss of individuality" and desperately wanted to be regarded by the island residents "as individuals and not 'G.I.'s."[79] Many war workers also found that they had traded in their individuality—and hadn't even gotten a uniform in return. Men longed to be treated as individuals. Men longed for that glance of recognition that did not stop at the uniform—be it the dirty work clothes of war workers or the khakis or whites of the services. Honolulu teased them with promises unfulfilled and possibilities unrealized. Honolulu seemed sometimes like a double betrayal: it was not the place of myth, nor was it home.

Feeling themselves in limbo, the men sought a sense of place in other ways. Hawaii was full of young men who did not belong there and who did not want to be there. That much, at least, they had in common, and they forged a culture based on their shared youth and shared destiny. There, some found a temporary home.

2
Culture of Heroes

Whether they had left home as volunteers or draftees, the men and women who came to Hawaii had to accept the fierce discipline of war and the nearly absolute authority of the war-making machine. In Hawaii, a place made strange to these men and women by its ethnic mix, its cultural differences, its startling beauty, its militarization, old ways had to be put aside, even if only partially and temporarily. In Hawaii, men and women from the mainland had to remake themselves in service to the war.

The life stories that follow make no simple argument about how the nexus of war and Hawaii changed Americans' views of themselves or each other. These stories are meant only to show how complicated the questions of self-identity and the meaning of Americanism became in the cultural caldron of wartime Hawaii.

In the last weeks of 1944, Fred Haynes watched the men of the 28th Marines, a regiment of the newly formed 5th Marine Division, run again and again through the maneuvers that had to take them up Mt. Suribachi on Iwo Jima. Haynes was an operations officer in the regiment and it was his job, among others, to train the men, to make them combat ready. Some of the 28th had hit other beaches, while serving with other units, but many, including Captain Fred Haynes, would be facing combat for the first time at Iwo Jima.

Hawaii was the perfect place to practice the 5th Marine Division's strategic mission. Command had identified a volcanic cone on the slopes of Mauna Kea very like the one the Marines would have to ascend. The beaches on the northern shore of the Big Island could be used to practice the landing. Scrubby, junglelike areas, similar to the kind that was believed to cover much of their target, were just a few miles east. The sprawling Parker Ranch that the Marine Corps had leased—at $1 a year—for the duration, was alive with combat training. The volcanic cone that so much resembled Mt. Suribachi and the surrounding scrub had been marked off by tennis-court tape into a mock-up of the northwest end of Iwo.

Very few civilians lived in this Hawaii. The men trained well away from unwelcome observation or possible diversion. They scrambled over abrasive lava rock and sandy scrub with live machine-gun fire just overhead, artillery bursts exploding around them. Far from home and from civilian eyes, they were trained to accept the fire of combat. Trained not to lift their heads, not to bolt and run but "to make that most agonizing and unnatural of moves, the advance into enemy fire."[1]

Their training grounds went by the name of Camp Tarawa. They were not the first Marines to be there. In December 1943, the men of the 2nd Marine Division who had taken Tarawa atoll, 2000 miles south and west of Honolulu, had come to the cool, deserted, windblown hills and stayed six months, recovering and then training for their next assaults.

Over a thousand Marines had died taking Tarawa; well over four thousand Japanese had been killed. They had fought for seventy-six hours. Marine Corps General Holland Smith had said that these men, when he saw them just after the battle, "looked older than their fathers, dirty, unshaven, with gaunt, almost sightless eyes, they had survived the ordeal but it had chilled their souls."[2] While the wounded men of the 2nd had been off-loaded in Honolulu for medical attention, those still fit for duty had been sent directly to the misty pastures high in the saddle between the dormant volcanoes Mauna Kea and Mauna Loa to build themselves a new base from which to start all over again. They had not been given shore leave in Honolulu for fear of how they might react to the sight of so many people of Japanese ancestry.[3]

When the 5th came to Camp Tarawa, it had been deserted for many months. The men of the 2nd were already back in combat. A thick layer of volcanic dust covered the rows of tents that had been built over rickety wooden decks. The mountain slopes were cold at night. It was a proud, haunted place that the men would have to remake as their own.

They were in cattle country, complete with cowboys or panio-los, as they called them locally; this was a Hawaii not known by mainland America. If you could ignore the massive black rock of Kilauea rising above the clouds to the south, the blues and greens of the Pacific visible in an occasional vista far to the north and west, and the wet jungle lands, Hilo way, you could almost imagine yourself in Texas hill country, familiar in some ways—at least to Fred Haynes.

Fred Haynes was from Texas. He looked the way people imagined a Texan—and a Marine, too—should look: tall, rawboned, ruggedly handsome. He'd been born and raised in Plano, Texas. His father had come to Texas to wildcat for oil but hadn't found any. Instead, he found the Great Depression. Fred Haynes' father's grand adventure, at least in part, had not panned out. But Fred's parents had weathered the bad time with grace and determination and Fred, with hard work and scholarships, had been able to attend college at Southern Methodist University in Dallas, graduating just before the war began. Haynes, a young man of imagination, had decided to be a scientist, and in the fall of 1941 he began a graduate program in biological sciences.

The war changed that forever. Even before Pearl Harbor, Haynes had seen it coming. A great many college students in the late 1930s, right up to the Japanese attack, had opposed American intervention in Europe. Students of the preattack years had protested, signed petitions, joined the "America First" movement, and been a part of the lobbying effort that had pushed Congress to pass—and forced Franklin Roosevelt to sign—a series of neutrality acts. But Fred Haynes had not been a part of those efforts. His father had served in World War I and the family believed in military service. When the war clouds blew in, Fred decided to volunteer, to be prepared for what he saw as the necessary and inevitable course of events. He chose the Marines. His younger brother became a Navy pilot.

Fred chose the Marines because of a book. He'd been in the

stacks of the university library, early in the fall of 1941, the coming of war on his mind. Purely by accident, his eyes fell on *Fixed Bayonets,* John Thomason's story of the Marine Corps in World War I. Standing there, he read the book straight through, and the spirit of the Marines moved him. He wanted to be a part of the Corps and he willingly embraced its traditions. Its ways, intertwined with his quickly developing sense of self, would guide his wartime actions.[4]

Shortly after Pearl Harbor, Haynes went to Quantico. He graduated near the very top of his officer candidates class. For the next year he trained incoming officer candidates, until his request for infantry duty came through.

He was assigned to the newly formed 28th Marines, the last regiment created to fill out the 5th Division. As a new regiment in a brand-new division, the officers and men of the 28th had to do at an accelerated pace what all the men and women in the service were supposed to do. They had to create respect, pride, esprit de corps, a sense of themselves as brothers-in-arms willing to die for one another. It sounds melodramatic now and it did then, too, so it was not much talked about; but that is how it was.

For Haynes, the first bond that had to be made, at a personal level, was with his NCOs. Many of his sergeants were of the old breed. They were prewar professionals, older men not predisposed to view an untested twenty-three-year-old officer with respect. Jim Harris, who'd seen action years before in the Marine Corps' campaigns in Haiti, was sergeant of Haynes' first platoon.

Harris tested Haynes early on, very publicly, casually lighting a cigarette during close order drill, just to see how the young officer would respond to a petty but glaring infraction by a more seasoned subordinate. That Haynes quietly chided Harris without hesitation showed the sergeant and everyone else what all needed to know: Haynes was comfortable with his command, age and relative inexperience not withstanding. Haynes knew the men needed him to be a firm, certain leader. He felt firm in his command and, in turn, believed in his superiors.

The most important thing in Haynes' universe in the months at Camp Tarawa was training, preparing the regiment for Iwo Jima. Haynes and the other officers were building on the time the men had spent in Camp Pendleton in southern California preparing for beach and jungle assaults. Most of the men had expected when they left Pendleton that they'd be fighting the Japanese in a few weeks or even sooner.

But Japanese tenacity in Angaur and Peleliu had slowed down the STALEMATE operation that the 5th had been sent across the Pacific to participate in. Command could not send the 5th forward. As a result, it was taken off alert and ordered to continue training. The men would have roughly another five months to prepare.

As an operations and training officer, it was Haynes' job to make the best possible use of that time. Haynes and other officers reviewed combat developments in Saipan, Tinian, Guam, and Peleliu and incorporated their lessons into training exercises. They pushed the men, worked them hard to gain an edge and keep the time from weighing on them.

The Marines took pillboxes under live fire. They formed boat teams and hit the beaches. They did it over and over again. A few men died in training, victims of an errant shell or a moment of uncontrolled panic. But exposure to the sounds and sights of war would help many others to survive. Haynes lived and breathed the training of the men; what could be done, would be done, he vowed to himself.[5]

At Camp Tarawa, men from all over the United States learned to trust and work with one another. While it might seem like a Hollywood film, it was nonetheless true; the immigrant Czech coal miner and the boy fresh from a West Virginia hollow and the New York City street kid learned to do their job together. Sergeants and corporals and even PFCs took turns leading and commanding groups of men. The Marines had learned that the Japanese would deliberately pick off combat officers, and other men had to be prepared to step forward and take command. Haynes himself learned to work with men far different and far less directed than himself. He learned to trust others. He came to believe very seriously in a simple lesson: normal men, very young men, if well trained, can do extraordinary things.

Haynes met men of unexpected temperaments. The regimental adjutant, thirty-four-year-old Joe Cason, was a "retread," an "old

man" who'd voluntarily thrown over civilian life to serve. Before he
joined the Marines, Cason had been an archeologist working on the
riddles of the Mayan civilization in the jungles of Central America.
He brought to the 38th Regiment a chivalric flair that Haynes, at
least, found perfect.

Soon after arriving on Hawaii, Cason met a deputy manager of
one of the local sugarcane plantations. The overseer, like many of
the managers on the island, was of Scottish descent. It turned out
that he had a set of bagpipes. Cason learned how to play the pipes
and he wasn't bad. Past nightfall at Camp Tarawa, when the day's
training had ended, Cason would play the pipes. Over the hills into
the cool night air, Cason would send the ghostly, martial notes. He
had the idea that he would pipe the men onto the beach at Iwo Jima
(he tried, but enemy fire almost immediately forced him to throw
the pipes over and hit the sand; toward the end of the battle the
mangled instrument was somehow turned over to G-2, who initially
thought they were some kind of secret Japanese weapon).

Sometimes as Cason played, Roscoe the regimental lion would
be moved to roar. The lion had come with the 5th Division from
their previous training grounds in southern California. Some of the
men had managed to convince a zoo keeper in Los Angeles to sell
them a lion cub for $25. The commanding officers let it pass and the
cub had sailed with the men to Hawaii, been quarantined for several
weeks and then, more lion than cub, rejoined the men at Camp
Tarawa. He was kept on a set of chains near the camp's center. The
men of the 5th, on their shoulders a scarlet shield and gold V
pierced by a blue spearhead, were pleased to have a lion for their
division mascot; it was one of those things that took your mind off
the deadly seriousness of the training, and what was coming after-
ward. Between Roscoe's occasional roaring and the bagpipes' mel-
ancholy wail, nightfall at Camp Tarawa could be a scene of strange
tranquility.

Not long before shipping out for Iwo Jima, Fred Haynes stood
on a hilltop with a fellow officer and watched thousands of his
Marines run through the maneuvers that would take them up the
left flank of Mt. Suribachi. He was, he understood with detached
pride, a small but vital part of a war that needed to be fought.

Fred Haynes was not typical. Among other things, his father had been a Shakespearean actor, and as he prepared himself and his men for Iwo Jima in the first days of the last year of the war, Haynes could find the distance and the intimacy to believe: "We few, we happy few, we band of brothers;/For he today that sheds his blood with me shall be my brother."[6] Most men trained for combat with far less appreciation of the historical resonance of their actions. Hollywood, not Shakespeare, supplied their images of heroes and the feelings of men going to war. So many of these young men knew little of the world beyond their neighborhoods. So many on their way to war in the Pacific were innocents. For most of them, Hawaii—a part of America, yet unlike the America they knew; in the war zone and yet out of the actual combat—was the first major step away from the protection of their old, familiar lives.

———

Bob Roberts was only sixteen when the Japanese bombed Pearl Harbor. It had been an unseasonably warm day in his hometown of Lorain, Ohio, where his father worked as a railroader; he and his pals were outside playing touch football when his little sister ran out with the news. None of the boys knew where or even what Pearl Harbor was. Bob had never been more than a couple of hundred miles away from home, and neither had anyone he knew.

He wanted to go to war. He wanted, he told his buddies, to be a part of the action. In his head, war looked like "a John Wayne movie."

Roberts had volunteered for the Navy as soon as he was old enough. He'd grown up by Lake Erie and liked the water. That was his main reason for choosing the Navy. He endured boot camp and gunner's-mate school, and then the hard work in advanced gunner's-mate training. But Roberts was bored. So he talked a friend into applying for sea duty with him. The war had been going on without them for more than a year-and-a-half and they were ready to fight.

Roberts was shocked by what happened after he put in his application for sea duty. He and his friend were ordered to appear before the base commander. The commander "reamed" them. In a fury, he shouted: "out there in the Pacific, people are actually getting killed!'' He said they should consider themselves lucky to be still in training school. Roberts went away with his tail between his legs but he was far more upset about being bawled out than about what his commander was trying to tell him. He was eighteen and "getting killed" was not real to him.

Just before he shipped out, Roberts ran into some old friends from Lorain, two brothers. The brothers had already been in combat. They wanted Roberts and his friends to understand. "You don't want to go out there," they kept saying. They were very emotional. Too emotional. Not shell-shocked or out of control; just insistent that the boys should understand. But they wouldn't really explain or describe anything, except to say that it was mean and rough and that you could come back with a piece of your self gone or not come back at all.

"When you hear this," Roberts thought, "it doesn't register because you are in one piece. You hear about it but you can't really have a feel for it. You have to go through it and then you can understand it."

Through all this, Roberts kept a diary. It was against naval regulations to do so since the enemy could make use of any information recorded therein if a diary fell into their hands. Few men in the combat zone kept them. But Roberts thought the diary helped him sort things out. There was much about the war he did not understand.[7]

He would understand soon enough. But first, there was more waiting. His training complete, Roberts and several of his classmates made the long crossing to Hawaii where they were barracked at Aiea, near Pearl, to wait for a ship. The men had only the clothes in their ditty bags and the money in their pockets. Their pay records were sealed and their sea bags were stored, all awaiting ship assignment. Roberts waited three months, broke and without a change of clean clothes.

To Bob Roberts, broke and uncomfortable, Hawaii did not seem like the place he had seen in the movies. It was filled with sailors like himself. And though the civilians who walked the streets and staffed the shops looked different from the people back home in Lorain, they were not particularly exotic or beautiful. Mainly, they were just not particularly interested in him. Time passed slowly. He felt neither here nor there.

Everyone, he came to realize, was after money.[8] And if you didn't have money nobody cared about you. This didn't make him angry; it was just a piece of new information.

The most important piece of information, the one for which he had been anxiously waiting, came July 3, 1944. Roberts was assigned to the U.S.S. *Enterprise,* the aircraft carrier that had been out on a shakedown cruise when the Japanese bombed Pearl Harbor; thus, the Lucky E.

Roberts was disappointed. He had wanted a destroyer, "something that would move fast and see a lot of action." In just a few weeks he'd be wiser, more experienced. Then he would know he hadn't known what he was asking for while he waited in Hawaii: soon enough he would understand that he didn't really want to be on a destroyer. But that knowledge would come only with experience.

Once he received his orders, everything accelerated. After months of having absolutely no money, he and his friends got their back pay and three days of liberty. They vowed to make up for lost time and headed down to Hotel Street, to see what they called the "pleasure palaces, cat houses, whore houses." Roberts didn't want to go in. They stared at the lines, long lines everywhere. Men lined up for the prostitutes, for liquor, for tattoos, for shooting galleries, for a bad steak. Jostling, laughing, bored men in sailor white crowded the streets.

They got their pictures taken with the hula girls, posing in front of a painted backdrop of palm trees. The girls wore grass skirts and low cut blouses. They were barefoot. For Roberts, that would be the only woman's embrace he would enjoy before going off to war. He sent the picture home, of him and his hula girl.

They went drinking. For Roberts, it was his first taste of beer. It made him feel good even as he realized, finishing his fourth bottle, that the beer was making decisions for him. Roberts, all of a sudden, became a drinking man. Everyone around him, it seemed, drank as much as they could as often as they could. Roberts joined the many men who would use beer and liquor and whatever other alcoholic beverages they could concoct to help get through the boredom and the tension and the flashes of horror they would have to endure.[9]

Roberts and his shipmates had their three days. After all the schooling and waiting, it was time to go. A battle waited for them in the Marianas. Roberts noted, "Our last fling, our only fling in Honolulu. So now we're headed for the South Pacific to see what it's all about. None of us knowing what to expect."[10]

When the *Enterprise* left Pearl Harbor, carrying Bob Roberts, Tony Capanna watched from where he was working on another ship. He'd seen the *Enterprise* leave before and he'd seen her come in for repairs after she had been hit in the Eastern Solomons in October 1942. He knew what the *Enterprise* had done and what she had weathered and he had great respect, even a kind of love, for her.

Like the tens of thousands of other men and women who came to Hawaii as war workers and spent their war years there, Capanna never saw combat or faced enemy gunfire. But he, like others at the shipyard, did see the wounded come off the ships. As a fellow worker wrote home:

> I seen something yesterday that made my heart ache, the hospital ship pull in from the big Battle at the Marshall Islands. I wish some people back there could have been there to see it. . . . They give their lives, arms, legs and eyes. God have mercy on them. I know I will never lose a days work while the war is on.[11]

Tony Capanna saw the men come back and he worked on their ships, readying them for what they had to do, repairing them after they'd been hit; and the war, though distant, was real for him, too.[12]

He had been working at the Kaiser shipyards in southern California before the Pearl Harbor attack. Twenty years old then, he was making more money than he had thought possible and his parents, "peasants from Italy," in his words, were proud of him.

Capanna was a highly skilled welder. He'd been working on cars and engines since he was a kid and he had a gift for mechanical work. In his off-time, he built and raced hot rods. When Pearl Harbor was attacked, he'd been tinkering around with a crazy car he'd gotten hold of, a sixteen-cylinder limited-production limousine. Fixing up cars was what he loved best and it was where he felt most comfortable. He had a harder time mixing with people; Tony was extremely shy.

Pearl Harbor had not meant much of anything to Capanna when he first heard about it. But by the end of the next day, after listening to the radio and the president's declaration of war and to other people talking, he began to understand the full seriousness of what had changed in the world, and decided to enlist. He would fight for the country that had given him and his family opportunity and a home. Every day for the next week, after work, he went to the recruiting station to sign up. But each day, standing outside, he felt so shy and nervous about going in and talking to the recruiters and mixing with all the other boisterous men who jammed the little station that he couldn't make himself do it. He was working up his nerve and probably would have gone in, when December 14th, the Sunday after the attack, he saw a notice up on the bulletin board at the Kaiser shipyard. Welders were desperately needed in Pearl Harbor. Without really thinking about it, Capanna signed up.

Just days later, Capanna was scheduled to leave for immediate assignment at the Pearl Harbor shipyard. He almost didn't make it. A couple of nights before embarkation Tony went out hot-rodding one last time. As had happened many times in the past, the police came after him for speeding. Tony had already accumulated a good many tickets, so he decided, in a questionable call, to make a run for it in the high-performance limo. The police, assuming the car was stolen, made a major effort to bring him down. Brought before a judge the next day, he received a sentence of thirty days in jail. After the sentence was passed but before Tony was hauled away, a Navy officer whom the Capannas had contacted came forward and explained to the judge that Tony was needed for the war effort and that, if released, he would be gone from Los Angeles a lot longer than thirty days. Capanna was released. He was on his way, he thought, to Pearl Harbor.

One more delay remained, however. In an indication of the need for speed, the Navy flew Tony and other skilled shipyard workers up to San Francisco to catch a transport ship to Honolulu.

The First Strange Place

While the men waited there, with hundreds of other war workers and armed forces personnel, they were bused to a shabby hotel to spend a night or two. At the hotel, the men paired off for room assignments.

Tony hung back out of shyness until just he and one other man were left. The remaining man was black. Tony, who'd worked with black men at Kaiser, thought nothing of this. And when he was introduced to another black war-worker who hit him up for a five-dollar loan, he shook hands on the deal without thinking about it.

After several days of waiting, with all the men he'd flown up with from San Francisco long gone, Tony screwed up his courage and asked the navy officer in charge when he was going to get on a ship. The officer looked at him with distaste and in a strong southern accent asked him why he had elected to sleep with a colored man? And why, the officer continued, did Capanna give five dollars to a second Negro? In the officer's opinion, the only reason Tony could have roomed with one Negro and then given money to another was that he was "queer." Capanna was being held in San Francisco, despite the critical need for his skills at Pearl Harbor, because his conduct with black men was beyond the pale of this officer's understanding of decent behavior.

Tony, though mystified, tried to explain. Whether he was believed or not, at any rate he finally found himself in Hawaii. When he first saw Pearl Harbor, he was horrified. Partly burned and sunken ships still lay in the harbor and the signs of destruction were everywhere. The people back at home, he thought, have no idea how bad it is here. Capanna was furious with President Roosevelt who, he felt, had somehow let the attack happen in order to push America into the war.

The first few months in Hawaii were tough. Both civilians and the military feared that the Japanese would come back. There was a rigid curfew at night, as well as a total nighttime blackout. People were scared, and military dependents and many of the island's well-to-do haole women and children were being evacuated to the mainland. At the shipyard, with tension so high, workers were pushed— and pushed themselves—to repair the damage and strengthen the fleet's offensive and defensive capacity. The yard was working around the clock for months with only two shifts. Capanna often worked from six at night until seven-thirty the next morning. It was several weeks before he got a single day off, and then for months his schedule was eight days on and one day off.

Tony's job was grueling. All shift long, he worked with the torch. That meant dragging a heavy gas cable, his mask, and the heavy steel box filled with his tools wherever he went. Mainly he welded gun mounts down and affixed the half-inch plates that shielded gunners from the enemy. But he also did whatever other welding repair work was needed. He came to know the ships with which the Navy waged war and he marveled at the engineering genius that went into their construction. He did not just feel he was doing a job because it paid well; he felt pride in his work and a personal obligation to do it as well as he could.

Still, some things bothered Tony. Sometimes, it seemed that a third of his time was spent repairing ships that had run into each other. One time the *Washington* came into Pearl with practically no bow left after a major collision with the *Indiana*. It just seemed so unnecessary.

Worse accidents occurred, however. One time a British plane, practicing dive bombing close to the Navy Yard, failed to pull up in time and exploded into a train full of arriving workers. Many died. The worst accident happened in May 1944, right in the harbor, when a string of LSTs with loaded ammunition somehow caught fire and exploded. One hundred and twenty-seven men died in the conflagration; 380 were injured.

The facts of the LST explosion were horrible enough. Because of censorship and secrecy, few in Hawaii trusted that they really knew what happened or how many were hurt, despite an official announcement detailing the casualties four days after the explosion. As one worker wrote, in a censored letter, "Maybe a year or so from now the real story will appear and it will knock your ears off when you hear it. It may come out sooner as no doubt our pal Tokyo Rose will have the details on it and will broadcast it and then the OWI will release the story." Some of the war workers felt betrayed by the military's decision to keep so many important things from them—the LST catastrophe was just one of many—and horrific rumors about the explosion continued to circulate.[13]

Tony Capanna, though sad and angry, took the explosions and

the other Navy Yard accidents in stride. There were many disquieting things in war that he felt obliged simply to register and accept. Right from the start, for example, he was shocked at how many prejudices the men had. Most of the anger flared between white men from the South and the increasing number of black men who came to work in the yard. Though the Navy hired local men and women to work in and around Pearl Harbor, they relied overwhelmingly on mainland recruits for their civilian work force.

The Navy, too, worried over the level of racial and ethnic antagonism. The authorities had intelligence agents in the yard, looking not only for saboteurs and spies but also for racial and ethnic provocateurs. The Navy also instituted elaborate procedures to sample the tens of thousands of outgoing letters in order to measure the war workers' social attitudes. Naval intelligence charted wartime race relations, and devised strategies for easing racial and ethnic antagonisms.[14]

Despite the angry words that flew around the yard, only a few major brawls or riots erupted and Tony always had the good fortune to be far away from them. Capanna simply did his best to ignore the slurs and epithets that passed for normal conversation. He worked alongside a full-blooded Hawaiian pipefitter and did a rough job in tandem with a black boilermaker. He had worked in integrated settings before and felt comfortable with all those who could pull their weight. Most men, he knew, worked well with each other. The prejudices were unfortunate but rarely got in the way.

Mainly, Tony worked. And when he wasn't working, he was usually at Navy Housing just a mile from Pearl Harbor. For ten dollars a month he got a bunk in one of the units where he lived with a dozen or so other men. They had maid service every day and within a few hundred feet was an all-purpose store, a laundry, and the cafeteria. Tony thought it was fine.

Tony himself was something of a rarity. He didn't drink or smoke or chase women. He did, however, get some vicarious thrills from his bunk mate Billy Morrison,[15] who seemed to be involved in every scam and hustle on the island. Morrison was an excellent welder but he got away with things nobody else even dreamed of. He had a brand-new Harley-Davidson sold nowhere on the island. How he got it, nobody knew. Stranger yet, despite tight rationing, he seemed to have unlimited gasoline. And against all regulations, he parked the motorcycle right on the unit's front porch. The naval officers who oversaw the housing area just gave him a wink when he hauled it up there.

One night, Tony came home with his flashlight on. Morrison hissed at him, from the darkness, to turn it off fast. The next morning, he told Capanna that he'd busted up a big card game, run by a navy chief, at the recreation center, when he'd noticed they were using a marked deck. He showed Tony the deck which he'd grabbed off the table. When he'd said the game was rigged, the chief went after him; Morrison was hiding in the unit when Tony had come in.

On a regular basis, during his rare days off, Morrison used his motorcycle to take prostitutes from the Hotel Street brothels over the Pali to the beaches on the windward side of the island. He spent a lot of time in the vice district and somehow had gotten to be a trusted friend to some of the women. More than once, Tony saw Morrison with a fat roll of hundred-dollar bills that he had gotten from the prostitutes. Morrison told Tony that he banked money for a few of the women.

Tony and some of the others decided that Morrison worked for naval intelligence and that was how he got away with breaking so many of the housing rules. It explained, too, how he knew so much about the vice district and why he was always looking into scams being pulled off in the Pearl area. Tony, who made it his business to keep his nose clean, got a kick out of his mysterious bunk mate who traveled in such strange circles.

Tony lived in a world made up almost completely of men. Only a very few women worked in the Navy Yard and none lived or ate at the housing area where Tony spent most of his time off. Tony's world was different from the one of the sailors and soldiers he saw so often in that he did not face the possibility of combat and his off-time, what little he had, was his own. But like theirs, his was a world without family and overwhelmingly without women. In Hawaii, he had to, in many ways, make a new life—a life overwhelmingly shaped by the war.

He correctly saw his work as being critical to the war effort and his role as a patriotic one. He was angry when a Marine officer, off-loading a large group of Japanese prisoners, yelled at him and other men who were gawking to get back to work "and earn your money." He felt the insult, the contempt the Marine felt toward him and the others who were not in uniform. Capanna knew his risks were much less than those men in the armed forces who had to face enemy fire, but he also felt that in signing up to work at Pearl Harbor, just days after the attack—when no one could have said whether or not the Japanese would come back—he had proved his mettle. Tony Capanna, like Bob Roberts as he headed out of Pearl Harbor on the *Enterprise,* could not know in advance what his war would be like. He had done his best in his time in Hawaii to do right by himself and his country.[16]

The women who came to Hawaii did not know what their war would be like either. Until the last few months, when WAVES and WACS and other women in the armed forces were stationed there, almost all of them were volunteer war workers or nurses. They came, overwhelmingly, in a spirit of adventure and patriotism. Most of the women worked as clericals in the hundreds of offices serving the Central Pacific war machine. Despite the tedium of much of their work, they found a new world that offered them an extraordinary, though often difficult, time.

Madelyn Busbee was from Lilly, Georgia, a town of 300.[17] The Depression had hit her hometown hard. She knew how lucky she was that her father had managed a steady income during the bad times; he was one of the few in her community to do so. Still, if it hadn't been for her grandmother, who'd managed to save during better times, even food and clothes would have been uncertain during much of the 1930s.

By 1942, life was much better for the Busbees. Madelyn had learned to type through a special school program made possible by the New Deal's National Youth Administration. The same program had also supplied her with a job cleaning the school where she studied. The NYA course and job had inspired her to go on for more education, and with the help of her older sister, she'd finished a two-year-college teaching degree by the time the war began. The teaching job paid $540 a year.

Madelyn dreamed of going on to a regular college. She wanted more than Lilly, Georgia, could offer her. As Madelyn saw it, "life was very simple in my home town. The people I knew were church-going, hard-working, small-town people." She knew little about the larger world and about what she could accomplish, given the chance. The war would help her free herself from the limits of her background. Like most working women, Madelyn gave up her "respectable" and poorly paid "lady's" job as soon as she could, and became a typist at much better pay at Warner Robbins Air Force Base, a sixty-mile commute from her small town.

The world of Robbins Air Force Base was shockingly, excitingly different. Tens of thousands of men came and went, preparing for war. Though combat was thousands of miles away, the feel of the war, the reality of people sacrificing their old lives for what was to come was palpable and pressing. Patriotism was not just an abstract idea. It consisted of the things that people around her were doing.

When a notice came around asking for volunteers willing to go into the war zone and work at Hickam Field and the Hawaii Air Depot, Madelyn and some seventy-five other women workers at Robbins stepped forward. Madelyn wanted to be of service. She also recognized the chance for adventure. (It would be several months between that time and her actual embarkation for Hawaii; waiting for orders was an experience millions of Americans—civilians and enlisted personnel—would have during the war years.)

Madelyn's parents didn't want her to go. Even after she and her grandmother had together overcome their objections, they still feared for her safety. Her father went so far as to call on Georgia's Senator Walter George in an attempt to have Madelyn's troop transport ship stopped and his daughter sent home when he learned that enemy submarines were operating in the Pacific. But Madelyn and her ship were out of his control.

Busbee crossed the Pacific in a group with the other women from Warner Robbins. Their ship also carried hundreds of soldiers. The men and women were barred from visiting with one another.

To insure the segregation of the sexes, the young women could not leave their staterooms without Marine escort. And because of the real threat of torpedo attack, the women had orders to keep their Mae West life jackets on at all times, even while they slept. The constant zigzagging of the ship combined with high seas made almost all of them seasick for the entire tense week of travel. It was no cruise ship.

Upon arrival, Madelyn and the other women were surprised by what they saw. As Madelyn's friend, Marcene Giddens, wrote, "I looked out and wondered where are the palm trees, flowers and hula girls? Instead it was dirty green and tan camouflage tents, quonset huts and streets filled with heavy equipment . . . trucks, ammo carriers, jeeps, gator tanks." Men were everywhere; the landscape was awash in khaki and white. There "must have been millions. It was awesome," wrote Marcene.[18]

The women war workers were immediately sent by bus to a barracks right on Hickam Field. The women expected, based on the recruitment notices they had read, to be housed in one bedroom apartments. Madelyn, like the others, drew a tiny room with a cement floor just big enough for an army canvas cot, a wooden chair, and a two-drawer chest. The entire barracks area was surrounded by an eight-foot barbed-wire fence, with twenty-four-hour patrol at the gates and around the perimeter. Since the threat of Japanese attack was nonexistent by the time they arrived (November 1944), the wire served only one purpose: it kept men out. A large wooden sign inside the gates made matters clear: "OFF LIMITS TO MEN."[19]

Madelyn wanted to use her spare time in Hawaii toward furthering her education. As soon as she got her regular work schedule, she decided to begin night courses at the University of Hawaii. To get to UH she had to make a long bus trip which meant, she knew, that by the time she got back it would be dark: before curfew, but definitely dark. Busbee thought little of the late hour. She was "still in the world where there was no need to be afraid. Didn't we ride the train at home and walk home alone in the middle of the night? Didn't we sleep with all the windows and doors open?"

Busbee did notice, on her first bus trip back from the university, that she was the only woman on the bus. Still, the bus left her off right in front of Hickam's guarded main gates. And from there she had only to walk on the field, then through the guarded gates at the barbed-wire fence. It seemed of little consequence compared to the thrill she felt about starting her new degree program.

Her "bubble burst" the very first night. Waiting in a jeep at the front gate was a soldier Busbee had befriended. He had found out from her barrack mates that she was coming home alone. He was furious at Busbee. Didn't she know how dangerous it was for a woman alone to go anywhere after dark! He gave her an angry tongue-lashing that left Busbee feeling lucky to have made it safely as far as the front gates and convinced that night classes were out of the picture. He drove her the few hundred yards through the dark, still base, to the barbed-wire enclosure of her home away from home. College would have to come after the war.

Was the soldier right to issue so severe a warning? Certainly, no orders had been issued by military command restricting women's travel before curfew. No rapes of women walking home through Hickam Field were reported during the war years. But despite evidence that women were not physically molested on the base, some of the men had good reason to fear for their women friends' safety. The soldiers in and around Hickam reveled in rough talk about sex. They carried on constantly about the lack of women, especially white women from "home." All the talk and griping contributed to a mood of angry desperation in which women figured somehow as both cause and cure.

In large part, the anger and solicitude of Madelyn Busbee's soldier friend reflected less the literal danger of rape than his concern that Madelyn, a woman walking alone through the dark, would be harassed and propositioned, taken as an "amateur" prostitute, subjected to gross vulgarity. She might be grabbed and fondled. It was important to him, as it was to the men who had guarded the women on the ship and at their barracks, that their "respectability" be protected and preserved.

Though women, especially white women, were in extraordinary demand and would be courted in extravagant ways, Hawaii during the war was also very much a man's world. Many of the men understood this and meant to protect women from the dangers and unpleasantness of a world in which drunk men with "war nerves" were a potentially explosive fact of life.[20] Both the risk and the protection put limits on the life that mainland women could make for themselves in Hawaii.

Madelyn, partly due to the solicitude of her many male friends, and partly due to the fact that she restricted herself to very few adventures without male companions, went through the war years without unpleasant incident. In fact, very little of the war's unpleasantness reached her at all. The soldiers she dated, she slowly came to understand, kept from her "the horror and heartache of the war." And thanks to her many suitors, whose access to a jeep was the prerequisite for a date, she saw much of the beauty of Oahu—as much as her six-day workweek at the Hawaii Air Depot allowed.

As she had done at home, she started every Sunday by attending a church service. However, she allowed her Sunday morning date to take her, in his jeep, to the church of his choice. Part of Madelyn Busbee's Hawaiian adventure was a multidenominational tour of Protestantism. She collected many of the church programs just as she collected the exotic menus from the Chinese restaurants she came to adore in Honolulu.[21] They marked her passage to a larger world.

Most of the people she worked with were whites from the mainland. But her supervisor was a local woman of Chinese descent, and the two women became lifelong friends. Madelyn's duties included teaching typing to enlisted men. To her surprise, her class included black as well as white soldiers, a situation which had never occurred when she was teaching school in Georgia. The class went fine, without incident; all of the soldiers were polite and treated her with respect. It was a learning experience for her, too. (As a teacher in Georgia after the war, Busbee—by then Laidler—would not have black students again until 1976.)

Madelyn Busbee felt herself change in Hawaii. She became stronger and more sure of herself. Hawaii had welcomed her and taught her much. Few women left wartime Hawaii without feeling that their sense of the world and how they fit into it had irrevocably changed.

When Rosie Altieri decided to leave home for Hawaii, it was with a slightly different sense of her possibilities than Madelyn Busbee.[22] Born in 1921, Altieri had grown up in and around New York City. Her father was a successful lawyer and her mother, in Rosie's words, was a "southern belle and very ladylike." Rosie decided, midwar, that she wanted to do something special for the war effort, partly out of patriotism, partly because some of her friends had signed up to go to Hawaii with the Red Cross, and partly because she wanted to do something terrifically adventurous and exciting. Rosie was already doing volunteer work with the National Catholic Community Service, a component of the U.S.O., and she found out through them that she could work for the U.S.O. in Hawaii. Her only concern was convincing her mother and father to let her go.

She waited until her mother was lying down before she broke the news. She expected a long argument and perhaps a few tears. Instead, her mother sat bolt upright and announced that one of her few regrets in life was that she hadn't gone to France during World War I to help the boys and that she thought Rosie must let nothing get in the way of her patriotic adventure. Rather than an argument, Rosie received a new tropical wardrobe from her excited parents.

Altieri was horribly seasick on the way over, and also very scared when her transport ship broke down—still hundreds of miles from Hawaii. When at last the ship reached Honolulu, she decided to make herself up with extra care and to put on one of her more spectacular new outfits: a black sundress, black high heels, a very fashionable black hat, and a pair of slim, very dark sunglasses. The dress had a tight-fitting bolero jacket that in the midday heat, she carried over her arms. Twenty-three years old and very attractive, she looked far more sophisticated than she really was.

As she took her place in line to disembark, a woman sidled up to her and hissed in her ear, "You're not going to wear that disgusting dress!!??" Taken aback, Altieri told the older woman, a kamaaina returning to the islands, that she would put her jacket on. She thought little of the incident, until later, as she stumbled in her high heels down the gangway and into her new life.

The First Strange Place

Waiting for Rosie and the three other, much older, new U.S.O. volunteers were two cars and drivers. The volunteers were greeted enthusiastically with many hugs and leis. With much bustling about, the drivers loaded all of the suitcases and trunks into the back seat of one of the cars. The driver asked Rosie to sit up front in his car while the others were escorted to the backseat of the second car. Rosie was completely charmed; the aloha spirit, the smell in the air, the landscape of mountains and ocean—it was everything she had imagined and more. Even the car was magnificent, an old-fashioned convertible touring car complete with running boards and wood-and-leather interior.

As she and her driver moved into downtown Honolulu, just a couple of blocks from the pier, sailors and soldiers began pointing and gesturing toward the car. Suddenly, dozens of men began running alongside. Some jumped onto the running boards and pressed in, waving scraps of paper and pens at Rosie, yelling and calling out. Rosie was startled and amazed and didn't understand.

"What do they want?" she asked the driver.

"Your autograph," he told her.

Dressed as she was, with her looks, being driven through town in the U.S.O.'s most luxurious automobile, the men assumed she was a Hollywood starlet in town to entertain the troops. She signed dozens of autographs. She loved it.

After a whirlwind tour, Altieri was taken, of all places, to the Army-Navy YMCA until regular housing could be found. An officer who'd met her on the ship had already asked her out for dinner that evening, so she ran up to her little room and showered and changed. Since the officer had promised her the best dinner Honolulu could offer, she put on one of her prettiest new outfits: an elegant off-one-shoulder white and pink flowered dress. She had a pair of pink high heels to match.

Since her officer was not allowed upstairs, she came down into the large front lobby to meet him. By the time she reached the bottom, a human wall of soldiers and sailors besieged her from every side. She was mobbed by what seemed like hundreds of men, all of whom wanted to talk to her, touch her, be recognized by her. She found it very pleasant but frightening, too. She thought later that there ought to be a special medal for resisting the advances of American soldiers.

Soon enough, Rosie was posted to a U.S.O. club and began her work. Over the next few months, she moved around some and took on a variety of tasks before settling in at the King Kam Club near Schofield Barracks and Wheeler Air Field. She was in charge of the library and writing room, and floral arrangements. At the regular dances, Rosie oversaw the young women who came to help out.

At the Club she became close friends with an older married couple, the Spurlocks, black Catholics from Georgia. "Imagine being black *and* Catholic in the South," they laughingly told her. She admired their spirit and their abilities. Mrs. Spurlock taught arts and crafts to the men at the Club and she took Altieri on as an assistant. The three of them became close and went to church together. She had other good friends. She loved her work.

On free nights, Altieri went on a whirl of dates. She went out with sailors and marines and men from the Army. She dated officers and enlisted men. Her only rule was that the man who asked her out must be a gentleman, well-behaved and well-mannered. Luck was with her and she never had a problem. Instead, she met a great many delightful men who showed her the town.

Altieri lived back in the mountains in a U.S.O. house. Two older single women who also worked for the U.S.O. lived in the little house with her. Rosie was fascinated by her neighbors and talked and mixed with them frequently. She noted that many of the couples came from different ethnic backgrounds. They had intermarried, sometimes across racial lines. Rosie took this as another part of the wonder of Hawaii and delighted in meeting people whose ways were so unlike what she had known at home.

Rosie even found herself mistaken for a "local girl." She took the bus to work and the drivers had taken to greeting her every morning as the "portagee girl." She had dark curly hair and the locals assumed she was of Portuguese descent, making her in island terms more like a "local" than a "haole." Altieri found the label endearing. She saw nothing wrong in being mistaken as kin to the Portuguese community in Hawaii that had come to the islands as plantation workers rather than as a member of the far more powerful haole class who controlled much of the islands' economy.

But some people viewed Altieri's island adventures with suspicion—particularly her seeming disregard for conventional boundaries. Altieri's supervisor at the King Kam Club, an older haole woman, did not approve of her young worker's ways. Altieri assumed that her boss was simply jealous of her youth, good looks, and social calendar. But it's also likely that Altieri's ready acceptance of Hawaii's mixed society, her social friendship with her black co-workers, her flamboyant style of dress, and her willingness to date men without regard to rank, struck her haole boss as signs of "unrespectability."

After Rosie had been working very happily at the King Kam Club for several months, her boss, without warning, ordered her to take a new assignment as a secretary at the U.S.O. offices in downtown Honolulu. Rosie trudged over to the U.S.O. offices where her new boss greeted her very coolly. She was an older woman, a member of the Hawaii U.S.O. board, and—most importantly in Hawaiian terms—a senior member of the all powerful "Big Five" that in many ways ran the islands.

"We understand you have been running a house of prostitution at your little house in Wahiawa," her boss announced to Rosie.

Rosie was flabbergasted and tried to defend herself against the cruel charges. She lived with two older women in the house, she said. She was an observant Catholic who went to church every Sunday with the Spurlocks. It was ridiculous, she said.

A few days later, in a misunderstanding that seemed simply incredible, she was forced out of the U.S.O., charged with being a liar and a woman of bad reputation. Her boss informed her that she and her friends would make sure that Rosemary Altieri would never find another job in Hawaii—"We'll starve you out!"

Rosie was distraught: her wonderful job, her grand adventure, the Hawaii she had come to love were all blowing up in her face. At a very practical level, she was suddenly without housing in a city in which a vacant room was harder to find than a good bottle of mainland scotch. Pulling herself together, Rosie called one of the men she had become particularly close to and asked him to pick her up.

Sergeant George Brownlee, who like Rosie had made friends on the island, came and arranged for Rosie to stay temporarily with a Japanese-American woman he knew.

Though shaken, Rosie got into gear. She wrote her father, telling him everything. She then plotted her immediate job future. The private sector, she figured was out—her old boss might be able to put the squeeze on there. But the U.S. Army, she decided, would be too big for even the Big Five to pressure. Supported by Sergeant Brownlee, Rosie applied to the Army for work. She was interviewed by Emma Chalker, a white-haired, blue-eyed, smiling woman. Rosie told her story, explaining how she had lost her job and how none of it was true and that all she wanted was a chance to work hard and stay in Hawaii.

Rosie would never forget Emma Chalker's response.

"I believe you, my dear," she said. And then, after a short pause, she asked, "Who do you date? Officers or enlisted men?"

Rosie, not sure what she was being asked, answered truthfully, "I date both. I date everybody who asks me as long as he's a gentleman."

Emma Chalker beamed at her, "You got the right answer! I've got one son who's an officer, one son who's an enlisted man! Where do you want to work?"

Rosie was posted to the 13th Replacement Depot Service Club. She worked and lived with seven other women right at the post, all of whom became lifelong friends. A few weeks later she married Sergeant Brownlee at the chapel on the base. Their local friends lined the walls and ceilings of the chapel with gardenias, the civilian cooks at the club made them a huge wedding cake, the club musicians serenaded them. And for a wedding gift, so to speak, she received a beseeching letter from the top U.S.O. official in the Central Pacific, apologizing for her mistreatment and asking her to please come back to the U.S.O.

Altieri's father had gone to the head of the U.S.O. in New York, presented the facts Rosie had given him, and demanded that matters be put right. The U.S.O. director had pulled rank on Rosie's former boss. It was a small symbol of the declining reach of Hawaii's Big Five.

But Rosie never answered the letter, nor the one that followed. All had worked out for the best, she believed.

———

Sgt. Robert Cowan saw little romance in Hawaii. For most of 1944 and through the war's end in 1945, he was an MP in Honolulu. He worked Waikiki and Hotel Street.[23]

Cowan was raised in a small town in North Dakota. His family, like so many, suffered during the Great Depression. During the bad times, he found government work clearing trails at Yellowstone National Park. Then he went off to California, looking for work, sometimes finding it and sometimes not. By the late 1930s, things started to turn around for him. He was in the California National Guard. He'd found and married a good woman (she'd been on the Queen's float in the 1931 Rose Parade). Then, just before the Japanese attack on Pearl Harbor, his unit was federalized. Robert Cowan would serve every day of the war.

A few months after the war began Cowan's division, which had been sent up to Fort Lewis, in Washington, to train, was told they were shipping out. They got a three-day leave. Cowan just had time to hitchhike down to his wife in Pasadena, say goodbye, and hitchhike back. He had no idea where he was going.

Cowan came to shore on Kauai, which was not much more than one big plantation. As far as the soldiers could tell, the biggest thing doing on Kauai was a little restaurant in Lihue that featured pineapple pie, pineapple pie, pineapple pie, and pineapple juice.

Cowan worked on trucks for nine months on Kauai. Then the division went forward, into combat. Cowan went on a couple of landings. He saw men hit by shrapnel, blown up, shot. It was so bad that he came not to talk about it. He stayed in the forward area for about a year. Almost from the first day, he had a feeling that he wouldn't come back. But it got so that it didn't bother him. He became hardened to his feelings and to other things, too. He "lived for the day and took things as they came." He was a sergeant. He talked with other sergeants.

Cowan became an MP by a quirk of fate. The division had been sent back to Schofield for reassignment. While waiting for orders, Cowan received word that his mother had had a heart attack; he received a thirty-day leave to go to her. When he returned to Schofield, his division was gone. After letting him kick around Ft. DeRussy for a few days, command decided not to send Cowan forward to his unit but to make him an MP.

Before the war, Frank Steer—an iron-willed major known to every madam and a nightclub operator in Honolulu—had been in charge of the MPs. Steer, himself a tall and powerful man, took only the tallest and biggest men for the job, men whose size alone intimidated drunks and rowdies.[24] Cowan never would have become an MP in those days. Cowan—though powerfully built—stood only about five foot eight. But during the war, conditions were different. And something about him commanded respect.

From several angles, being an MP was good duty. Cowan had a jeep to drive around in and he was allowed a lot of leeway in what he did and how he did it. Only rarely did the need for prompt action or rough duty occur. Being an MP meant that you stayed away from Task Forces and you stayed in Honolulu. Of course, men didn't like you—strictly by virtue of the band you wore on your sleeve—but that was not something to bother Cowan.

Cowan used to drive over to Hotel Street, park his jeep, and just sit there and watch. He'd watch older Japanese ladies in tight dresses walk with little steps in the street rather than fight for space with all the sailors and soldiers and concessionaires on the sidewalk. He'd watch the men lined up, hundreds of them, waiting to go upstairs to the brothels. He'd watch thousands of men step in and out of the four-drink-only bars that lined the strip.

Many of the men were drunk. Sometimes they'd start fighting or yelling or causing a nuisance. Then Cowan would have to step out of the jeep and have a word with them. If a man could talk sense, he wasn't too drunk. Cowan would tell him to quiet down and be on his way. But if a man couldn't talk or leave well enough alone, Cowan took him in. Sometimes, the men he pulled over to the jeep for a conversation would slip a little money onto his seat and Cowan would look away and tell them not to do that.

Cowan liked a drink himself, from time to time. But for an

NCO, decent liquor took some finding in Hawaii. At the NCO Club, all they had was locally brewed beer, which left a bad taste in your mouth. The one time they'd received a big order of American beer it all turned out to be flat. As an MP, Cowan confiscated a lot of liquor from drunks but it was almost always locally bottled whiskey, too awful to drink. However, as an MP, Cowan also had free access to the Officers' Clubs while they were closed—to check them out. And while he was there, he'd take a short drink from all the different bottles of good liquor, being sure to put a new mark on each one.

Officers were one of the annoyances of his job. A host of second lieutenants—ninety-day wonders—were constantly coming through Hawaii on their way to the war. Every time, it seemed, they'd pull Cowan or some other NCO up on the street with a petulant "Soldier, why didn't you salute me!" Officers seemed to be a different breed.

One day, out on pass, Cowan was heading down King Street, near Bishop, when he noticed a major's coat folded over the seat in a parked jeep. The jeep's driver told him that the major had a girlfriend down the street and had left the coat in order to be less conspicuous on his way to her apartment. Cowan, after a brief negotiation, managed to borrow it. Thereafter, for the rest of the afternoon, Cowan became an officer. He strode into a bar and clapped men on the back and acted the part of a true, if noble, democrat. The soldiers treated him like a prince and bought him drink after drink. The uniform makes the man, people always said.

If he had been caught impersonating an officer, he would have lost his stripes and probably done time. Cowan understood that but he didn't care. Dozens of times he'd caught soldiers doing stupid things. Anything for a change, they'd tell him. Maybe that's why he did it. He didn't know. It happened.

Cowan saw and learned many things. He became friends with the man who ran the slot machines in all the NCO and Officers' Clubs, and he learned how to fix the machines to control the payoff (you put a little block on the back of the winning combination to make it skip past). So many things were hustles of one kind or another.

Culture of Heroes

Sometimes, Cowan had to do things he didn't like, things that nobody liked doing. Once, he had to take a good friend to jail. A couple of times he'd had to pull his gun on soldiers in a brawl. He'd arrested some young soldiers who thought they were being funny by playing peeping tom at a nurses' quarters. One time, he'd been assigned to go up to the mountains to check over the site where two military planes had crashed. He found the guts of dead men hanging all over the telephone wires and body parts scattered around. He'd seen this before, but that didn't make it any better.

Cowan had gotten married just before the war began but on the streets and at the bars, clubs, and stores he watched over, he became friends with a number of young women. This entrée to civilian circles was a traditional perquisite of the MPs in Hawaii. When Frank Steer took over command of the Military Police, before the Pearl Harbor attack, he pulled a surprise bed-check one night and discovered that not a man was to be found; every one had a "shack job" going with a local woman. Steer put a stop to that. But access to local women, and to civilians in general, was something that made the hostility directed at MPs by most of their fellow soldiers more tolerable.[25]

Cowan had a lot of good times on the islands. He went to luaus with civilian friends. When he got a pass, he and some of the other sergeants would sometimes take women to the beaches across the Pali from Honolulu. He was able to get decent liquor, at least more often than most. Cowan even worked out a deal with a high-level civilian from Washington, D.C., to share an apartment and a car. Cowan made his time in Hawaii count but somehow much of it never really touched him.

All of it was connected: the combat, the long waits between action—any action at all—the isolation, the years away from his wife, the hostility he took just for doing his job, the sordidness, the drunkenness, the brawls, the strain of being caught between the ignorance of the enlisted men and the arrogance of the officers. The way it added up, the beauty of the Pali and the friends he made were trumped by the stupid brutality of the war and the petty ugliness of the vice he policed. Robert Cowan felt himself get hard and bitter in Hawaii.

Bob Roberts' feelings when he came back to Hawaii on the *Enterprise,* after months at war, were not, in the main, like Cowan's. True, he was harder in some ways, but for him there was really no bitterness; only a sense that now he knew how things really were and what everything meant. So much had changed for Roberts out at sea. He had seen more of the war than he ever imagined.[26]

He had watched his ship's gunners take on dive bombers and kamikazes with the five-inch guns, then the 40 mms, and then when the deadly planes started to loom overhead, the 20 mms. In the drilled chaos of fighters landing and taking off, he'd fit out his planes and then anyone else's planes, working over their 50-mm and 30-mm guns and rocket launchers. He'd learned to move with skill and economy. In weeks, he was an old hand who knew how to work under deadly pressure.

The Lucky E took considerably less damage than many of the ships around her, but in little more than a year Roberts went through seven major engagements. He saw what his friends from home had been trying to tell him back when he was at gunners'-mate school. A bomb exploded ten yards from him and seven men were blown apart. Somehow, for no reason, Roberts himself was not touched. Planes he had worked on never came back; the men, with whom Roberts had traded jokes, were dead. Off Okinawa, a kamikaze kept coming and coming through the antiaircraft fire and took the lives of fourteen men.

"In the service," Roberts realized, "you live a lot closer with shipmates than actual family. You're eating, sleeping, horsing around together, you're with each other continuously, twenty-four hours a day, you know their good points, their petty irritations. When you lose one of them it's really something."

Roberts watched his shipmates "go over the side, buried at sea, on a slab of wood, an American flag laid over them, put in a bag, a five-inch shell put in the bag so they'll sink. When they tip that board and your body slips out from under that flag and that bugler starts to play taps . . . there is not a dry eye on that ship."

The kamikaze that had killed fourteen of his shipmates forced

Culture of Heroes

the *Enterprise* to sail back to Pearl Harbor for repairs. For Roberts, time back in Honolulu was brief but very welcome. He drank and looked around and remembered when he'd been stuck at the barracks at Aiea, still more a kid from Lorain, Ohio, than a sailor in the U.S. Navy. By the time he came back to Hawaii, the *Enterprise* had become his real home, the war his frame of reference. Hawaii, so strange and exotic on the way to war, felt familiar, even comforting, on the way back. Hawaii, in the words of another returning man-at-arms, had been made new. It was no longer seen only in contrast with home or even simply a place of "rest and relaxation." For the men who'd been to war, Hawaii had become "a kind of sanctuary."[27]

3
Hotel Street Sex

The new crossroads of the world . . . it starts at the Y and ends at the
River. Long after the war is over, the boys from Podunk and Blue
Goose Hollow will tell their families with bated breath how they won
the war on Hotel Street.[1]

—Hotel Street Harry

If Hawaii was a sanctuary for some men returning from combat,
then—in the profane logic of wartime—Hotel Street was the sanc-
tum sanctorum. Hotel Street, the vice district, sat in a corner of
Honolulu's Chinatown tightly bound by River, Beretania, Nuuanu,
and Hotel Streets. People on the islands called it "the Serviceman's
Domain." It was where the men came to get drunk, to have their
pictures taken with an ersatz hula girl, to get tattooed. Hotel Street
was where the brothels were.

Within months of the attack on Pearl Harbor, 30,000 and more
soldiers, sailors, marines, and war workers killed time in the vice
district on any given day. Close to 250,000 men a month paid three
dollars for three minutes of the only intimacy most were going to
find in Honolulu.[2]

Hotel Street during the war was a rush of reeking fish markets,
overflowing tattoo parlors, dinging pinball games, sing-songing concessionaires and pushing, shouting, elbowing men in uniform and

95

out. Men stood in lines everywhere, for everything. The district had been crowded before the war swelled Hawaii's population but during the war Hotel Street pulsed with money, sex, and occasional violence.

On every corner, photographers crowded the sidewalks with their box cameras, grass huts, and cardboard palm tree backgrounds: "Two pictures with Hula Girl—75 cents." The rumor was that for $20 you could get an overnight deal with the girl of your choice. Like most rumors, it wasn't true. But the men lined up.

Barefoot shoeshine boys swarmed through the district, jibing at the soldiers and sailors in a pidgin the men could not begin to understand. The shoeshines cost a quarter. On any given day, there were more than a thousand boys on the streets looking for business. Teenage girls, most of them Hawaiian, sold flower leis. They went in and out of the bars, up and down the lines of men waiting to buy a drink or a steak or something else. The leis cost two and three times prewar prices.

In every nook and cranny of the district, men and women set up stands to sell watches, jewelry, popcorn, postcards, keepsakes. Some worked the street full-time; others, part-time. They came to catch some of the free-flowing money. Most of them were Chinese; it was Chinatown, after all. With few exceptions, every person on the street selling or posing or hawking wares and services to the haoles from the mainland was of pure or mixed Chinese, Japanese, Puerto Rican, Hawaiian, Portuguese, or Filipino descent.

Winding this way and that over the few square blocks of the district was the protean mass of khaki and white upon which the small-time operators and hustling entrepreneurs depended. Every day (including Sunday), the troops waded down the street looking for good times, money weighing down their pockets. Because of curfew and blackout regulations, every buy and deed transpired in the bright sunshine of "paradise."[3]

Kenneth Burch, a farm boy from Oklahoma, was dazzled by the scene. To him it was like a foreign country, another world. He had not known what to believe about Hotel Street or what to expect when he got there. He came, though, until he learned. When he got liberty from the Naval Air Station, he hung out at the bars; though with the long lines and terrible liquor, no one stayed at any one bar for too long. Signs were posted, warning: "WE LIMIT our customers to 4 DRINKS PER PERSON." Your four drinks often came stacked all at once. If you took too long to drink them, the bouncer, usually a big Hawaiian, moved you out to make room for the next paying customer. As a result, men often guzzled their drinks. Many men became instantly drunk.

Burch walked the crowded streets. He learned the ways of the brothels and he came to know some of the women who worked in them.[4] It was the brothels that gave Hotel Street its dark magic. The prostitutes offered the men sex, simple and uncomplicated. And for many of the boys, that was enough. Ken Burch, standing in line or watching from a bar, knew that some of the young men going up the steps to the brothels would die, never having had any other woman than the three-dollar whore they had bought while drunk in broad daylight in Honolulu.[5]

Most men didn't come to Hotel Street just for sex. To many, it seemed the only place to go to break the routine or to find some kind of human exchange. Hotel Street Harry, the columnist for the *Midpacifican*—the Army newspaper that served the Central Pacific—wrote week after week about the district. He called it the "Street of Lonely Hearts." "I don't think there is a worse feeling in the world than to be lonesome in a crowd," he wrote. "The Street is filled with men whose hearts are aching."[6]

Sometimes the emotions overflowed. Arguments turned into fist fights; a man turned away from a bar suddenly pulled a knife. Once, just outside the district, a drunken young soldier smashed a department store window and stabbed a blonde-wigged mannequin. He shouted to the fast assembling crowd, "I like the smell of blood, let me at her."[7]

Moving through the landscape of cheap souvenirs (cellophane hula skirts, silk pillow covers inscribed "I Love You Dear Mother of Mine," and "art" photos), past bars with names like "Trade Winds," "Two Jacks," and "Just Step Inn," all serving the same imitation rum and gin at the same high prices, into penny arcades (Shoot Hitler's eyes out with a slingshot; eight shots for ten cents), the men looked for something to do.[8] Anything to break the routine. Most of the time, the overwhelming experience of Hotel Street was one of boredom and disappointment. The men were looking for intensity or contact with another human being. By and large, they found neither.

For the women who owned and managed and worked the Hotel Street brothels, the men's boredom and neediness provided an inexhaustible gold mine. The men lived with scarcity: a scarcity of money, liquor, women. Many also faced a scarcity of time. The prostitutes lived—for the moment—in a time of lubricious plenty. Their story is a fascinating window on the political struggle, economic velocity, gender turn-about, and social chaos created by wartime necessities. The women of Hotel Street fought hard to keep what they felt they had earned and they enlisted an unlikely group of allies—including the provost marshal and the military governor of Hawaii—in their efforts not only to make money but to gain respectability and security. They made it their business to gain what control they could from the men who needed them.

Between 1941 and 1944, about 250 prostitutes were registered as "entertainers" with the Honolulu Police Department. Each paid $1 a year for her license and was expected to report her earnings and pay taxes on them. Approximately fifteen houses of prostitution operated in Honolulu.

Prostitution was illegal in Hawaii as it was on the mainland. Not only were there statutes against it in Hawaii, but there were federal laws against it as well. In July 1941, in preparation for an expanded armed forces, the May Act had been signed into law by Franklin Roosevelt. The May Act had broad-based support. It was meant to control the venereal diseases that had had such a significant impact on World War I manpower, but it also was a part of the political campaign to smooth out America's unpopular peacetime draft. The act clearly stated that where local officials were either unwilling or unable to do the job themselves, the federal government would stamp out any and all prostitution aimed at servicemen. With the avid support of the Women's Christian Temperance Union and many other reform groups who did not want to see a wartime loosening of morals corrupt America's youth, the May Act had been rigorously enforced. According to the Office of Defense Health and Welfare Services, 292 red-light districts were shut down almost immediately. By 1945, over 700 vice districts would be closed.

In Hawaii, the May Act had been assiduously avoided, although enforcement provisions specifically applied to American territories as well as states. Some people in Hawaii did want to take advantage of the federal act to move on the Hotel Street district, including at least one member of the Police Commission. But most of those in control of the police and the military decided to ignore the act, as they had long been ignoring local laws against prostitution that should have applied to the regulated brothels.[9]

The regulated brothels existed for many reasons. The military and many people in Hawaii approved of them because, in the face of what they saw as unstoppable urges and acts, the houses seemed to keep venereal rates relatively low. But by far the most important reason "respectable" people—including the majority of the members of the Honolulu Police Commission—not only looked the other way at regulated prostitution but approved of it, was a very simple one. An editorial in *Hawaii,* a magazine supported by the haole elite, stated it clearly:

> If the sexual desires of men in this predominately masculine community are *going to be satisfied,* certainly not one of us would rather see them satisfied in regulated brothels than by our young girls and women—whether by rape, seduction or the encouraging of natural tendencies.[10]

The brothel district, in one form or another, had existed for decades to serve the huge deployment of marines, sailors, and soldiers attached to Pearl Harbor, Schofield, and then Hickam, and also to service the disproportionately male population of plantation workers who made Hawaii's prewar economy go. The brothels, many believed, kept those mainly lower-class white and dark-skinned men away from the island's "respectable" white women. Many believed that wartime Hawaii, swollen to the bursting point with members of the armed forces and war workers, needed its buffer of whores more than ever.

George Sumner, the Chairman of the Police Commission and a

leading conservative businessman on the islands (after the war, he was president of American Factors, Hawaii's largest business), argued the point strongly in a private meeting. There were too many men in and around Honolulu, he said, who were "just like animals" to even permit thinking about closing down the brothels.[11] During most of the war, the brothels were a regulated enterprise supervised by the municipal, territorial, and federal authorities.

———

The women of Hotel Street worked hard. Each prostitute normally serviced about 100 men a day, at least twenty days out of every month. Some women did more. Their bosses—the madams—kept count, and shirkers were treated harshly. The women paid for their perseverance with disease and broken health. In 1943, 120 prostitutes were hospitalized 166 times for a contagious venereal disease. Bad cases put women into the hospital for at least two weeks. Women with "the clap" had to be hospitalized and treated before they could go back to work; the health officials charged with overseeing the brothels made sure of it.

Few women had the stamina, will, or desire to keep at their trade, uninterrupted, for the duration of the war. But for those who could and did, the money was astounding. Prostitutes kept two dollars of every three the men paid. During the war many of the brothel prostitutes made thirty and forty thousand dollars a year at a time when a working woman was considered very fortunate to make two thousand. The madams cleared upwards of $150,000. All told, the houses took in over $10 million each year during the war. The amount approximated the revenues lost when tourism was halted for the duration.[12]

The "sporting girls," as some of them preferred to be called, did have fixed costs which lowered their incomes. Most of them lived and ate (or at least maintained a residence) in the brothels, generally in a ground-floor section of the house known as "no man's land." Room and board came to about $100 a month. The girls also had to tip the housemaids who cleaned up the cubicles where they took care of business. They paid for the laundering of the prodigious amount of linens they went through, and they also gave generous tips to their regular "maids," who shepherded the men in and out and kept them orderly. The prostitutes also had to pay for their own weekly gynecological examinations, regular testing for venereal diseases (the VD tests alone were $13) and hospitalization costs. Many of the madams padded the bills they levied against their "girls." Still, the chance to make a fortune was there for the women of Hotel Street, and many made a killing.[13]

At most of the brothels, the routine was the same. Kenneth Burch and many others knew it well. Every day, from before 9 a.m. until after 2 p.m., sailors and soldiers lined up for admittance in an orderly fashion, a sea of white and khaki that wound down the district's alleys and narrow sidewalks. Over their heads, neatly lettered signs read "Bronx Rooms," "The Senator Hotel," "Service," "Rex Rooms," "Rainbow Hotel." Many felt it was best to get in line as early as possible, "before the women were all wore out."[14]

To the great amusement of all, sometimes men (and on far fewer occasions, women) thought they were in line for some other scarce commodity and instead found themselves at the brothel doors. A favorite wartime joke (and the joke was played out for real) told of the little old lady halfway up the line who thought she was on her way to a rare bottle of mainland scotch. So many lines formed on Hotel Street that it was easy to become confused.

From beauty parlor windows and souvenir shops, Chinese and other local women watched and giggled at the lines of white men. Shoeshine boys, in their pidgin, kidded the soldiers and sailors, many of them ill at ease.[15] After the long public wait—which might last a couple of hours—the men reached the brothel door. Many arrived drunk, although no liquor was allowed on the premises. If men were too drunk, they were denied entrance. Some men took the news in stride, other became belligerent. For the women at the door it could be funny, if also a little dangerous.

Adeline Naniole, a Hawaiian woman, kept the door at the Rex for a while. Working the door and then later as personal maid to the prostitutes was the best money Naniole ever made, up to $125 a week. It was steady and far better paying than the dead-end jobs she'd done at Honolulu's pineapple canneries.

Naniole liked the work. She got along well with the prostitutes.

The First Strange Place

To Naniole, what the prostitutes did was a job, and her job was to make their job go as smoothly as possible. The smoother she made it for them, the better they tipped her.

Men who came to Naniole's place of work falling-down drunk found her blocking their way: "I won't let them come in. They're just a humbug." Naniole's friend and fellow doorkeeper had a quick reply for the white men who came to the door too soused, a reply that always made Naniole laugh. "I'm sorry," she'd say. And when the man said, "Why, why not?" She'd say gently but firmly, "Well, I don't think you can make business."[16]

Few men, however, went to the houses without some fortification. Alcohol was the preferred aphrodisiac but some men found another route to arousal. For over a year and a half, at the movie palace just outside the vice district, Hedy Lamarr sizzled in *Ecstasy*—the film that had been banned even in New York City for its sexual explicitness. You could watch the servicemen make the trek from Hedy's performance to their own.[17]

If found suitable—and almost all of the men were—the man climbed the stairs to the brothels' second-floor beehive. At the head of the hall that led to the prostitutes' cubicles, the madam stood behind a money booth, sometimes caged. Each man, in turn, paid her $3.00. She gave the man a ticket or a token (usually a poker chip). By 2 p.m. every day, most of the madams had stacks and stacks of dollar bills. At the Senator, the Bronx, and some of the bigger brothels, the madams collected thousands of $1 bills every day.

Once past the booth, the men sat on benches against the wall, waiting their turn. Usually the men were quiet. They smoked unfiltered cigarettes. The smoke mixed with the men's nervous sweat, the stink of cheap liquor, and the heavy sweet-sour odor of disinfectant.

The brothels were stripped down. They were devoid of sofas and comfortable chairs. No drinks were served, no entertainment was provided. The operation was assembly-line efficient.

Before the war, when the brothels offered more services, most of them had used a two-door policy, one for whites (mainly soldiers, sailors, and marines) and the other for local men (almost exclusively plantation workers). Even then the system was aimed at keeping the servicemen peaceful, for many of them were contemptuous of the men of color and easily moved to violence at the thought of dark-skinned men having the same white women as they had. During the war, with the demand so high from the white servicemen and war workers, most of the madams removed all chance of racial conflict by simply refusing to serve men of color.

In the rushed atmosphere of the brothels, many of the men went to the first available woman. Some men had favorites, and some wanted to choose. Sometimes little lines formed in wait for a certain sporting woman. Several of the houses were set up with blondes operating out of the rooms on one side of the hall and brunettes working out of the rooms on the other side. Men could pick a woman by her hair color. Some men, with money to burn, bought two tickets and went first with one and then the other.

Most of the women were so busy that the waiting servicemen and war workers had little opportunity to look them over. The men made their choices based on past experience or friends' recommendations. Most just took a chance. A sign in one of the houses reminded all concerned about the rules of engagement: "Men are very fickle and until a man is in the trick room he has a right to change his mind." The sign was just one indication of who was in charge and at whose expense most jokes in the brothel were played.

Maids carrying small towels, dirty or clean, brushed past the men. The women, in various states of undress, dashed in and out of rooms. When a man's turn came, he went into a cubicle—the trick room—often a regular room divided into half by a flimsy sheet of plywood or wall board which sometimes reached only two thirds of the way to the ceiling. The room was bare except for a single cot, a table with a wash bowl and a wastebasket. Often the man undressed or waited alone for a minute while the prostitute finished up on the other side of the partition. The man could hear what went on on the other side and he knew he would be heard in turn.

Most of the brothels used what was called a "bullring" setup. The bullring consisted of three rooms. In one room, a man undressed, in a second the prostitute engaged her customer, in a third a man who had finished put his clothes back on. In the brothels, time was money. The prostitutes wanted to move the men in and out as quickly as possible.

For many of the men, sexually inexperienced and fresh from months at sea or long weeks in a battle zone, the three minutes they had bought was more than enough. As one veteran noted, "they put it in and they're gone. Sometimes they're gone washing off in the pail. . . ." For those who could hold back, the women used their expertise; they were professionals at getting men to come fast. One patron of another brothel explained the modus operandi of the professional in action:

> . . . The routine was standard . . . I think the girls could diagnose clap better than the doctors at the time. She'd have a way of squeezing it that, if there was anything in there, she'd find it. Then she'd wash it off with a clean wash cloth. She'd lay on her back and get you on top of her so fast, you wouldn't even know you'd come up there on your own power. She'd grind so that you almost felt like you had nothing to do with it. Well, after that, she had you. She could make it go off as quickly as she wanted to . . . and she didn't waste any time, I'll tell you . . . I'd say the whole thing, from the time you got in the room until the time you came didn't take three minutes.[18]

To insure that no one tried to prolong matters, many of the prostitutes set an alarm clock before each encounter. You were through when that alarm went off, no matter what.

The women, their minds on the lines outside and always looking to control the situation, often used fellatio to move the men along. That was fine with many of the men. According to Lt. Commander Carl Stockholm, the Senior Shore Patrol Officer who regularly patrolled the district, at least 30 percent of the young men who went to the brothels for their first sexual experience let the prostitutes take them in their mouths. (Lt. Commander Stockholm, whose job it was to keep sailors on shore leave on the right side of the line that separated permissible from unpermissible vice, believed that young men who found sexual release in the mouths of women were more likely candidates for shipboard behavior which, if discovered, would result in undesirable discharge from the Navy. As he told a roomful of avid, reform-minded listeners meeting just a few blocks from the district: "it is not a far cry from such sex perversions ['buccal coitus,' as it was called in the room that day] to homosexual acts.") As soon as the man came, the woman went; she moved to the other cubicle to process the next waiting man. A maid insured that the man who had finished hurried along.

The war-time brothels hummed with a can-do spirit, though no one claimed they provided high-quality sexual experiences. Many of the men left feeling gypped. One marine, his duty done, cracked up the men waiting by announcing, "A guy might as well use a dead fish." Another three-minute man commented with deep disgust, to the rich amusement of the more jaded, "Some of these gals act like they think they're frozen to their jobs."[19]

Despite the impersonal efficiency of the system, it could break down. One regular customer told his favorite at the end of his three minutes, "Judy, you're the bummest fuck I ever had." As he tells it, she was so angry she spent the rest of the night proving him a liar—for free. (It meant a lot; he named his daughter after her.)[20] This experience was not common.

After their three minutes or less, the men trooped down the same steps they'd gone up. Some of the men, especially young sailors who'd celebrated their first act of coitus to the cheers of their shipmates, went off to the next step in their initiation as full-blooded men. They got tattooed.

For many of the men, Hotel-Street sex and tattooing went together like peanut butter and jelly. Once again, the men waited in long lines. Almost without exception, they arrived at the tattoo parlors drunk—either still drunk from their prebrothel imbibing or newly fortified for the painful experience. Even the standard prices for the often-linked experiences were the same, $3.

During the war years, Honolulu led the world in tattooing. The thirty-three tattoo artists (all Filipinos) at the eight Hotel Street parlors needled 300 to 500 tattoos a day, with some men receiving more than one tattoo at a session. "Remember Pearl Harbor" was probably the best seller. Anchors, American eagles, hula girls, and women's names—heart optional—were also extremely popular. The most prominent parlor, just a few steps from several of the brothels, featured Eugene Miller, a very shy, fey-looking boy, who in 1944 was just fifteen years old. A huge sign over his parlor announced him as the "World's Greatest and Youngest Tattoo Artist." Miller used Listerine in his dyes to prevent infections and was well-respected for his artistry. His price went as high as $25.[21]

Getting tattooed was not what the men were supposed to do after their three-minute affair. They were supposed to go posthaste to the prophylaxis stations set up by the Army and Navy right in the Hotel Street district. Inside the stations, they were asked to urinate, wash "exposed parts," "instill colloidal silver solution into the anterior urethra," and apply ointment to "all exposed parts." Before the war, the prostitutes, as part of the ground rules of the system, were to apply prophylaxis to the men—this had been the idea of an army officer who had helped rationalize the regulated brothels. But during the war, the prostitutes were simply too busy to take time out for post-coitus care.

The armed forces were trying to learn from the past. During World War I, the federal government had fallen prey to hysteria over the subject of prostitution and venereal diseases. The progressive reformers who ran the antivice campaign put most of their resources into keeping suspicious women away from the doughboys. As a result, some 30,000 women suspected of too-amorous relationships with members of the armed forces (the vast majority not commercial prostitutes) had had their rights seriously abridged, with thousands incarcerated and forced to undergo humiliating physical examinations. The treatment of the draftees by the moral reformers was quite different. The emphasis was on continence and the maintenance of a manly male virginity. Lecturers explained to the men that "sex organs do not have to be exercised or indulged in . . . forget them, don't think about them." The results were not good: more American men left the armed forces with a contagious venereal disease than were wounded by the enemy.

The Army and Navy, never pleased with the federal government's official policies, had toward the end of World War I already shifted their energies toward prophylactic treatments. By World War II, the Armed Forces did not punish men for failing to go through prophylactic rituals since they did not want the men to hide venereal infections. The Armed Forces tried to make prophylaxis as easy as possible. A large sign informed all passersby, military and civilian, that they were welcome to make use of the prophylaxis facilities, absolutely free of charge. Each and every brothel had an informative sign posted in the waiting room reminding the men where to go and why they should. The Hotel Street prophylaxis stations were, by mid-1943, able to handle 1,500 men an hour. They were busy places with their own long lines.[22]

Men usually went to the brothels nervous, keyed up, and looking for a human touch, even one that had to be bought and administered assembly-line fashion. They wanted stimulation and release. The women of the houses were not looking for stimulation, just the opposite. They wanted distance. Many shot morphine. Some smoked opium. The morphine went for about $10 a shot. One of the prostitutes, Jean O'Hara, estimated that about a third of the women were addicts. The madams controlled the dope supply. Jean O'Hara, who faced her life with open and unclouded eyes, explained the situation:

> Madames resort to many and varied measures to keep their girls from leaving them. Morphine is dope that promotes a false and high feeling. It creates indifference, disdain for everything. . . . The madames would rather their girls had the habit! Then the Madame has a hold over the girl. It was all a masterpiece of simplicity. Madames dissatisfied with the girl, could threaten the girl by threatening to cut off the girl's supply of dope. And then a girl under the influence of dope can work longer. Yes, the madames approved of "hoppies."

The dope helped some of the women get through their hundred men a day but it cost them—cutting into their income and their health. But as Ms. O'Hara, a prostitute since she was seventeen, said, there was nothing special about the dope scene in Honolulu: "with any red light district goes dope. . . ."[23]

Most of the women who worked Hotel Street were haoles. Most came from San Francisco. Before the war, madams in Honolulu would pay San Francisco pimps $500 to $1,000 for the procurement of a white woman, depending on age. But it was not "white slavery";

the women came voluntarily. They were professionals after the money Hotel Street promised. Most of the madams had also come into the business in San Francisco, the capital of American vice. Everybody knew everybody.

It was a rare prewar liner between San Francisco and Honolulu that did not carry at least one Hotel Street prostitute, either coming or going. During the war, of course, it was much harder for a prostitute to secure passage to Honolulu on the priority-only transports. To get across, some of the women signed up as war workers, others as entertainers.[24]

A favorite joke among the smart set, which at least one woman seems to have played out, went like this: right after the attack on Pearl Harbor, a young, well-to-do haole woman finds herself stranded in San Francisco, separated from husband and children. She is told by the authorities that due to the emergency only high-priority personnel could be granted passage to Honolulu and, at a time when the wives and families of most servicemen and thousands of the island's haole women and children were being evacuated from Hawaii, there would be no room for some time for a woman seeking to return to her family. So with a wink and a wiggle, the woman announces that she's an entertainer, seeking to help boost the morale on the island. Naturally, she's booked onto the next departing ship. Perhaps the real joke is that—listed as "entertainers"—at least six prostitutes did cruise into Hawaii at a time when passage was highly restricted.[25]

The women of Hotel Street celebrated the end of their daily grind of buccal and vaginal coitus differently, and unpredictably. Their leisure-time activities were actively discussed by their patrons, as well as their enemies on the island.

Before the war, the women of Hotel Street faced extremely limited opportunities for recreation or any kind of life outside of the brothel. As a condition of their employment in Hawaii as licensed "entertainers," they had to follow a cruel and complex set of rules or face severe punishment. For most of the war years, the women were able to flout these rules and thumbed their noses at their enforcers—the vice squad and Chief William Gabrielson of the Honolulu Police Department.

The rules established by the Hawaii police in the years before

World War II were mainly meant to keep the "sporting girls" out of sight and so out of mind of "respectable citizens," and to keep the women powerless and in thrall to the men of the Vice Squad. Every prostitute brought over from the mainland, before she received her license and after she was fingerprinted, was personally instructed by a member of the vice squad in the rules that would govern her stay on Hotel Street:

> She may not visit Waikiki Beach.
> She may not patronize any bars or better class cafes.
> She may not own property or an automobile.
> She may not have a steady "boyfriend."
> She may not marry service personnel.
> She may not attend dances.
> She may not ride in the front seat of a taxicab or with a man in the back seat.
> She may not wire money to the mainland.
> She may not telephone the mainland without permission of the Madame.
> She may not change from one house to another.
> She may not be out of the brothel after 10:30 at night.

The vice squad had many rules that served to isolate and humiliate the highly paid women of Hotel Street. To break these rules was to risk a severe beating at the hands of the police and possible removal from the islands.

Before the war, few mainland women served in the houses for more than six months before they returned to the West Coast. The rigidity of the system put some "sporting girls" on the boat home. They found their lives in Paradise a boring, degrading routine ruled by often brutal masters. A few months was all they could take. Some probably earned what money they needed in those few months and left the trade. Others were ordered by the vice squad to return to the West Coast. Jean O'Hara, who would fight the rules and pay a price for it, said the police forced girls to leave the islands after about six months "whether the girl's record was up to standard or not . . . [because] she got to know too much in that length of time."[26]

Jean O'Hara was one sporting girl who never intended to quietly accept the gender politics (a highly anachronistic term and one Jean O'Hara would not have used but too suggestive of her feelings to leave out) of the rules of her profession as she found them in Honolulu and she would contribute to the changing of those rules. O'Hara's background and character were not what most people would expect of a woman who would spend, by her own account, fourteen years in the business of prostitution and a large chunk of the war years taking on more than a hundred men a day.

In the mimeographed memoir she distributed in Honolulu in the fall of 1944, she states—and a grain of salt is in order—she was born in Chicago in 1913 to a strict Catholic family. Her father was a doctor, her mother a devoted mother. She was an only child, full name Betty Jean O'Hara, fawned over, "happy and normal . . . given the best schooling in preparation for a career." She was good with words and at writing. As a teenager, she thought she'd like to become a doctor, like her father.

Her parents, she says, "were strict in the regimentation of my life," but she was allowed to attend movies and parties. At one of these parties in Chicago, she met a spellbinding pair: "The girl was bedecked in jewelry and clothing that had me fascinated, and interested to know how to go about getting such finery. I was young and easily led. . . ." The girl's boyfriend, her pimp, taught Jean how to earn such jewels and clothes for herself. She was seventeen.

If she was indeed the daughter of a doctor, Jean O'Hara was a rarity among Chicago prostitutes, most of whom were native-born progeny of poor, immigrant families. In her calling, however, she was far from a singular "fallen flower." Despite periodic campaigns against prostitution, in 1930, when Jean O'Hara started, about 5,000 prostitutes worked Chicago, "the city on the make."[27] While prostitution was declining in Chicago and elsewhere from its height at the turn of the century, and "sporting guides" to the houses were no longer openly sold, brothels and streetwalkers were no secret in Chicago or in any other city.

Jean O'Hara was a pretty girl who became a handsome woman.

December 7, 1941. In the early moments of the attack on Pearl Harbor, people gathered on a corner to watch the planes fly overhead. Many thought they were watching American war games.

The fears of invasion were very real at first. Martial law was declared, and citizens practiced evacuating downtown Honolulu (above). Almost 20,000 civilian men formed Home Guard Units to defend the Islands. Even boys' games (below) looked to wartime realities.

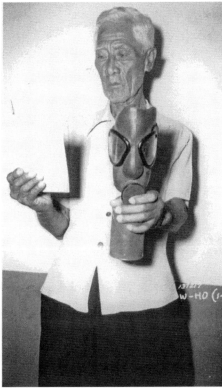

Frank Napookiwi Kiko, an 84-year-old Hawaiian (left), studies instructions for the gas masks that were issued to all island residents. In the early days of war, Elizabeth Beach Brown (below, left), a new mother living on the Big Island, served dinner in the bathroom because it was the only room she could black out. Eloise Ornelles (below, right) was almost eleven when war broke out. Her family entertained lonely servicemen at home.

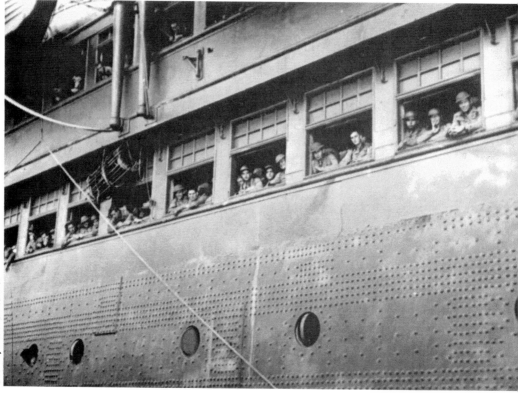

Over a million servicemen and war workers came to Hawaii during the conflict. Above, men wait to get off the troop transport at Matson pier in Honolulu, April 1942. Below (from left to right) are William and Joe De Fossett of the 369th Coast Artillery, war worker Gene Simonson, and Frank Branigan of the 98th Infantry.

The servicemen and war workers who came to Hawaii found the beaches of "paradise" strung with barbed wire (above). Below (from left to right) are Robert Roberts of the USS Enterprise, M.P. Robert Cowan, and Fred Haynes of the 5th Marines.

Courtesy Robert Roberts; Robert Cowan; Fred Haynes

Courtesy National Archives

The war brought together men and women from many different backgrounds. The men in the photo above of the 64th FA Brigade, Battalion A, hail from Pawtucket, Rhode Island; Harvard, Nebraska; Johnstown, Pennsylvania; Hiram, Georgia; Gloversville, New York; St. Paul, Minnesota; and Newark, New Jersey. Below (from left to right) are Rosemary Altieri, U.S.O. staff member and war worker, of New York City; Madelyn Busbee, a war worker from Lilly, Georgia; and Mildred ("Kit") Carson, a war worker from Ohio.

Courtesy Rosemary Brown; Madelyn Laidler; Mildred Lott

Many servicemen trained for combat in Hawaii. Above, the 34th Infantry moves up the Waikane Trail during maneuvers. Below, infantrymen practice bayonet charges over rough terrain.

Hawaii was for most a place of waiting, and men from the mainland were often anxious and lonely. Above, men crowd for the first mail they have received since leaving the States. Fred Borgerhoff (below left) passes time in the barracks while his mother (below right) waits at home in Cleveland Heights, Ohio.

In the grim humor of war, Hawaii was called "the Rock," midway between Heaven and Hell. The sign at KauKau corner in downtown Honolulu evokes the common sense of being at a midpoint in Hawaii, in suspension, by showing the men *exactly* how far they were from places strange and threatening as well as those that were familiar and comforting.

Minutes away from battle, Marines who had trained on the Big Island approach the smoke-obscured island of Tarawa.

Casualty rates in Pacific island battles sometimes approached 100 percent.
Few prisoners were taken by either side. Above, war dead line the beaches of
Saipan in the Mariana Islands. Below, American wounded arrive in Pearl
Harbor.

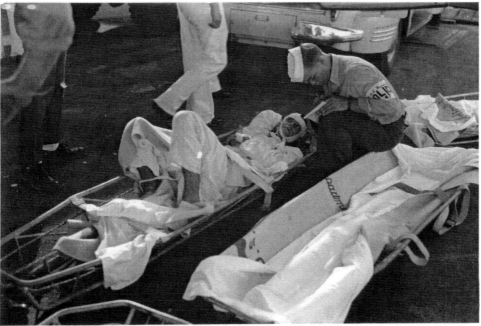

The pressures of war altered sexual
mores and challenged established
ethnic and racial boundaries. At left,
men in a Hotel Street shop look
over photos of nude women. Below,
a Navy pilot on leave from combat
shares a meal with a volunteer at
Chris Holmes Rest Home.

In the Hotel Street vice district, men lined up for everything: from buses to liquor and tattoos, and the infamous brothels (above). Not all vice was confined to the District, however. Below, an abandoned vehicle served as a "shackup house." The Army Signal Corps originally captioned this photo: "Side view of junked body of an auto, used as sleeping quarters for the enlisted men."

The common estimate of 500 men to each woman in Hawaii was exaggerated, but most believed it anyway. Mabel Thomas (above left), director of the Army recreation center Club Maluhia (above right), sometimes oversaw dances attended by thousands of men and only thirty or forty women. Below, enlisted men from the USS Enterprise wait their turns to dance with Navy Yard employees during a rare shore leave.

While the armed forces remained segregated in Hawaii, the semi-professional Aiea baseball team (above) had a Hawaiian manager, a Japanese-American coach, and players from across the racial spectrum, including the De Fossett brothers of the 369th. At right, the wedding of John Runkle and Thelma Liborio exemplifies the way wartime encounters between people of different backgrounds could have permanent results.

World War II forever changed the social, sexual, and racial landscape of American society, both in Hawaii and on the mainland. Above, an impromptu victory parade on Hotel Street, August 14, 1945.

She was "black Irish," fair-skinned with a clear complexion which set off her dark eyes, raven hair, and even features. She stood about 5'4" and at 120 pounds was slender by that era's standards. Her good looks and classy bearing would serve her well.

Between 1930 and 1938, O'Hara took her business around the mainland. She did not like to dwell on those years and tended to blur them together. Like much of what O'Hara told most people, this was an account of her past that satisfied her own sense of what needed to be said, rather than an exact record of what happened. Jean says that a month after turning pro, she and a new girl-friend skipped out to San Francisco, where they both gained employment at a high-class brothel. As she tells it:

> I became definitely committed to the practice of prostitution. My mother and father tried every means available to frighten me into going home, but being headstrong, and enticed by the seemingly fabulous earnings, I resisted their every effort. Although I actually loathed the life, my sense of shame and sin aroused in me a perverse independence.

Jean O'Hara's police record, as put together by her enemies at the Honolulu Police Department, shows that she was arrested on the mainland three times for prostitution between 1934 and 1938. The Chicago Police arrested her—she was using the name Jean Burk—in June 1934. She got off. Three years later, she was tried at the county courthouse in Ottawa, Illinois, ninety miles southwest of Chicago. She had probably been caught in one of the perfunctory roundups that went on in LaSalle, a wide-open town a few miles outside of Ottawa that catered in the prewar years to gangsters, locals, and Chicagoans who liked to gamble. She was ordered out of the county. April 1938, the police in Monterey, California, a Navy port of call, hauled her in and the judge gave her ninety days suspended and ordered her out of the county for two years.

Did Jean O'Hara ever work that high-class brothel in San Francisco? By the time she showed up in Honolulu she looked as though she could have. She was neat, well dressed, and worldly. She was also independent, ambitious, and had a fiery temper. And unlike most prostitutes, she used no drugs and had no pimp.

The First Strange Place

Jean O'Hara came to Hawaii to make money—and because she had to leave the Bay area. She liked the money she found, but like almost all of the women on the Street, she didn't like the conditions under which she earned it.

When she showed up in Honolulu in mid-1938, the brothels were in full swing and highly regimented. O'Hara went right to work. And though conditions were far different from the war years—only on Army and Navy payday would the prostitutes have men lined up down the steps and out the door, and normally it was closer to ten minutes for $3—after a few months, she had built up a sizable bankroll and started thinking about moving from prostitute to madam. She learned who lent money to the madams—a haole loan shark with a respectable storefront on the hoity-toity Merchant Street. She watched the madams encourage their "girls" to buy expensive jewelry from the two hucksters who made regular trips up the brothel steps, sample bags packed with diamond watches, jeweled earrings, and other gaudy items that helped keep the money running through the prostitutes' fingers and tied them to their work. And she watched the madams push dope. "Some of the madams here in Honolulu," O'Hara came to believe, "are the most hard hearted women I have ever met in my fourteen years experience. They are greedy. They are money hungry, and they drive the girls to the very breaking point."

O'Hara also learned about the monthly payoffs the madams made to the vice squad to keep from being closed down—upwards of $30 a woman. During the war years, she claims, it cost the madams $50 a woman in payoffs. She learned that the chief of police, William Gabrielson, had direct control of the vice squad and the personal power to grant the madams the right to open a place and to close them down, and further that there was no appeal to his judgments. And since all of the houses broke at least some of the rules some of the time, they had to pay off the vice squad to keep open. For example, it was against the rules for the women to take drugs. To stop the drugs, however, was to stop at least some of the women from working, or from working as hard as the madams wanted them to work. The madams also found that the vice squad provided good muscle, keeping their "girls" in line and their customers orderly. So the madams paid. They had sizable investments and incomes at stake. And to keep on the Chief's good side, the madams tried their best to live by his rules and to punish those women who challenged the setup.

Such setups, with their built-in corruption and payoffs, were far from unique to Hawaii. At the turn of the century, regulated—if illegal—vice districts operated in most big cities. Payoffs to police and politicians were a natural part of doing business. In Jean O'Hara's hometown, Chicago, First Ward Democratic Party bosses and world-class characters Bathhouse John Coughlin and Hinky Dink Kenna had flouted Victorian morality at the turn of the century with a wide-open annual costume ball to honor the prostitutes, pimps, madams, gamblers, and other denizens of the thriving vice district they protected in exchange for cash.

The mainly middle-class moral reformers of the 1910s and World War I years, in towns and cities around the country, had shut down many of the most open, regulated brothel districts. Still, most major cities, and all towns and cities near military bases and navy ports, had some kind of system of prostitution. None, however, were as open as Hotel Street. And because they were not open or regulated they were more likely to spread venereal diseases, a problem the military fully understood; they were more also likely to be rife with pimps, procurers, and other men who used violence to enforce their criminal order on both the prostitutes and their customers, thus creating much unpleasantness for any police department.

In full recognition of the trade-offs, and with some extra twists that wouldn't have figured in mainland cities, Honolulu's system had survived the reform campaigns of other cities and had even grown more open and intertwined with the police department and government officials. Too many people saw the setup as too valuable to lose.[28]

Jean O'Hara, who'd gotten on the wrong side of the system in Chicago, LaSalle, and Monterey, also got in wrong on Hotel Street. After a few months at work, bankroll in hand, O'Hara decided to take time off and figure out what to do next. She and a co-worker named Betty, violating the rules that had been so carefully spelled out to them by the vice cop who had met them dockside at their arrival in Honolulu, leased a place just off the beach in Waikiki.

The vice squad reminded her that she was not allowed to live outside the district: a resting whore, in their book, was still a whore. O'Hara and her friend moved. Quietly, they found a place up on one of the rises, Pacific Heights, overlooking Honolulu. Three weeks later, the vice squad found them and again forced them out.

Furious, O'Hara and her friend left Oahu for the slow-paced garden isle of Kauai. They went back to tricking at a little house there set up for plantation workers. Then, with the money she saved up, O'Hara decided she would open her own place on Maui, where only two houses competed for the local trade. She was told, however, that even for a house on Maui it was necessary to get permission from the Chief of Police in Honolulu.

O'Hara went back to Honolulu. After talking to the people who seemed to know, she decided there was no way around it. She had to ask Chief Gabrielson for his permission to open up a place in Maui. So she went to his office and asked him.

But the Chief knew about O'Hara's attempt to live outside the district, to break his rules, and he wasn't having any of it. Gabrielson was a tough cop. He'd come from the mainland back in 1932 to put some iron into a police department that many in the white elite believed was reeling from too much politics and too little law enforcement.

As O'Hara tells it, Gabrielson practically spat at her: "No girl in Honolulu can have my permission to open a house anywhere when she has violated my rules like you and Betty have. Who do you think you are, anyway? . . . If you don't watch out, you'll find yourself back in San Francisco." O'Hara had a notoriously short fuse and it went off. It was the Irish in her, she said later. She exploded, cursed at him, said that she was a citizen and a taxpayer and had violated no laws, "only his dictates." She said she'd do what she damn well pleased.

Jean O'Hara had made a serious enemy. She'd also begun to break down the rules of the game. She opened her house in Maui, got arrested immediately, and paid her fines. Then she started paying off the local police, bypassing Gabrielson's authority. She stayed open for about a year until the end of 1939, when she'd had enough of being a madam and enough of living in the sticks. She sold the place to one of her own girls for a tidy profit and moved back to

Honolulu. Maybe she thought with a year gone by that things would have cooled between her and the Honolulu police. If that's what she thought, she was wrong.

Back in Honolulu, just after Christmas, she checked into the Rex and started tricking. As she tells it, a week after she went back to work on Hotel Street, her husband called.

She had a legal husband. Soon after she arrived in Hawaii, she'd married a "local boy" who worked on the docks. Maybe she married him for protection, maybe for good times, maybe for both. Maybe she fell in love. It was never clear and it hadn't stopped her from working her trade or taking off to Maui for a year.

Her husband, she said, wanted her to stop working Hotel Street and come home to him, and she'd decided to take him up on it. She told the madam of the Rex, Lillian Martin, that she was checking out and wasn't coming back. Martin told her that it was after 10:30 and that if she wanted to leave that night she had to get the permission of the vice squad. So Martin called the police and Robert Kennedy arrived with members of the vice squad. Kennedy knew what Jean O'Hara had done. He knew about the house in Maui opened after the Chief had said no. He knew about the swearing and the insults that O'Hara had thrown in the face of his boss.

Robert Kennedy stood over six feet, a big man. Kennedy told O'Hara that whores could not leave the houses after 10 p.m. and that she couldn't leave until the next morning. O'Hara said she was leaving just the same. Maybe—probably—she swore at him.

He punched her in the face. He hit her again and again until she fell down. Then he kicked her in her ribs.

While he punched and kicked her, the two cab drivers who'd come to collect O'Hara and her suitcases watched. Lillian Martin, madam of the Rex, stood by and said something like, "I hope that this will be a lesson to the rest of the girls not to break Chief Gabrielson's orders." Martin needed to stay open and, in her case, business came before sisterhood.

Kennedy dragged O'Hara to a patrol wagon—by her hair, O'Hara said. For the next three days, she was held in a cell and denied medical attention. She had two broken ribs on the left side. Her bridgework was busted. She had two black eyes and bruises up and down her body. She was charged with assault and battery on a police officer and with using profanity. The real charge was simple: she was a whore making waves. The men who ran Honolulu, like the men on the mainland, did not look kindly on any woman, let alone a prostitute, challenging the rules of the game.

But O'Hara did not scare. She sued Kennedy and Chief Gabrielson for $100,000 for what they'd done to her. She had photographs taken of her black eyes and bruised body. Her husband, who went back a long way with Kennedy, wanted to kill him. But O'Hara wanted to get him herself with the weapons the courts and the laws provided for any citizen, man or woman, prostitute or otherwise. The newspapers picked up the story and suddenly Jean O'Hara was a "demi-mondaine" to be reckoned with in Honolulu.

After a fair amount of dickering, the police agreed to drop the charges and O'Hara dropped her suit. The police department regulations affecting the Hotel Street prostitutes, while not revoked at this time, suddenly could not be enforced with the same enthusiasm. The police department's absolute control of the brothels had begun to crack.

Jean O'Hara had stood up for her rights, and if her victory was incomplete, her battle with the authorities left her feeling in command of her own life. For all to see, and flagrantly breaking one more rule, Jean O'Hara drove the streets of Honolulu in a brand-new Lincoln Zephyr sedan. To set her imposing vehicle off from any other Lincoln on the road, her Zephyr came fully equipped with fog lights. It was a decorative touch in fogless Honolulu, perhaps inspired by her San Francisco days. Honolulu had clearly not heard the last of the indomitable Jean O'Hara.[29]

After the Pearl Harbor attack, like much of the town, the brothels were shut down for a few weeks. Soon after they reopened, with the troops pouring through Honolulu and the men's pay upped from the prewar scale, the women jumped their prices to $5 for three minutes. As they saw it, market conditions had changed.

What a meeting it must have been, when the madams gathered to raise their prices—some of the toughest women in America plotting their move. Women like Nickey Allen, Ruth Davis, Lillian Martin, Patricia De Corso, Peggy Staunton, all of whom had fought their way to the top of their business, all of whom were on their way to being among the most successful businesswomen of the war years.[30]

Word of the price hike immediately reached Frank Steer, at that point an Army major who had come to the islands in September 1940 to head the Military Police. Steer, a West Pointer born and raised in the Oklahoma Territory, was for most of the war provost marshal under the post-attack state of martial law in Hawaii. By virtue of martial law he had final authority for the control of vice, among many other things, on the islands. Steer already knew all the madams "by first name," as he liked to say. He knew them because as prewar commander of the Military Police, he had already had many a dealing with them. He had no problems with the idea of the brothels and no problems with any of the inhabitants—his was an attitude of live-and-let-live, so long as order was kept and nobody was being put through the wringer. But as he saw it, raising the price on the fighting men was wrong.

He ordered the prices dropped. "The price of meat is still three dollars," he informed the madams. Steer was not a man to be crossed but, more than that, he was a fair man. The madams, not a trusting lot, trusted Steer, and they backed down. But like the rest of Hawaii, Hotel Street business would not go back to normal after December 7th.

Right after Pearl Harbor, the women of the houses, who were far closer to the injured sailors and enlisted men than most of the island's residents, hurried to help. Some of the women who rushed to the hospitals and temporary facilities set up for burned and wounded men were turned away when they admitted their occupations or gave their addresses. The official reason was fear of infection. But several of the prostitutes nursed the men and did what they could to help. The madams turned over their brothels' living quarters to the overflow of wounded. Hotel Street, for a few days, looked like a Red Cross annex. It was war and the women of Hotel Street showed a commitment to the men in line to fight it that few outside the district would have expected. Word of their concern and of their deeds soon got around.[31]

With their beds filled—and with normal lines of authority disrupted—the sporting women chanced it; they moved out of the district and out of the shadows. They bought and leased houses all around Honolulu, up the rises, down by the beaches, in fashionable neighborhoods. They told anyone who asked that the district seemed too risky; it was a firetrap in the event the Japanese came back. They weren't just talking. Like many others on the islands, some of the women believed invasion was imminent. Several prostitutes passed up the promised boom times and joined other women, many of them wives of army and navy officers, who had arranged passage on the December 20th special-evacuation transport bound for San Francisco.

For several weeks, even as the brothels reopened and long after the wounded had moved out of the prostitutes' living quarters, no one seemed to pay any attention to the women's quiet movement out of the district. The women of Hotel Street, treated with such contempt by those in authority, had reason to hope that the long and brutal reign of the Vice Squad was over.

At first, the women who'd moved out of the district behaved like model citizens. Feeling no heat, some began to explore their new freedoms. Not surprisingly, Jean O'Hara both led the way and paid the price for the adventure.

O'Hara—long back at work—and two of her friends had vacated their brothel sleeping-quarters and taken adjoining rooms at the Moana, one of Waikiki's three luxury hotels. Her two friends were probably Carmen Akina and Bernice Kimbrel. Carmen Akina, alias Carmen Lopez, alias Carmen Lee Hall, alias Carmen Akina Hall, had an arrest record a mile-and-a-half long. She'd been before the judge about sixty times since 1930, mainly for being drunk, for soliciting, and for profanity. She liked to have a good time and she didn't mind letting other people know about it. If she'd been a man, she would have probably been called the life of any party. But she was a woman who made her living selling her body and the police ran her in every time she gave them lip, got too loud, or too obvious—which was often. She was a walking insult to the regulated system that was supposed to keep the Hotel Street harlots out of sight and out of mind of respectable Honolulu.

Kimbrel was a different case. A long-time prostitute, she had a few aliases and she'd had some run-ins with the police, but nothing compared to Akina. Back in the fall of 1938, she had shown up at the Hawaii Republican Party Convention, which was attended by the haole elite who ran Hawaii, and picketed them, seemingly over their hypocritical prostitution policy. She was hauled into jail. Like O'Hara, she was an ambitious and independent woman, and like O'Hara, she'd pay dearly before the war was over.

That night at the Moana, the three women were having a party. They'd invited some men over and all hands were doing some serious drinking. They jitterbugged across the floor, music blared, the men threw the women around the rooms.

The house detective of the once-exclusive Moana came to quiet things down. At his knock, Akina and Kimbrel and the men ran into the adjoining room and shut the door. O'Hara plopped on the bed and opened a book before asking the house detective to come in. When he saw who he had on his hands, he called the Vice Squad.

The cops came, took down the names of all the women—not the men—but arrested only O'Hara. Since her public fracas with Chief Gabrielson and the Vice Squad she'd been tagged several times by the police: for speeding in the car she wasn't supposed to own, for disturbing the peace in the outside-the-district homes she wasn't supposed to live in, for assault and battery against the police who watched her every move. O'Hara blamed Chief Gabrielson for her troubles with the law. And there is no doubt that he did take a personal interest in the Moana case, asking that the rap sheets on Akina, Kimbrel, and O'Hara be sent to him for review.

O'Hara went before a provost court. With martial law in effect, the civilian courts were shut down. The provost court judges, military men who had little or no legal background, were fierce in their sentencing. As they saw it, there was a war on and no mischief of any kind by civilians could be countenanced. O'Hara got six months for creating a disturbance at the Moana, an outrageous sentence, even taking her priors into account, that flabbergasted the military officer handling the prosecution. Maybe Gabrielson had put in a word with the judge; that's what O'Hara thought.

When the sentence was passed, O'Hara, her temper for once firmly under control, told the prosecutor that she had no hard feelings against him. As he remembered it, "Jean did not seem to resent this sentence particularly." She finished her chat with him by saying that "she was going to take a nice, long, well needed rest." She served four months, her first jail time ever.[32]

O'Hara had gone down, but all around Honolulu, her co-workers tested their limits. In their own private homes, they began to make up for lost time. They had parties, wild parties. Men came and went freely. They began to do what they wanted. The military police just gave them a wink and a nod.

The local police, especially their chief, were more than a little annoyed by the new order of things. Prostitutes had invaded every neighborhood. Hawaii's carefully calibrated system of social stratification was being mocked. Mainland whores, white women, were out in public, demonstrating daily how little white skin meant in the way of moral superiority or some sort of "natural" right to lord it over the vast majority of Hawaii's people of darker hues. Already the hordes of working-class white soldiers, sailors, and war workers had damaged the racial equilibrium that gave stability to the island's ruling white families who had seemed nearly indestructible for some forty years. Now the white prostitutes made further mockery of the whole racialist setup. More ominously, the invasion of the "whores" indicated how easily the tables could be turned—a foreshadowing of what could happen on a larger scale after the war.

Supporting this new laissez-faire approach toward the prostitutes was General Emmons himself, the military governor. The military had long been the wildcard in Hawaii's odd social structure. Before the war, enlisted men had been scrupulously ignored by the majority of the island's haole population. High-ranking officers had been carefully included in a limited way. The Navy, overwhelmingly the most important branch of service in Hawaii's Territorial history, was for so long itself an exemplar of racist practices that it had found no grounds to challenge the nearly absolute control of Hawaii's haole elite over island affairs (indeed, before the war, the white elite's "mild" racism and strict exclusionary policies stood in well-remarked contrast to mainland America, where rigid legal segregation and extreme racial discrimination were taken for granted by most white people). Still, the Navy and the Army had far different priorities than the local elite, especially with the war on.[33]

For General Emmons and for Major Steer, keeping the boys orderly, venereal disease rates down, morale as high as possible superseded long range worries about racial or ethnic boundaries or the haole elite's postwar control of the islands. Their immediate concerns about maintaining Hawaii's internal security and meeting the enlisted men's simpler needs came well before enforcing what seemed to them the somewhat bizarre and corrupt practice of hiding the prostitutes in plain view.

The boys, judging by the hundreds of thousands who went up and down the Hotel Street brothel stairs in the months after Pearl Harbor, wanted prostitutes. The regulated brothels supplied them and insured that they would be relatively disease free—and the Hawaii military district had the lowest VD rates in the armed forces. The prostitutes had done their part after the attack to repay the men. They had accepted the command not to raise their prices. Many high-ranking military officers believed that "any man who won't fuck, won't fight"; they saw the women of Hotel Street as useful in maintaining morale and a manly spirit among the boys. All in all, Emmons, Steer, and others who played a part in enforcing martial rule figured that keeping the prostitutes safe from needless harassment and exploitation seemed to be a commonsense way of keeping the better houses operating smoothly under what were obviously extraordinary circumstances.

The matter came to a head quickly. In April 1942, Police Chief Gabrielson ordered his men to evict four prostitutes living together in a Waikiki house. He expected his orders to be obeyed as they had been in the arrest of O'Hara, who had also been pinched in Waikiki.

Before the war, the Vice Squad had been very specific in telling prostitutes that Waikiki was absolutely, without exception, off limits. Waikiki before the war was not the hustling, bustling worldwide tourist center filled with conventioneers and package tours it would become. Waikiki was an exclusive resort for the well-to-do. Jews and people of color knew better than to try to stay in its three luxurious hotels. And though a mixture of Hawaii's many ethnic groups lived in its residential section, the area was carefully maintained as respectable and welcoming for the moneyed mainland visitors. Of course, the war had changed much of that. Tourism had stopped. Servicemen and war workers had taken over the hotels and cafés, and at least a few Hotel Street prostitutes meant to be a part of the new Waikiki.

Gabrielson's man told the women to leave Waikiki. The women complained to Captain Benson of the Military Police, who seemed to be acquainted with their affairs. He told them to forget it, that the police didn't run things anymore and that his commander didn't care where they lived just so long as they did not ply their trade outside the Hotel Street district. The women were quite pleased and essentially told Chief Gabrielson's officer to stuff it.

Gabrielson exploded. He got hold of Lt. Colonel Melvin Craig, who at this point still had the formal title of Provost Marshal, and asked him what the hell was going on. Craig backed up his man but responded vaguely about who had actual control of vice in Honolulu. He said something like, well, from now on if you want to have any of the prostitutes moved, contact the military police and we'll investigate it and get back to you.

Gabrielson stayed mad. A few days later, he issued Administrative Order Number 83, putting the vice district under the direct control of the military. He had the memo leaked to the Honolulu *Star-Bulletin*. He wanted to watch the Army squirm.[34]

Emmons promptly threw the hot potato back to Chief Gabrielson. In a letter that would remain classified for the next forty-seven years, General Emmons made his position clear:

> I desire to inform you that your understanding regarding the responsibility for vice conditions in the City and County of Honolulu is in error. . . . No directive has been issued to the Police Department in any way limiting its responsibility for any phase of law enforcement. . . . Cancel Administrative Order No. 83.[35]

Chief Gabrielson resumed control with pleasure. But Colonel Steer and the Military Police did not play ball, and a quiet skirmish began between the MPs and the Vice Squad. Vice did its best to round up the scattered denizens of Hotel Street and restore the strict supervision of prewar times. The MPs assured the women that they were within their rights to resist and that, appearances aside, it was the Military Police who had the final say in their disposition. [36]

The women of Hotel Street were caught in the middle. They did not want to go back to the deliberately demeaning conditions of prewar days. It was one thing to choose to service 100 men a day; it was another to abide by rules that denied their basic freedoms.

By June of 1942, the Hotel Street prostitutes had already given in to Major Steer's demand that they keep their prices to $3. But they were damned if they were going to allow the police to bully them and force them to miss the good living that their profits could afford. And some wanted to take advantage of the wild times that hundreds of thousands of footloose, bored, and free-living young men offered. In response to the police department's efforts to push them back into the district, into prewar conditions, the prostitutes of Hotel Street went on strike.

For close to three weeks a group of prostitutes walked a picket line outside the police department headquarters, which was just a few blocks from the district. The police department was also Major Steer's headquarters and the home of the MPs. The women carried placards protesting their treatment; they wanted to be allowed to live where they pleased and to go where they liked when their day's work was done. They struggled not for better pay but better treatment, for full rights of citizenship. They gambled that the Military Police would keep the police department from using force against them and that their military supporters would back them up. What they did took courage and, of course, a certain amount of brass. [37]

Establishment Hawaii did its best to ignore the strike and the newspapers carried not a single word about it. General Emmons, however, personally fought to find a solution to what was for him an embarrassing situation. Major Steer and others in the Military Police, advising Emmons, seemed to sympathize with the plight of the prostitutes.

Emmons held a series of meetings with the Police Commission and Chief Gabrielson. At first, the police responded stiffly to General Emmons' request for a new plan for controlling the district. They submitted an updated but essentially unchanged version of the prewar rules: all prostitutes must live in the brothels; prostitutes had no right to be outside of those brothels except under very specific conditions. Prostitutes were to remain out of sight; in choosing to practice their trade, they sacrificed certain rights and freedoms. Emmons studied the proposal and came back with a dramatically amended version. In Emmons' plan, the women would have the right to live outside the brothels and appear in public so long as they kept their business to the brothels and behaved in an orderly fashion both inside the district and out.

Emmons did not attempt to ram the plan down the police department's throat. He did not want a repeat of the Administrative Order 83 fiasco. He argued his case in a "most constructive and cooperative" manner, according to one participant. His arguments were simple and straightforward, avoiding the complicated terrain of morality and the political implications of regulated brothels in order to focus on the women's working conditions. His was a liberal perspective. He said that "the girls are overworked and need periods of rest; that their work is now during daylight hours; that formerly they could go to the Coast for a rest and could be replaced by new girls arriving by steamer; that this is not possible today."

Emmons also said that the military, with the assistance of the Hawaii Board of Health, would take over the onerous and somewhat unpleasant task of insuring that the women maintained their regular medical checkups and that the houses maintained proper sanitary conditions. The police department, he assured all concerned, would have the right to enforce all other laws and regulations that applied to Honolulu's prostitutes.

The Police Department accepted the compromise. It was not clear how much choice they had since General Emmons, under martial law, had the right to order them to obey. The prostitutes cheered the decision and ended their "strike." Their right to appear in public and to live outside the brothels, while fragile, was nonetheless established in principle.[38]

The increased public presence of the Hotel Street "sporting girls" was noticed by the more observant. "Hotel Street Harry," the bon-vivant columnist for the *Midpacifican,* naturally followed the doings of the "ladies of the evening," as he called them, observing that "most of them conduct themselves most properly and their

presence adds a little glamour to an otherwise drab joint."[39] "Harry"
also told a story of one soldier and a "proper prostitute"—a story that
seems too perfect to be true, though Harry swore by it.

A lonely GI, educated and not a skirt chaser, goes to a bar, not
on Hotel Street, to have a few quiet drinks. A near miracle occurs;
a woman strikes up a conversation with him. "She was charming
and glamorous . . . brilliant and cultured, she loved good books."
They have a long and delightful conversation. They part amiably, he
delighted to have found a thoughtful woman who made him feel
special. In loving detail, the GI describes the woman to Harry. You
can guess the punchline. The next Sunday (and a certain twisted
joy seems to go into stressing that it is the Sabbath) Harry, who was
one of the very, very few men during the war to admit in print that
he frequented the brothels, goes "to visit some of the ladies on the
Avenue." Naturally, on the second floor of one of the brothels there
is Miss Charming and Glamorous: "Hello Honey," she greets
Harry.[40]

Fred Borgerhoff tells another one. Borgerhoff was a smart, tal-
ented kid from Cleveland Heights who liked to talk to people.
Drafted in May of 1943 right out of Cleveland Heights High, he was
in Hawaii with an anti-aircraft unit by early 1944. He had plenty of
detached duty, playing drums with an Army big band that did gigs
around Oahu. One rainy afternoon, late in 1944, he and some other
musicians stopped in a Hotel Street bar to kill a few hours before
their gig. Borgerhoff struck up a conversation with a young, attractive woman, a highly unusual occurrence for him and for most every
other enlisted man in Hawaii. He does get the feeling that she is a
prostitute but that means little to him. The conversation drifts
around to the woman's life and she says that she's going to be a very
well-known woman someday because a guy is writing a book that's
got her in it. Borgerhoff kids along with her, but she says she's not
joking. She goes into a back room and comes back with a box filled
with typed pages. She tells Borgerhoff to take a look.

For the next couple of hours, engrossed, he reads a series of
sketches and parts of stories about army life in Hawaii. Sure enough,
there are descriptions of Hotel Street and several prostitute characters figure in; much of the action takes place just before and after
the attack on Pearl Harbor. Borgerhoff thinks it's terrific stuff, true

to life, enough so that he'd rather keep turning the pages than talk up the good-looking and maybe obliging woman who gave it to him. Eight years later, he saw a version of what he'd read on the silver screen: *From Here to Eternity.*[41]

Hotel Street Harry and hipster GI's were not the only ones to notice the public presence of the increasingly well-to-do women of Hotel Street. Home owners, small businessmen, and law enforcement officers found prostitutes and madams, with cash in hand, all over town. By mid-1943, FBI special agent Joseph Thorton was horrified to find prostitutes and madams loaded "with one dollar bills to the extent that they can make cash payments for residential property on the Ala Wai, Pacific Heights and Kahala ranging from $28,000 to $60,000."

At least one prostitute discovered a nice little real-estate sideline. She had an agent buy her a property in a exclusive residential district. After moving in, she made sure her neighbors learned about her line of work. The neighbors then bought her out at a substantially higher price than she had paid. Other prostitutes, looking for a more legitimate angle, began investing their money in rental properties. Madams began diversifying, buying up beauty parlors, commercial property, restaurants, and stores. In Hawaii's go-go wartime economy, they became important players.[42]

The prostitutes' riches and much higher visibility did draw some unwanted attention. Thieves came after them. Twice, brothel safes were cracked. A number of the prostitutes' new homes were broken into: thieves always knew when they'd be out. Jean O'Hara, who by midwar had somehow managed to open, and keep open, her own brothel on Hotel Street, known to the men as "The Betty," had a $3,000 diamond watch stolen. Another time, her house was ransacked and several pieces of jade were taken. O'Hara's beloved fog lights were even stolen from her Zephyr. According to O'Hara, the police did nothing about the thefts: "they took the attitude that the girls could get more, anyway."[43]

Jean O'Hara was infuriated by the police department's indifference to the thefts and loosed a complaint any of the city's businessmen might have appreciated: "We pay some of the highest taxes in this town. Where, I ask you, are the beneficial results of our taxes?"

As O'Hara and some of the other women saw it, they were doing vital war work and they wanted to be treated as good citizens. Indeed, the prostitutes and madams contributed to the war effort and not just in the obvious way. They had acquitted themselves well after the Pearl Harbor attack. They were notoriously soft touches for enlisted men in need of a loan and, on a larger scale, proud participants in war-bond drives. Midwar, one madam received a special citation from Secretary of the Treasury Henry Morgenthau for selling $132,000 in war bonds. The bonds were sold, no doubt, to fellow sex workers.[44] The prostitutes and madams, as homeowners, patriots, and entrepreneurs, were becoming an open part of life in Honolulu.

This openness was seen as an open wound by some. Police power was being mocked. Hawaii's social order—which put white women on a pedestal and white men in power—was being subverted by the class-confusing operations of the white madams and prostitutes. Accordingly, with the powers that remained to them, the police went after the most conspicuous offenders against the prewar order.

Jean O'Hara's Lincoln Zephyr was repeatedly pulled over for moving violations, and on March 17th of 1944—St. Patrick's Day—a squad of police opened fire on her after a not-so-merry chase that began when she was whizzing some Army flyer friends back to Hickam Field. She lost her license after that affair, but lack of a license did not stop her from using the increasingly well-known Zephyr to try to kill the husband of one of her friends (a co-worker) during a violent confrontation near her Pacific Heights home. The police convinced the victim, a gambler with his own problems, to press charges against O'Hara and she was brought to trial for second-degree attempted murder and a string of other charges. Her trial became one of the great celebrity events of the war, though the coverage sometimes made it seem more like a society lunch than a murder trial. Breathless descriptions of her clothes appeared in the papers:

> The defendant has changed into a light beige suit. . . . During the morning session she had worn another black town dress, this

one with a square inset yoke of rose-beige lace with matching lace
medallions on the pockets. Her shoes and bag were black.

The standing-room-only crowd at the courthouse, which included rows of army and navy officers, as well as Hawaii notables
like Duke Kahanamoku, the Olympic swimmer, seemed to be wholly
in her corner. So was the jury. It took ten days to try the case. The
jury took less than five minutes to return a verdict of not guilty on
all counts. O'Hara's exploits alone insured that the multimillion
dollar business of regulated prostitution was a subject about which
few could feign ignorance or, increasingly, indifference.[45]

By August 1944, with Jean O'Hara's adventures in the news
and prostitutes living happily in Honolulu's most exclusive residential areas, respectable Honolulu began a serious counterattack. The
haole elite and the armed forces had permitted the open secret of
regulated brothels for years. The Army had accepted the brothels
primarily as a means to control venereal disease and to maintain
morale. The elite had used the prostitutes as a sexual buffer. Those
reasons had seemed important enough before the war. By mid-1944,
with Hawaii completely out of harm's way and American victory all
but assured (though fierce battles still lay ahead), some in Hawaii
had already begun to look to the future, toward statehood and economic development. They did not see free-living, ungovernable prostitutes (who somehow fleshed out mainland images of Hawaii as the
primitive, licentious home of brown-skinned "natives") playing a
role in that future. The gradual restoration of civil control over
governmental affairs gave impetus to the effort to demolish the un-
bridled vice district.

The Social Protection Committee of the Honolulu Council of
Social Agencies led the way in fighting the regulated brothel system
that had been formalized in the early 1930s and had run amuck
under martial law. Unlike the police, who simply wanted to regain
control over the women, the Social Protection Committee wanted to
shut the brothels down completely.

The Committee was a mixed group of haoles, most of whom, in
the context of 1940s Hawaii, were liberal to progressive. One member of the committee was Miles Cary, who more than anyone in

Hawaii had fought the haole old guard in building real educational opportunities for local people in Honolulu. To some extent, the group resembled the kind of well-educated, modern reformers who had closed down regulated brothel systems in dozens of American cities at the height of the Progressive Era.

On August 1, 1944, the Committee issued a bulletin titled "Prostitution in Honolulu" that described (in exceedingly untitillating prose) the Hotel Street system. As a bonus item, a map showed where every known prostitute in Honolulu lived. The message was clear: the prostitutes live in YOUR neighborhood.[46]

Riley Allen, editor of the *Honolulu Star-Bulletin*, the daily associated with the liberal faction of the haole elite that controlled the government and economy of Hawaii, helped lead the fight against prostitution. He'd been involved in a much earlier and temporarily successful effort to close down the brothels just before World War I, and had never supported the regulated system that had grown up by the 1930s. He wrote:

> We have all been remiss, for many years . . . sincerely convinced that some catastrophe, some crime wave, some orgy of sex fiends, would follow from the closing of the houses. . . . Well we have finally waked up. We finally saw conditions become so shameful that in moral revolt we said, "This scandalous violation of the law and this open invitation to tens of thousands of fine young men is all wrong . . . morally indefensible and totally against decent and sound public policy."[47]

With civilian control of the vice district won back from the military by the summer of 1944 (the Japanese threat to Hawaii was long gone and finally so acknowledged by the military governor), the first phase of the antiprostitution campaign went into effect. All prostitutes were ordered to vacate all residential areas and to move back into the regulated houses in which "they carry on their trade." The town was being taken back by the men who meant to run Hawaii after the war.[48]

One month after the prostitutes had been more or less successfully forced back into the district, Governor Stainback, who had been angrily fighting military control of the islands since 1942—

after the Battle of Midway had made invasion of the islands extremely unlikely—joined foursquare with the antiprostitution campaign. Stainback had shown little interest in the subject through the war and his jumping on the antiprostitution bandwagon can be seen, at least in part, as a further attack on military control, since it was the military that acted as guardian angel of the women of Hotel Street. He was also looking ahead to the end of the war.

Stainback, a Democrat appointed by Roosevelt, was linking his interests with the progressive elite. He was distancing himself from the old guard, Republicans all, who used the "whores" as a buffer between "respectable" whites and the "disreputable" lower-class white soldiers and sailors with whom they shared the island.

The "sacrifice" of lower-class white women from the mainland had been a price the old elite had been willing to pay. The progressives who lined up against the brothels, while far from radical, marked off class and racial boundaries less strictly. Even gender lines, though far less so, would be softened and then rethought in the postwar years.[49]

On September 21, 1944, Governor Stainback, in one of his first major reversals of military policy, ordered the regulated brothels shut down. The leaders of the armed forces offered no resistance. A public debate about the issue, in the face of a determined campaign by an influential group of civilians at a time when wartime censorship was at a low ebb, was not something anyone in the armed forces could weather, and the leaders of the antiprostitution forces knew that. The military's decision not to fight the brothel closings might well have been influenced by the fact that penicillin had just become available to cure whatever venereal diseases servicemen picked up as a result of a less controlled sex-for-money racket.[50]

The actual closing of the brothels went smoothly. On September 22nd, three members of the Vice Squad in full uniform visited the brothels between 11 a.m. and 1:30 p.m.—working hours. The madams had already gotten word of the governor's order, made the day before, and so had the customers; business had already come to a virtual stop in most of the houses. The Vice Squad officers told the madams that after 2 p.m. any acts of prostitution committed on their premises would subject them to arrest. The prostitutes were told not to practice their profession in the brothels or outside them and that they should move out of the houses as soon as they had found places to live.

A good many of the prostitutes welcomed the end of an era, and not without humor. One woman greeted the announcement with the old witticism, "I don't practice, I'm an expert." Another woman, wearing "an abbreviated red apron, short-short skirt and a pair of cowboy riding boots," gave out a loud "whoopie" when the news broke.

Madams took the news in a variety of ways. One, "a portly, motherly type of woman, clad in holoku," told reporters, "Okay, boys, now I can go home and take care of papa. I have nothin' to worry about. We'll be closed right up. Thanks for everything." Other women were more annoyed, especially those only recently set up, who'd made substantial investments getting into the business. But the madams, in general, seemed to feel that they had little to complain about. One madam, and probably not the most successful, had voluntarily paid taxes on an income of $383,000 for 1943. As another madam said, in summary of her years in business along Hotel Street, "Well, we really got no kick coming. We really have been well treated in Honolulu." No one had expected the wartime situation to last; the women had only meant to get the most they could out of the ride. With the clampdown in effect, some prostitutes left Honolulu as soon as they could arrange transportation back to the mainland.[51]

Jean O'Hara, in line with her demure and fashionable courtroom appearances, had announced even before the order was finalized that she was leaving the business. Her plan was to follow in her father's footsteps. Close friends told an eager reporter that O'Hara was going to "resume" her study of medicine and surgery. No record of Jean O'Hara's medical school application has been found but neither does she reappear on the court docket in Honolulu. After her sensational trial for murder, Jean O'Hara disappeared from the public eye.[52]

Of course, not everybody took the news so well. Prostitution did not stop with the closing of the brothels, just as it had never been limited to them. Several of the women set up shop elsewhere to meet the incredible demand for their services. They were able to charge up to $100 a session and regularly insisted on $25 for little more than the old three-minute routine. Pimps and procurers naturally became a bigger part of the action.[53]

Bernice Kimbrel neither turned in her "entertainer's" license nor took up with a pimp. Instead, in the face of the closing up of Hotel Street, she opened a brothel. The police shut it down. She struggled to stay in business. Three months after Governor Stainback ruled that prostitutes no longer had the right to operate freely in Honolulu, Kimbrel was murdered, probably by a man who wanted a cut of her earnings.

After all the worry about the men's needs and urges, the closing of the brothels seemed to make little difference. There was no epidemic of sex crimes and the servicemen put up no fight. According to officers who were informally surveyed by their superiors about the brothel shutdowns, the men were fine: "If the troops miss the prostitutes, nothing has been said about it," reported the officer with the dubious distinction of exploring the question.[54] For the three-minute men, it was just one more gripe, one more piece of "chicken-shit" to put up with in a war that had demanded far worse sacrifices.

4

Strangers in a Strange Land

No one found Hawaii stranger than did the 30,000 black soldiers, sailors, and war workers who came through the islands during World War II. In Hawaii, African-American men found themselves in a racial hothouse. Everything seemed possible and nothing seemed certain. The meaning of their own racial identity and the boundaries of racial relations seemed fluid and mutable. Most black men (very few black women came to Hawaii before the war's end) discovered on the islands a more welcoming environment than the one they had left behind. In letters home to family and friends, sweethearts and wives, they mused about its unfamiliar possibilities and explained how they were fighting to claim and to keep what new dignity and hopes Hawaii's wartime racial fluidity offered.

A shipyard worker penned a private note of thanksgiving: "I thank God often for letting me experience the occasion to spend a part of my life in a part of the world where one can be respected and live as a free man should." In a chatty letter home to his girlfriend, a young man tried to explain: "Honey, it's just as much difference between over here and down there as it is between night and day." He concluded that Hawaii "will make anybody change their minds about living down there."[1] "Down there" was the Jim Crow South, the place about which a third man wrote, "I shall never go back. . . ."[2]

White men and women from the mainland also saw these implications. A few expressed excitement about the racial harmony they were witnessing. "They have come as near to solving the race problem as any place in the world. I'm a little mystified by it as yet but it doesn't bother anyone who has lived here awhile," wrote a young nurse. A teacher found it world-shaking: "I have gained here at least the impulse to fight racial bigotry and boogeyism. My soul has been stretched here and my notion of civilization and Americanism broadened."[3]

Most whites felt differently, however.[4] One hardened soul, in Hawaii with her husband and children, wrote the folks: "Down here they have let down the standards, there does not seem to be any race hatred, there is not even any race distinction . . . I don't want to expose our children too long to these conditions."[5] A white man wrote home with racist bemusement: "Imagine that the South will have some trouble ahead when all the black bastards return. Over here they're on the equal with everyone and I mean they live highly. They're in paradise and no fooling."[6] Other white men clearly did not believe the trouble would keep: "Boy the niggers are sure in their glory over here . . . they almost expect white people to step off the streets and let them walk by. . . . They are going to overstep their bounds a little too far one of these days and these boys from the South are going to have a little necktie party."[7]

Thus, if Hawaii sometimes seemed like Paradise, it was not without a serpent in the garden. Black men watched in dread as white southerners proffered the bitter apple: "As you know, most sailors are from Texas and the South. There are most[ly] Navy men here, and they have surely poisoned everyone against the Negro . . . with tales of Negroes carrying dreadful diseases, being thieves, murderers and downright no good."

White southerners did more than spread racial calumny; they campaigned to restore racial hierarchy. Just a few months after the first black war workers and only weeks after the first black troops had arrived in Hawaii, a black war worker wrote his wife:

I've told you before perhaps of this inter-racial conflict and how each little incident was adding a little more fuel. Well . . . it seems that it's becoming a roaring inferno. And if I die, I want you to know that I went down fighting, with a prayer on my lips and your memory in my heart, fighting to break down those racial hatred and prejudices.[8]

For some African Americans, Hawaii was a place of eye-opening possibilities, but it was also a place in which racial struggle would become a necessity.

———

The federal government's presence was more extreme and totalizing in the Territory of Hawaii than in any other part of the nation, except for Washington, D.C. Hawaii was in the war zone; and for almost the duration, from shortly after the surprise attack on Pearl Harbor until late in 1944, the islands were under martial law. The majority of mainland whites and blacks served under military authority in one form or another. How the military chose to enforce its rules and regulations therefore helped determine rights and privileges for all.

Black Americans in Hawaii wanted the military to choose sides in their struggle for respect and justice. As they saw it, military order required that rank and not race, regulations and not custom, should govern how white and black service personnel treated one another.

The peoples of Hawaii, too, helped shape the struggle between mainland whites and blacks. Their alternative assumptions about race were disconcerting for both groups. African Americans took hope from what they saw as a more egalitarian racial order and tried to find a place for themselves in the multiracial "rainbow." Conversely, a good many white soldiers, sailors, marines, and war workers tried to teach local people their racist ideas. Hawaii's people, both local and haole, often found themselves obliged to choose sides in this alien battle. Prefiguring the wars for public opinion fought by the civil rights activists of the 1950s and 1960s, also against a backdrop of increasing federal intervention, mainland blacks and whites struggled for the support of Hawaii's multiethnic society.

———

Racial struggle, especially during wartime, was hardly new to the American landscape.[9] During and just after World War I, even as American forces fought for territory in the European countryside, on the homefront African Americans had literally fought and died for the right to live on certain city blocks, swim at certain beaches, and work in certain places. By that war's end, little clear ground had been gained.[10]

At the dawn of World War II, black Americans knew racism as their daily bread. In the South, where over 75 percent of all African Americans then lived, few blacks were allowed to vote, to serve on juries, or to earn a decent living—let alone learn and practice a skilled trade or profession. Black men and women knew that to walk down the street in the white parts of a southern town with head unbowed could risk a beating, jail, or worse.

In the North, almost all blacks, whatever their incomes, lived in ghettos. Most were restricted to low-paying work, regardless of their education or ability. Black men and women in the North lived in a world of circumscribed dignity. "If you're black, step back, step back," went an old blues song. With the rarest of exceptions black Americans, North or South, were not permitted to tell white Americans what to do.

Because racism was so ingrained in American life, President Roosevelt deliberately decided that the free and democratic country he led, notwithstanding its claims to equality and world leadership, would fight its enemies with segregated armed forces. And despite some efforts to the contrary, it would not be a "separate but equal" military force but one in which African Americans would be overwhelmingly restricted to a lowly caste of mess boys, stevedores, and common laborers.

The rationale for such segregation was clearly stated: "The War Department administers the laws affecting the military establishment; it cannot act outside the law, nor contrary to the will of the majority of the citizens of the Nation."[11] The majority of citizens approved: a wartime survey of five major American cities, north and south, showed that nine out of ten white Americans supported a segregated army. Eight out of ten African Americans did not.[12]

Black Americans faced official racism as best they could, with calm reason and with reasonable rage. John Hope Franklin, who later became a distinguished historian, learned from the racist selective service system in North Carolina that "the United States, however much it was devoted to protecting the freedoms and rights of Europeans, had no respect for me, no interest in my well being, and not even a desire to utilize my services. . . . I concluded that the United States did not need me and did not deserve me." Franklin used his considerable talents to avoid serving in an army run by "those who draped themselves in the flag and sang the national anthem even as they destroyed the nation's ideals and its people."[13] Franklin's choice not to serve was the one white America did not want African Americans to embrace.

The threat that many black Americans might take this path was the one—very risky—trump card black activists could play as they struggled to gain justice during the national emergency. Walter White of the NAACP, A. Philip Randolph of the Brotherhood of Sleeping Car Porters, and other leaders of African-American organizations, in different ways, took their fight to Washington, D.C., and used threats of disunity, international embarrassment, and street heat to win important, if limited, victories. Just before war broke out, in response to pressure from black Americans as well as from the First Lady and other liberal intimates, President Roosevelt appointed William Hastie, a black civil-rights paladin, Civilian Aide to the Secretary of War.

Hastie fought to gain black service personnel a place of respect in the armed forces. During the crucial first year of the war, he struggled against his antagonistic boss, Secretary of War Henry Stimson, to keep issues of social justice for African-American servicemen before the President and a few other sympathetic officials. Though he resigned in frustration little more than a year after Pearl Harbor, Hastie gained black Americans a little more room in which to maneuver.[14]

During the war years, hundreds of thousands of black southerners moved North. Competition over housing, jobs, and recreational facilities fueled America's racial fires. The balance of American race relations was shifting. In wartime Detroit, New York, and elsewhere, thousands of African Americans, many of them newly arrived defense workers, fought pointed battles against white racism during violent riots. The civil rights *movement*, though still inchoate, was enjoined during the war.

In the end, though, few African Americans battled in the streets, looked to Washington for help, or took John Hope Franklin's defiant stand against the war. Overwhelmingly, they served their country and embraced the war effort.[15] However, many did define the goals of the war differently. They championed the "Double V" campaign called for by the nation's largest black newspaper, the *Pittsburgh Courier*: "Victory over our enemies at home and victory over our enemies on the battlefields abroad."[16] As Robert L. Vann, publisher and editor of the *Courier*, wrote just after Pearl Harbor: "We call upon the President and Congress to declare war on Japan and against racial prejudice in our country, certainly we should be strong enough to whip both of them."[17]

Only one of those wars would be officially declared. Black Americans would have to carry their fight to the second front. The question many pondered as the two wars raged, was whether some white Americans would support them in their struggle.

Long before the strains of World War II had become visible, W. E. B. Du Bois had written:

> One ever feels his twoness—an American, a Negro; two souls, two thoughts, two unreconciled strivings; two warring ideals on one dark body, whose dogged strength alone keeps it from being torn asunder. The history of the American Negro is the history of this strife—this longing to attain self-conscious manhood, to merge his double self into a better and truer self. . . . He simply wishes to make it possible for a man to be both a Negro and an American, without being cursed and spit upon by his fellows. . . .[18]

The tens of thousands of African-American soldiers, sailors, and war workers who came through Hawaii to fight America's enemies knew those emotions.[19] In their letters home, they dwelled almost obsessively upon their double obligation to race and country, to their senses of honor and duty.

A young war worker at the Pearl Harbor shipyards admitted his confusion about the war: "It's awful hard for one to concentrate all his efforts toward the war when he has such a great battle to fight at home. Yet they tell us we are fighting for freedom, maybe I am too young to understand." An older man, less sure of pen, but clearer in his thoughts, wrote: "When I read of the way they were doing Colored people in the South I wondered am I doing right for helping with the war. I get pretty hot some time the way they do. But I will do my best to help save it. But if they don't do any better when the war is over, I am making a change."

One of the better educated black men wrote a friend with the questions that haunted much of black America: "Our people are dying in the far flung battle fronts . . . for what? We are little better than slaves now, opportunities are withheld from us, in fact, we are outcasts of society. What benefits will this war bring us?"[20]

African Americans in Hawaii felt the twin pull of race and nationality. But in Hawaii, African Americans felt another pull as well. In Hawaii, race and ethnicity, racism and prejudice came bundled in unknown quantities and in unfamiliar shapes. In the mysteries of this radically different cultural configuration lay possibilities for African Americans as yet unexplored in mainland America.

Hawaii had no "Negro Problem" before World War II, in part because few people on the islands recognized that any "Negroes" lived there. In 1940, by one government estimate, approximately 200 "Negroes of American birth" lived on the islands. But there was no social group identified as Negro in any territorial document, though there were some people of African descent, ethnically Puerto Rican, who made up a "small statistical (census) group." Census data on race and ethnicity was notoriously hard to gather on the islands because there was a great deal of intermarriage and because the racial categories of the mainland did not necessarily make sense. In Hawaii's census data in the early twentieth century, people of African descent were classified as Puerto Rican while Puerto Ricans were classified as Caucasian. Thus Hawaii's so-called "Negro" population was classified as Caucasian.[21]

The white elite was proud of the ways in which their race relations differed from those of the mainland. And though their statements were often self-serving, the haole elite was at least partly right; race relations were different in Hawaii. Samuel Wilder King, the delegate from Hawaii to the U.S. Congress before the war and Governor soon after (himself proudly part-Hawaiian), explained this view in a 1939 magazine article, "Hawaii Has No Race Problem":

> Today the races of Hawaii live together as one people, owning one common allegiance to their American nationality. Racial origin means nothing to the individual in his status as an American. Among the racial groups there is mutual understanding and friendly sympathy. The spirit of Old Hawaii governs, and "race prejudice" as such is not countenanced.

King concluded with words that would echo through wartime Hawaii: "That Hawaii should ever lose its happy freedom from intolerance because of a new philosophy brought into the islands from elsewhere, would be indeed a tragedy."[22]

To an extent, the haole elite really believed their Hawaii to be a paradigm of racial harmony. That they had economically excluded Asian and Pacific Americans for decades, that they had done their best to keep them out of real political power, that they spoke of them in prejudicial terms, and refused to mingle socially with Asian Americans; all this was omitted from their view of Hawaii as the land of racial and ethnic *Aloha*. To many of islands' peoples, such a view seemed ridiculous, a malicious coverup.

Still, King was more right than wrong, since he was describing the general attitude of the peoples of Hawaii. Most local people did not bring the racist ways of the mainland into their daily lives. They did stereotype one another: many Japanese Americans looked down on the Chinese; the Chinese looked down on the Filipinos, and so on. Each ethnic group had their suspicions of the others. But such prejudices did not reproduce the mainland's rigid caste society. Even many of the white elite did not by World War II manifest the depth of racist thinking that was essentially pro forma on the continental U.S. Much more than the rest of the country, Hawaii did represent, as many on the islands claimed, the possibility of a rainbow society.[23]

The African-American servicemen and war workers who came to Hawaii had not come to a racial utopia, even though some saw it that way. But they did discover there an alternative to the America they knew.

Before a single black soldier[24] arrived in Hawaii, military command had wrestled with the question of whether to send "colored" regiments to the islands at all. G-2, or Army Intelligence (a contradiction in terms, went the obvious joke), had thought that black troops' "propinquity" with whites would be unavoidable and dangerous in Hawaii. Intelligence officers also feared that existing tensions between white troops and local people might be worsened by adding mainland blacks to the already precarious balance of Hawaiian race relations. Thus they argued that no black troops should be sent to Hawaii.

Of course, G-2 had argued that sending black troops just about anywhere outside of the mainland United States would be extremely problematic. America was not the only Allied nation with a race problem. The British had India and their Caribbean possessions, Australia had its Australia-for-whites-only policy, France and Belgium had their African colonies—indeed, black troops could create political problems throughout the colonial world. Racism was not just an issue of local prejudice, nor was it America's "peculiar" problem. It was integral to the political and economic order of much of the globe.

American military commanders had generally decided that deploying troops where they were most needed would come before the specific racial concerns of allied nations. American military planners did not repudiate racism or the racial policies of Allied nations but they did insist that such racial concerns be a secondary concern. Most American allies, in the end, agreed.[25]

So, within the rigid framework of a segregated armed forces in which blacks were systematically denied equal treatment or opportunity, African-American troops and war workers came to Hawaii as military necessity required them.

—

The African-American men who came to Hawaii were far from a homogeneous group. In most ways they were almost as diverse as their white counterparts—though far more of them were poorly schooled, came from rural areas of the deep South, and had been denied specialized civilian and military training.[26]

When it came to their attitudes about white racism and their responses to racist practices, the most significant divide was between those from the rural South and those from the urban North. A poll taken on the mainland showed that seven out of ten northern blacks thought segregation should be attacked during the wartime crisis but only one in ten southern blacks agreed.[27] Southern blacks lived with the fear learned from experience of the massive, deadly retaliation white southerners could visit upon them if provoked. A good many northern blacks, while not unaware of these dangers, simply felt obliged by their traditions and their experiences not to accept traditional southern racism. Nor would they keep their objections to themselves.

Leading the charge against racism in Hawaii were the men of the 369th Coast Artillery (AA) Regiment—known as "The Harlem Hellfighters." The entire organizational structure and history of the 369th leading up to their deployment in Hawaii reads like a primer in how to foster pride, integrity, and esprit de corps in young men. During World War II, the men of the 369th would use their training, their character, and the opportunities of wartime Hawaii to change the racial boundaries of white and black.

Not that fighting racism was seen by the men of the 369th as their primary duty. They saw themselves first of all as outstanding soldiers who meant to be treated as such. Fighting racism was simply something that came with the territory.

The 369th was an elite New York National Guard unit that had been federalized for the war effort. In 1941, they were one of the very few all-black regiments: officers, as well as enlisted men. They were based in the heart of Harlem—their armory overlooked the Harlem River at 142nd Street—and they were a beloved and respected community organization.

The 369th had won its place in the heart of black America during World War I. The unit had fought in the Meuse-Argonne offensive attached to the French army, and they had been among the first Americans to fight their way into German territory (fifty-five of those men were still with the 369th in Hawaii). Their courage under fire had been exemplary and the French government awarded the Croix de Guerre to the 369th regimental colors and to over 150 of the men. When they returned from "over there" at war's end, all of New York turned out to pay their respects as the regiment marched up Fifth Avenue. As one of their officers remembered it:

They did not give us their welcome because ours was a regiment
of colored soldiers—they did not give us their welcome in spite of
ours being a regiment of colored soldiers. They greeted us that day
from hearts filled with gratitude and with pride and love, because
ours was a regiment of men, who had done the work of men.[28]

Proponents of black combat forces during World War II mobi-
lization—espousing a far from universally accepted idea—pointed to
the unit as compelling evidence against racist charges that blacks
were inherently poor soldiers. One of the most outspoken white
champions of black soldiers during World War II, Hamilton Fish,
Jr., the fiercely anti-New Deal, conservative Republican congressman from New York, had been a company commander with the
369th during the Great War.[29]

Approximately 1,800 men went to Hawaii with the 369th during World War II. They included men from all five boroughs of
New York as well as from the southern states. But the core of the
group came from a ten-block radius within Harlem. Many of the
men had gone to the same schools together—P.S. 5, 89, 139, 194—
and were from the same churches and family networks. They knew
and trusted one another. Few regiments in World War II were
drawn from such a coherent group (though the reasons for the
369th's coherence are not all positive).

Joining the 369th, before it was sent up for training as a coast
artillery regiment, was not a simple matter. Before the war mobi-
lization, members of the 369th were carefully screened by the regiment. First, you had to have a sponsor in the unit who'd vouch for
you. Then the recruiting team interviewed you and visited your
home and employer, primarily to see if you were responsible and to
make sure that you could have two weeks off each summer to go to
training camp. Several of the younger men had to apprentice to the
unit and prove their self-discipline before they made the ranks.[30]

William De Fossett is fairly representative of the kind of young
man who was attracted to the 369th, and his experiences in the
Army explain much about the possibilities of race relations both
during and after the war years.

William Kenneth De Fossett was born in New York City in
1920. During the Great Depression, at a time when black unem-

ployment in New York approached 50 percent,[31] De Fossett's father held on to a job with the Southern Pacific Steamship Company. Although she was a college graduate, his mother, like most working black women in the North (and most married black women with children worked), was a domestic. Opportunities were limited and racial prejudice was a fact of life. But both of De Fossett's parents had been born in New York City and had little personal knowledge of the worst aspects of racism—of Jim Crow, of political disenfranchisement, of bowing and scraping before white people, of lynch mobs. Instead, they enjoyed a life in one of the most vibrant and culturally rich communities in the nation.

When De Fossett was seven and his brother eight, his family moved to Harlem's Paul Laurence Dunbar Apartments, a model housing development financed by John D. Rockefeller. Little William's neighbors there included some of the giants of black America: Paul Robeson, W. E. B. Du Bois, Bill "Bojangles" Robinson, A. Philip Randolph, Mat Henson, and many others. As a kid of nine and ten, he and his pals played in Henson's apartment, dressing up in the very mukluks Henson had worn when he—and not Commander Peary, Henson told them—had become the first American to reach the North Pole. Paul Robeson, whom De Fossett thought of as "just the singer on the third floor," taught him how to throw a football.

De Fossett grew up feeling proud of his people and his community. His parents, by their example and through instruction, pushed him intellectually. His father used to tell his boys that a day should not go by without their learning a new word and that they should not associate with people from whom they could not learn. The De Fossett boys grew up expecting to be somebody.

From childhood on, playing in the shadows of the Polo Grounds (home of the New York Giants), and well coached by his father, De Fossett was a standout athlete. By the time he was fifteen, he and his brother, Joe, were playing professional ball, part-time, in the Negro Baseball League. William was a tall, well built, dark-skinned, good-looking young man who could hit a long ball. His friends called him "Babe." Both De Fossett boys played for the New York Black Yankees, the Pittsburgh Crawfords, the Baltimore Elite Giants, and with Alex Pompez's Cuban Stars. For a kid and a fill-in, the pay was small—nobody made real money playing in the Negro Leagues—but in the midst of the Depression, it was a pleasant way to earn a few dollars.

Like a good many other teenage boys in his neighborhood who had something on the ball, De Fossett wanted to be a part of the 369th. He'd been watching them drill and parade outside the Armory since he was a little boy. Everyone knew what they had done in France during World War I. Joining the 369th was something he and his friends could do together as a sign of maturity and as a way to earn respect in their community. Best of all, it meant two weeks every summer in the mountains, getting paid to have fun. De Fossett was known to be an outstanding athlete and when he was sixteen he was sponsored into the 369th. You were supposed to be eighteen to enlist, but De Fossett and his baseball-playing friends were big for their ages and nobody thought anything of it.

Before the war, young men joined the 369th through the individual companies. I company was made up mainly of men from the West Indies, Barbados in particular. C Company, too, had a lot of young men from the Caribbean. Another company had men who almost all hailed from South Carolina. G Company was drawn from the blocks just uptown of the Armory. De Fossett thus became a private in G Company, a young man surrounded and supported and watched over by other young men from his own neighborhood.

The men of the regiment had each other to live up to as well as the proud name of their troop. If you failed your company everybody on your block, in your family, and all your friends were going to know about it. The prospect was a spur to the men's dedication. Attendance at the prewar training camps was usually 100 percent. [32]

The 369th boasted some of Harlem's finest young athletes and musicians. Olympic track star John Woodruff (holder of a master's degree in sociology) served as a first lieutenant. Dozens of top professional jazz musicians filled the ranks and made the unit's band among the best in the country. People in Harlem did not focus much attention on the 369th in the years before the war; but like graduating from P.S. 5 and P.S. 139, being in the 369th was a sign of being promising, a young man of note. [33]

The 369th was federalized in January 1941 in an early phase of the war buildup. The Army command, under the watchful eyes of interested whites such as Congressman Hamilton Fish, as well as those black Army officers and civilians fighting for a combat role for black troops, slated the unit for one year of anti-aircraft artillery training. Though the men of the 369th did not know it, the training represented a kind of compromise between the military command's basic racism and its need to demonstrate some commitment to a nondiscriminatory policy.

Since anti-aircraft artillery regiments were fighting units of high status and skill, the Army was showing good faith in the ability of the 369th and four other black combat regiments trained in 1941 for AAA status. On the other hand, anti-aircraft artillery units were, as War Department Civilian Aide William Hastie wrote in protest to Secretary Stimson, "in a special category" of combat units.

> Such a unit could be given a separate and more or less permanent defensive station in the theatre of operations. It need not be integrated with other combat forces. So the utilization of Negro anti-aircraft units in the theater of operations was adopted as a device best calculated to confound the critics of any policy as to Negro combat troops without basically changing that policy. [34]

The 369th was very purposefully slotted for the kind of combat training that would keep its champions satisfied, but would minimize its integration into combat operations with white soldiers. The issue of race structured everything military command did to, for, and with the Harlem Hellfighters.

Also purposefully, Harlem's finest were not sent south for training. The southern training camps were hellholes for black troops. In them, Jim Crow reigned; the white citizenry heaped abuse; and southern (and not a few northern) officers devised elaborate rituals of degradation for the black men under their camp command. [35] It did not even take Army Intelligence to point out the explosion likely to occur if Harlem's armed pride were sent down *en masse* to the land of cotton. In fact, when a reporter from a black newspaper read to a group of these soldiers a letter from a friend of his stationed at Fort Bragg in North Carolina, detailing the camp's racist practices, the reaction was swift: "They all in concert declared that the day they are assigned to the South, they will go prepared for any and all emergencies" (later, cadres from the 369th were sent to Camp Stewart in Georgia and the results *were* explosive).[36]

Instead, the 369th was sent north to Oswego, New York, the land of deep snow. They'd marched out of the armory to the Mott Haven Railroad Yard with full packs, rifles on shoulders, surrounded by family and friends. Mothers, fathers, sweethearts, and wives were emotional but the men of the 369th went out stoically.

Samuel Phillips was a very bright, sparkling twenty-one-year-old who was also one of the better point guards in Harlem. He was new to the regiment, one of the draft-eligible men who had volunteered just a couple of months before the regiment was federalized. He'd been personally welcomed by the troop's sergeant major, who was one of his ball-playing buddies.

Phillips had quickly picked up the regiment's esprit. "Nobody cried or said anything," as they marched off, he remembers. The men knew that there was a war on the horizon, and nobody could say when they'd be back. But everyone treated the move to Fort Ontario as just another training session. As Phillips saw it, he was "going away with friends-for-life." Morale was outstanding.[37]

Like almost all the troops that went to Hawaii, the 369th put in long months training on the mainland before they got overseas orders. Their preparatory experiences helped define and focus the race consciousness and racial pride their Harlem days had taught them.

At Fort Ontario the men became expert at handling anti-aircraft weaponry. Lieutenant Woodruff would be able to tell the white press, with no brag: "they're dead eyes . . . and I don't mean with the galloping dominoes." White officers agreed: "They were crackerjack at parade and weapons."[38] In almost a year's time, the 369th, under black officers' command (though two white artillery officers had been assigned during training as advisors) had been transformed from part-time soldiers into professional warriors.

In racial terms, the time in Oswego went well. The town was "lily white" (De Fossett's term) and people had greeted the 369th with more than a little concern. Soon enough, though, the townspeople got to know the young men and became friendly. De Fossett and most of the other nonpolitical men saw this as the way of the world. They believed that once you got past rumors and stereotypes and got to know each other as people, everything would be all right. And, in general, the Oswego experience proved them correct.

But one incident belied these simple hopes. The incident influenced the men's understanding of life beyond Harlem and also indicated how they would handle racially charged situations in Hawaii.

As happens the world over, the servicemen soon made the acquaintance of the local women. Since there was only one black family in Oswego, those local women were white. And as is wont to happen, a young soldier and his girlfriend were discovered in a compromising situation. The soldier fled—in embarrassment and perhaps fearful of the immediate repercussions. The white woman, humiliated and under threat of social ostracism for breaking a major taboo of 1940s America, said she had been raped.

This was upstate New York in 1941, not Mississippi. No lynch mob came. But the police did, and insisted that the entire regiment be lined up so that the suspect could be identified and jailed. Within hours, all the men knew what had happened and they were angry. Until the charges were dropped, they decided, the city of Oswego would be boycotted. Many members of the 369th could remember the "don't shop where you can't work" campaigns that the Reverend Adam Clayton Powell had led in Harlem along 125th Street in the midthirties. A few of the young men, no more than boys at the time, had marched in the picket lines—mostly for fun and adventure. And among the older men were serious "Race Men," like the chaplain Robert B. Doakes and William Eubanks, a friend of Powell's who'd also fought against the fascists during the Spanish Civil War.

The officers fully supported the boycott; vehicles were provided so that the 369th could take its business to other towns. New York's Governor Lehman, partly in response to the concerns of Oswego merchants, agreed to mediate, and shortly the charges were dropped. The 369th thus defeated one of the saddest and most dangerous forms of America's racial sickness.[39]

After completing a year's training, the 369th was supposed to go home. But a little more than a month before their hitch was up, the Japanese attacked Pearl Harbor. A few months later, the men of the 369th found themselves, weapons at the ready, guarding Cape Cod from air attack. A few months later still, they were sent to defend the southern California coast, and American race relations took another odd turn.

Military command worked out the map coordinates and sent the 369th to emplot their guns. They must have known that they were sending the black unit to set up their anti-aircraft guns in the backyards of some of the wealthiest white people in America, including a few of Hollywood's biggest stars. There, in the midst of elaborately coiffed lawns and landscaped gardens, twelve black troopers pitched their tents in each yard and settled in for who knew how long. Not a few of the wealthy whites were aghast.

William De Fossett, by this time Personnel Sgt. Major of the 369th, heard some of the complaints: "We've never had Negroes living here and now they're in our back yards with those horrible guns." De Fossett thought it was hilariously funny, as did the men. Orders were orders, however, and they stayed where they were.

If some whites were appalled by the Army-style integration of Burbank, California, many others welcomed their defenders. White stars like Humphrey Bogart and Rosalind Russell befriended the troopers. Bogart told a group of the men that they were welcome to make use of his house and gave them the keys to show he meant it. Black celebrities like Leigh Whipper, Eddie "Rochester" Anderson, Lena Horne, and Hattie McDaniel came and visited the troops and provided them with generous hospitality. The 369th tried to repay these attentions with some generosity of their own. Every Sunday, they played a concert for their neighbors, featuring the finest big-band jazz sounds that Burbank had probably ever heard.

For almost a year, the 369th had trained in Oswego for cold-weather duty. They'd been issued snow boots and huge woolen union suits. Now, in another fine display of Army logic, after a few weeks in sunny California the 369th were loaded into a troop ship in San Francisco and zigzagged their way to Honolulu Harbor. The 369th was to be in charge of defending Hawaii from air attack. They came with their morale still strong, their commitment to a double victory unchanged by a year in the Army.

Sam Phillips, when told they were bound for Hawaii, could only think, "What the hell is it?" No one that anybody knew from Harlem had been to Hawaii. Of course, Phillips and the others knew Pearl

Harbor and, like many other mainlanders, he had listened at one time or another to the popular radio show, "Hawaii Calls." But that was about it. That Hawaii was a multiracial society, involving complex relations between the white elite and the Asian and Pacific peoples who made up the bulk of the population, was totally unknown to Phillips and most of the other men. The main thing Phillips thought about as they steamed into harbor was, "I hope the Japanese don't come back."

Ironically, as the 369th chugged their way to their initial base camp on the little sugarcane railroad, a noticeable number of people reacted to them as if they were some kind of invading force. In the fields the train cut through, inexplicably, people seemed to be running from them.

It didn't take long to figure out what had happened. Local people had been warned by southern white soldiers and sailors that blacks were, literally, dangerous animals.

De Fossett could scarcely believe the rumors that were circulating on the island about the black troops: "These people have tails. They're this far from monkeys," the rumor went. If a black man and a local woman had a child, "the baby would be a monkey." It was almost funny, but De Fossett and others couldn't help but notice that in their first few weeks on the island, people were actually looking for their tails.

A story quickly made the rounds among the men that verified the power of this calumny. A small group of the men were invited to a social gathering with some local people. It was very pleasant and nothing exceptional occurred until a couple of the men noticed that all of the chairs to which the black men were steered had pillows on them. When one of the men went to sit on a chair without a pillow, the host ran over and flung one under the descending soldier. The men asked what was going on.

Their hosts somewhat sheepishly explained that they had been told about the black men's tails and they imagined that without a pillow to sit on they would be subject to great discomfort. The hosts were only trying to be nice.

All over the island—especially to young women—the 369th calmly explained that the tail business was a racist lie, as was the rest. How could it be true, they sighed, that black men made monkey babies? But often enough, the explanation seemed to leave a residue of uncertainty. So the men offered physical proof. As De Fossett reported, "the 369th spent a lot of time taking their pants down" to show that they were "an anurous biological species." At the beginning of their stay, the 369th "dropped drawers all over Hawaii," as people actually looked for their tails.[40]

In letters home, black servicemen fumed about the spread of racial hatred:

> There are a great many southerners here that seem to think we Negroes have no place here of a right in the sun. They preach to the natives a nasty, poisonous doctrine that we must fight like hell to overcome. They tell the natives that we are ignorant dumb, evil, rapers, and trouble makers. They have the native women to a point they are afraid to even speak to our Negro boys.

Another bitterly complained: "The old settlers here tell me this place was once a paradise for Negroes. Since the war, a Negro finds things very unpleasant here."[41]

The men of the 369th did not take kindly to such provocations. The antiblack propaganda they could only fight indirectly by doing their best to set the record straight. Direct confrontations were another matter.

From their first liberties in Honolulu, the men encountered a practice that many had heard of but few had actually witnessed. The scene was often the densely packed sidewalks of the Hotel Street district, with thousands of men in uniform squirming through the long lines, the sidewalk concessionaires, and the darting importunities of hundreds of hustlers. From a distance, the men would watch as a group of white sailors or soldiers sauntered down the sidewalk right at them. And then, in their face, there'd be the words, the same words every time, "Nigger, get off the street!" And when the black men did not move, "Nigger, don't you know you're supposed to get off the street!" In the first few months, the 369th faced this set piece again and again—southern street protocol played out in the middle of the Pacific Ocean. But there were some very important differences.

The first was the 369th itself. As De Fossett says, once the "crackers" made their pitch, the 369th made their reply. A black soldier would punch the speaker in the nose. It didn't often take many punches, but he would make sure the man went down—and hard. "We were raised in New York," De Fossett says. "We were not strangers to street fighting." At least two white servicemen died in these confrontations. One died after striking his head when he fell (some say on a fire hydrant, some say on the curb). Another just collapsed in the middle of the fistfight (his death was later attributed to an aneurism or some other natural cause).

And here was the second difference between the routines of the South and the realities of wartime Hawaii. In the early 1940s, a black man who killed a white man in the deep South over a question of racial protocol would be lucky to see the inside of a jail cell.[42] But in wartime Hawaii, both Wentworth Morris and Preston Daniels, the two black soldiers who knocked down and killed the white servicemen, were cleared of all charges. That decision sent a potent message. A black man's right to self-defense was formally endorsed by the standards of military justice. The 369th made sure that the word got around. They intended to be treated with respect and according to military protocol—and they had shown that they were able to enforce these expectations.[43]

While incidents like these were never banished, the 369th had proved a point. The Military Police got to know the unit and reckoned that the black soldiers "did not seek trouble but . . . never backed up from trouble."[44] Some members of other black units in the islands sought protection in the mystique of the 369th. They wrote home, talking about their exploits and venting their own angry feelings about racial discrimination being "brought here by the white man." But black soldiers in Hawaii did not just talk about the 369th, they emulated their example, sometimes literally. Many members of the quartermasters corps, for instance, when on pass in Honolulu, replaced their blue-trimmed caps with the red-trimmed ones worn by the coast artillery. The caps insured a measure of respect. Within a few months (at least as the 369th saw it), most of the other black troops on the island, while on pass, walked the streets in the red-trimmed caps of the Harlem Hellfighters.[45]

Street protocol was a loaded issue for white and black southerners alike. It was a very public, everyday way in which racial
hierarchy was played out and reinforced in southern towns and
cities. The 369th had changed the rules, and the MPs and military
justice had affirmed their stance. But military protocol supported
the black troops in an even more explosive battle.

In the South, whites did not call blacks by titles of respect
regardless of their age, accomplishments, or gender. As a matter of
course, in 1940, many white people addressed black doctors and
yardmen alike as nigger or boy or any other demeaning term that
came to mind. Southern whites had been raised to patronize and
command blacks; never did they take orders from them.

The rules and regulations of the armed forces put these traditions to at least a partial test, as military intelligence had known
they would. In part out of concern about how white enlisted men
would respond to the presence of black officers, the Army had tried
to prevent white and black troops from serving even near each other,
let alone with one another. Black officers were few and far between
in World War I, not only because of racist assumptions about their
leadership abilities but out of concern with how to fit race protocol
into the military hierarchy. The regular Army, before war mobili-
zation began in 1940, had only five black officers (five more than the
rest of the active-duty forces had combined), and three of those
were chaplains. During World War II, black troops were overwhelmingly led by white officers. Even at the end of the war, less
than 2 percent of all officers were black and they were systematically denied positions not only where they would command white
troops but where they would directly outrank white officers.[46]

The 369th, like other federalized black National Guard and
reserve units,[47] was an exception to general rules governing black
troops. The unit was led throughout the war years by black officers.
These officers demanded the respect due them by military regulation.

Southern servicemen who had attempted to enforce their traditional race protocol in Hawaii had lost. They could try to overlook
the breach of behavior by ignoring the black faces they encountered
on the streets. But there was a problem with this tactic. Rank had

to be observed. In the United States Army, enlisted men saluted officers, lower-ranking officers saluted higher-ranking officers. Failing to salute your superior was a breach of regulations and could lead to disciplinary proceedings.

For many southern whites, raised to regard black men with feelings that narrowly ranged from vicious contempt to patronizing amusement, the intersection of military protocol and race protocol created a conundrum. One young private in a southern training camp believed he had found a solution. The white enlisted man explained his logic to the black lieutenant: "If you would take your clothes off and lay them on the ground I would salute them but I won't salute anything that looks like you." In the camp where this occurred, commanded by southern officers, and largely governed by local racial customs, the private got away with this offense to military regulations. The black lieutenant, who had asked his white superiors to discipline the private, was soon transferred out as a troublemaker.[48]

In Hawaii, the conundrum was similar, the proposed solution novel, and the outcome very different. Sergeant De Fossett saw it all come to a head.

Ever since the 369th had come to Hawaii, some white soldiers and officers had resented the necessity of saluting their black superiors. As De Fossett says, you could almost hear them thinking, "how can I get around this?" You could watch the wheels turning.

A plan was hatched, although whether it was literally a coordinated plot or just a bright idea that swept through a swath of junior officers remains unclear. The resulting scene was so bizarre that the officer corps of the 369th were, at first, too surprised to react. The scene was repeated on the streets of Honolulu, at Schofield Barracks, or anywhere a certain kind of junior white officer could not avoid a black officer of superior rank.

The white officer would start running, not away from the black officer, but right at him. He'd run right up to him, grab the officer's hand and start shaking it while chattering brightly, "Hello, hello, how are you," as if the men were old acquaintances. Then he'd walk smartly away.

The white men who did this were mocking the system. Perhaps

they assumed the black officers would be so pleased by the show of friendship that they would forget the breach of decorum. The white officers were willing to feign intimacy, even make physical contact, rather than have to salute a black man as their superior. It was so unexpected that it did, briefly, work—until a junior-grade lieutenant tried the routine on Major Edward I. Marshall, the Battalion Adjutant of the 369th.

Major Marshall was a stern, commanding, even intimidating presence. He was not amused by the lieutenant's insolence.

Marshall did not argue, he did not complain. Military style, in full fury, he exercised his authority.

"Do not shake my hand. I don't like you and you don't like me. But I am a major!!! You are a lieutenant!!! Salute me!!!!" He raged at the rigid junior officer. The lieutenant, in silence, complied with the order. Sgt. De Fossett watched from beginning to end, finally breaking out in laughter as the dismissed white officer scuttled off, and he made sure the whole unit heard about it. Word must have reached the rest of the handshakers as well; no more incidents of insubordination of this sort were witnessed in Hawaii.[49]

Major Marshall demanded respect, and he got it. Military protocol had been upheld by a black man answering to his own confident sense of dual obligation to duty and personal honor. But Marshall and the other men of the 369th did not act in isolation in Hawaii, and although they had enemies, they also had allies. Their most important ally was the military governor of Hawaii, Lt. General Emmons. While he may not have been precisely on their side, he was less opposed to improving race relations than he was to the prospect of race riots, which he saw as the only alternative.

On November 6, 1942, a few months after the 369th arrived in Hawaii, Emmons issued a confidential memo to each commanding general and to all commanding officers at every post, camp, station, depot, district, and service command in the Hawaiian Islands. Emmons was very unhappy about the increasing "instances of interracial conflict in the city of Honolulu." He wanted the incidents stopped and he laid blame squarely on white shoulders.

"The fact that such incidents have occurred indicates a lack of proper training, instruction, and discipline on the part of the per-

sonnel involved, and of the officers under whom they are serving,"
Emmons stated. He then ordered all commissioned officers to adopt
"every possible means" to eliminate the causes of discord and to
inculcate by personal example "a spirit of harmony and unity" among
their personnel.

> It is of the utmost importance that our ranks present a united
> front in the present emergency and that racial prejudice, jealou-
> sies, and discord be not permitted to create or foster internal
> friction. The reasons for the total elimination of such friction are
> so apparent and so compelling that they require no reiteration.[50]

The reasons Emmons found "so apparent and so compelling" were
not ideals of social and political equality, but the practical business
of winning the war. Simply put, he wanted all hands pulling in the
same direction.

Emmons' call for racial calm did not have uniform effects, however. His order was a kind of racial Rorschach test for his subordi-
nates, who could and did interpret it in different ways.

The editors of the *Midpacifican*, the official enlisted man's Army
newspaper, seemed to see the order as a call for better racial understanding. Prior to this, the *Midpacifican* had not been a beacon of
racial enlightenment. In one of its first issues after Pearl Harbor,
the editors printed a gratuitous cartoon of a white man stepping into
a cab (a horse and buggy) and telling the black driver that he wants
to go to a "haberdasher." The cabby answers: "No look a-here boss,
I be'en drivin' in dis town twenty years and I an't neber giv' nobody
away yit. Now you jus' tell dis nigger whar 't is you wanter go."[51]
Not untypical race humor of the time.

After the order, the paper's approach to black Americans took a
decided change. The 369th was featured in a glowing account (a
typical genre in the paper) exclaiming, "Their record on duty has
been termed 'excellent.' " In the next issue, the editors elected to do
a major profile on the 369th's Olympic champion, Lt. John Woodruff, who had been on the island, unpublicized, for many months.
No more racist jokes were printed. Instead, the *Midpacifican* became
a steady instrument for racial progress.[52]

Strangers in a Strange Land

At the Pearl Harbor Shipyard and other nearby work and housing areas, where thousands of black civilians and service personnel were stationed during the war, Emmons' orders had little effect. The shipyard and the Naval Cantonment housed many of the Pearl Harbor war workers. It was here that blacks and whites most often mixed, and more than any other places in Hawaii, the shipyard and the cantonment reflected the contradictions of the government's race policy. Housing for the shipyard workers was segregated. The barbershops were segregated. But the mess halls, the theaters, the commissary, and all other public facilities were not. Blacks and whites worked together alongside local people of color. Civilian workers were supposed to have the same opportunities for advancement, regardless of race, though black naval personnel were restricted to low-ranking duties. The mixed policy and the uneven enforcement of rules and regulations governing equal employment and fair treatment dramatically heightened racial tensions at Pearl Harbor.[53]

Many white southerners could not believe that they were expected to mix with black men, and they were furious over the government's call for racial equality. They also realized that they had limited space for fighting back. "I am in a place where niggers are treated just like they are in 'Yankey' land," wrote one war worker, "and I am so damn burned up with the S.O.B. that the first one that looks crosseyed at me, after I cross the Mason-Dixon line, well I won't say what will happen to him." Another man from the same work section added, "The government is sending alot of them out here and giving them all the privileges of a white man . . . we are going to have a war with the Negro[e]s when this one is over right in the States."[54]

Black men at the shipyard and other Pearl Harbor work areas did enjoy the relative freedoms the Navy provided. As one man observed about life in the cantonment: "I do wish some of the poor trash or crackers in the South could give a look. They would realize that the Negro does not want to socialize or fraternize with them but want equal rights to enjoy some of that freedom that they talk about every time we pledge our legence [sic] to this great flag." But others noted that while Navy policies were a decided improvement over what they had known at home, big problems remained, and they rankled.

One well-educated black man tried to explain his frustrations to Naval Intelligence Officers:

> I have no hesitation in saying that there is discrimination against the colored boys and they know it. The first point of discrimination is in the service. We have many boys at the cantonment who were anxious to join the Navy. Many are intelligent and cooperative. They couldn't get commissions . . . at best they become chief bandsmen or messmen . . . their skin inhibits their opportunities. How many Negro leadingmen are there in the Navy Yard? The paucity indicates they are either inferior in ability or else they are discriminated against. I can't help but feel that the latter factor is at least partially an explanation.[55]

The white Chief Master-at-Arms of a Navy base company agreed that the Navy's overall pattern of discrimination put his black sailors on edge: "The boys are not getting what they were promised. Many of the seamen are capable of doing electrical or mechanical work and yet are still doing stevedoring. . . . This complaint is pretty general and it is the biggest cause of dissension which exists here. It causes dissatisfaction continually."[56]

A number of white men at the shipyards and elsewhere aimed a steady drumbeat of racist remarks, insults, and slights at their black co-workers and fellow sailors. Black men already angry over the cap to their ambitions set by formal Navy policy and everyday, informal, and unpunished discrimination, were easily made to boil over. Between mid-1942 and 1945, dozens of fracases occurred between blacks and whites, including four small riots. The Navy, while constantly investigating race relations in the Navy yard and elsewhere—and even accepting, by late 1943, that black men felt rightfully discriminated against—did relatively little to defuse the situation.[57] General Emmons' order, which had been partly precipitated by a June 1942 racial confrontation at the cantonment, accomplished scarcely anything, except to encourage further investigations by the Navy's intelligence office.

The District Intelligence Office (DIO) of the Pearl Harbor

Naval District ran in a somewhat predictable direction with Emmons' order. Counterintelligence officers began to crack down on what they considered subversive materials responsible for agitating black servicemen and war workers. Their operatives first raided the University of Hawaii and removed from the library all copies of the *Crisis,* the official organ of the NAACP, which were found to contain "inflammatory matter."[58]

The counterintelligence initiative did not come out of the blue. Naval intelligence had long ranked "Negroes" as a primary suspect group of "subversives," right after the "Japanese" (even though the Soviet Union and the United States were wartime allies, the number-one target of military intelligence operatives was "Communists"). Not unreasonably, then, given their premises, Hawaii counterintelligence operatives' greatest fear was a meeting of minds among all three of the leading "subversive" groups—Communists, Japanese, Negroes.

African Americans were not subversive in and of themselves, according to the DIO. What made them potentially so was their anger over racism. Race agitation produced racial conflict, which in turn could weaken the American war effort. Thus, by DIO standards, to fight racism during the war was itself subversive (a dubious logic that other intelligence and national security agencies maintained throughout the Cold War era).

Naval District Intelligence officers did not agree with the spirit of Emmons' general directive that military commanders were somehow responsible for preventing racial conflict. At first, they were certain that "subversives"—Communists or Japanese or perhaps Japanese Communists—were responsible for African-American "agitation" against racism. The International-Communists-are-behind-it approach to African-American struggles against racism would be most famously championed by J. Edgar Hoover in the postwar years.[59]

A few weeks after Emmons' memo, post office censors reported a letter to the mainland, dated December 16, 1942, from a Japanese-American member of the Communist party in Honolulu. The letter described the Party's efforts to proselytize members of the 369th. It was almost too much—the black men charged with defending Hawaii from the Japanese were being subverted by Japanese Communists!

Of course, the letter was not exactly proof of treason. If anything, it was a little silly, expressing the American Communist Party's romantic approach to black people: "I secretly hoped that our visitors would be from New York and they were! The boys were the finest lads, splendid physical specimens, handsome, conversant, gracious. . . ." It seemed that a small group of Communists, of various ethnic backgrounds, was hard at work on these black servicemen and sailors, mainly inviting them to social occasions for cookies and cake and low-key politicizing.[60]

For the next several months, intelligence officers watched this relationship closely. Finally, on August 31, 1943, the intelligence agent in charge reported that, as far as he could tell, members of the 369th and other black servicemen enjoyed the cake and cookies but showed little or no interest in the politics. The unit's chaplain, Robert Doakes, though an outspoken opponent of racism in the military and on the mainland, candidly informed intelligence officers that while he was sympathetic to the Communist Party's approach to American race relations, he said he believed that the Party was just "using Negroes," and that he had told the troopers as much. The Communist Party, Japanese members included, reported counterintelligence, was having no impact on black men in Hawaii.[61]

"Enemy activity" and "communist inspiration" were the usual explanations for racial conflict in Hawaii. But for the DIO, "agitation directed by the mainland" was quite another matter.[62]

Without a doubt, black servicemen and war workers did relish news and information from an African-American perspective. Two Pearl Harbor workers had managed to get an irregular line on distributing the *Pittsburgh Courier* just after the Japanese attack, and for most of the war they sold 1,000 copies of every issue they received. They thought they could sell even more if they could get them.[63]

Naval Intelligence officers clearly disliked the black press. In a confidential memo which was widely distributed, intelligence agents characterized the four major black newspapers as "Communist . . . in a marked degree" and asserted that "hatred is their principal stock in trade." In sum, they warned that "treatment by the Negro press of much of the news about the Negroes in the armed forces constitutes . . . sabotage of morale."[64]

Although outside agitation, communist influence, and Japanese involvement were seriously investigated by counterintelligence throughout the war as major causes of black anger about racism, no proof of involvement by such outside forces was ever uncovered. The black men themselves could have saved the intelligence agents a lot of trouble. The problem as they saw it was imported, white racism.

Many black soldiers believed the biggest troublemakers in Hawaii were southerners straight from the mainland. According to Pearl Harbor war worker Ernest Golden, a keen observer of this radically new world, men who "had been on the front, came back and was seasoned people and they somehow or another had gotten a lot of that stuff out of them." War had seemed to dissolve, at least temporarily, some of the distance separating black and white Americans. As for the new arrivals, Golden thought, "they had to start calling names, and they had to start doing this, and there would be a fight."

Unsurprisingly perhaps, many of the racial fights broke out in the buses bringing men back from Hotel Street to Pearl Harbor before curfew—buses in which Jim Crow-style, back-of-the-bus seating arrangements were disallowed by military order. In the jammed buses, with people hanging out the windows, men of all colors jostling one another, white men with too much liquor in them would start a fight. Golden saw it happen again and again:

> The funny thing about it, at this time, the relationship between the local people, local men and the Black men was close. . . . There was what you would call an empathy from the local people as to what the black people had endured. They sort of, I guess, sympathized with us to a degree.

These sympathies had a direct impact on the course of the brawls between white and black men. After a fight started, the local bus driver, says Golden, would hold the bus doors closed as long as the blacks were winning. "When everything was over, he'd open the doors and let the blacks disappear. They were on our side. . . ."[65]

Of course, local men and women were not always on the side of the dark-skinned malihini. In letters from the islands, a strain of prejudice against black Americans often appears. Local women, who were repeatedly warned by white troops about black men, wrote frequently of their fears. "I am very scared of these Negro soldiers here in Honolulu. They make my skin shrivel and my self afraid to go near them," wrote a Chinese girl. A young Japanese woman wrote in almost identical terms: "They are so big and dark. . . . Seeing them around while I'm alone gives me the 'goose-flesh'."[66] Another Japanese woman was a little more reflective. After sharing a perfectly uneventful bus ride with four black soldiers she wrote a friend: "Gee, I was very frightened. . . . Funny isn't it how I am about them. One would be that way after hearing lots of nasty things about them."[67] These women had learned mainland racism.

But racist fears were not transmitted in a vacuum. They were given some small credence by real events. Some black men, mostly the ones from poor, rural backgrounds, pursued local women in a rough manner. One woman complained to a friend, "We are scared to go [swimming] always because some plenty soldiers. They go under water and grab our legs. . . . The white soldiers no make any kin[e] but the Blacks Whoo. They follow us thats why we always have to go."[68] Such things occurred, but the general suspicion of "negroes" helped to make even innocuous events seem vaguely threatening. A sociology student at the University of Hawaii recorded a story that circulated in the plantation community of Kahuku, Oahu: A Negro "walked into a girl's house while she was playing the piano and sat down to listen. The other occupants in the house were speechless with fright. Everyone looked at him as an intruder, but said nothing to him. He returned a few days later and asked the girl to play the piano."[69]

What really seemed to frighten local people—local women, especially—were the stories about rape. Very few cases of violent stranger rape involving mainland men were reported during the war: they probably number fewer than a dozen. But of those rapes, a larger number were committed by black men.[70] The stories of these rapes spread rapidly through local communities, the grisly details embellished in the retelling. One rape by a black soldier became through word of mouth "quite a lot of raping cases . . . the colored soldiers are causing quite a lot of trouble here."[71]

Military censors found that local attitudes toward black men changed dramatically after a brutal rape and murder occurred in Maui—so much so that they claimed "the Negro problem . . . became a major factor in creating poor morale among Island residents."[72] Though stories of rape by white servicemen or war workers did not make local people afraid of all whites, similar stories about black men confirmed their ugliest suspicions.

Shortly before Christmas of 1944, Walter White, executive secretary of the NAACP, came to Hawaii as part of his tour of the war zone. He was greeted enthusiastically by a group of 250 men and women, most of them servicemen. White had come in part to speak to the group about their desire to charter a chapter of the NAACP in Honolulu. A few months earlier, 105 of them had sent in membership applications and a note saying they hoped to have 500 members in Honolulu by the time they were chartered.

White gave the group two messages. At his public talk, he reminded the servicemen to obey their officers, and stated that "the high command of the armed forces are determined not to permit racial discrimination." Later, in a private meeting attended by an agent of Naval Intelligence, White recounted the many acts of racial discrimination he had witnessed or heard of in the armed forces. His underlying message seemed clear: black men and women would have to press the government to meet its own standards of fairness.[73]

By now, at least a couple of hundred black men and women thought organized resistance to imported mainland racism had become necessary. They particularly meant to fight racial exclusion at downtown restaurants, nightclubs, and dance halls. Before war's end and in the years just after, the NAACP in Hawaii sponsored picket lines against several establishments that refused to serve African Americans. They won these battles.[74]

When Walter White came to Hawaii, the men who had most publicly challenged racism in the streets of Honolulu had already left the islands. The 369th Coast Artillery Regiment had joined the forces invading Okinawa. William De Fossett had been reassigned as battalion supply officer to Task Force 58, an interservice unit that would fight in Saipan. Here, for the first time, he faced the kind of direct and degrading racism that he had so far been able to avoid. De Fossett was, of course, in an all-black unit.

Almost all other men were from the South, and when a white officer came into their area, his troops did something that offended and troubled him. They took off their hats. De Fossett explained that what they were doing was not in the Army regulations and said they should stop it. Salute an officer, he told them, but your hat stays on. They replied that this was what they had been brought up to do, and whites expected it. De Fossett said he didn't care; they had to stop. But the men appeared very uncomfortable about what he was asking them.

De Fossett was deeply pained by their submissiveness. Even more, he did not want to take his own hat off to any white man, and he knew that if the others did it and he didn't, there was going to be trouble.

Trouble came anyway. Some of the men complained to white officers about what De Fossett had told them. The battalion colonel called on De Fossett, and in a clear southern accent, asked why the Supply Officer had told his men to keep their hats on. De Fossett said, "Sir, I am following Army regulations." The colonel called him an "uppity nigger" who did not understand southern customs. Nevertheless, he did not tell De Fossett to rescind his order, and henceforth the men kept their hats on. It was a small victory, but a sweet one.[75]

———

After the war, some of the black men and women stationed in Hawaii chose not to go home. At least two men from the 369th demobilized in Honolulu and married local women. Many black war workers also stayed on, living out their fantasy of never going back to old Jim Crow. In 1940, only 255 Negroes were listed in the Hawaiian census; in 1950, the number had jumped to 2,651.[76] In the years just after the war, most of those black men and the small number of black women who stayed in Hawaii successfully blended into the community, giving up some of their own cultural identity in the process. As Pearl Harbor worker Ernest Golden remembers, "I often criticized us for that. [But] we were just so afraid of creating a black ghetto here."[77] Golden married a woman of Portuguese descent and found a place for himself in Hawaii. Though not without some incidents and personal adjustments, these African Americans tended to leave behind the bipolar racial system of the mainland and joined Hawaii's racial and ethnic experiment. To some extent, they gave up being "Negroes" in order to become "local" people.

But the Hawaiian experience also affected the men who went back to their homes, whether northern or southern. Some were bitter, having witnessed the spread of antiblack racism to a place that had not known it. Others never forgot the new friends of all races they made. Most saw their experiences in Hawaii as mixed— and complicated.

The African-American men who served in Hawaii also brought back a knowledge that was intriguing and portentous. First—at least sometimes—their government had backed them up. It was not as if military officials or government agents had gone out of their way to give black men a helping hand. But if the men pushed, federal authorities treated their situation seriously. And if they simply took—sometimes heroically—the rights and freedoms that rank and position seemed to promise, federal authorities (however unpredictably) tended to support them.

In Hawaii, the military's reliance on rank and protocol, on a clear set of rules meant to govern human interaction, provided a useful structure for social justice. Change, nonetheless, still depended upon individual initiative and courage and on the willingness of the federal government to enforce its laws. After the war, African-American activists would press hard to deepen federal involvement in their struggle. Based on the experiences of African Americans in Hawaii, one could argue that the struggle was one that some segments of the federal government (especially, though not happily, the military) were well on the road to joining.[78]

Secondly, the story of the 369th in Hawaii raises questions about racial identity and social change in America. The men of the 369th, by and large, possessed a strong and self-conscious racial pride; they embraced their identity as Negroes. But they also in-

The First Strange Place

sisted that their identity was not unidimensional. They were Negroes; they were Americans; and—first and foremost—they were combat soldiers. When they encountered conflict in Hawaii they called upon all these identities. They insisted that their status be measured by criteria other than race. In so doing, they furthered their cause of racial justice and equality.

Few black men carefully weighed all of the political implications of their wartime Hawaii experiences. But many returned with fond memories. William De Fossett, who saw so much, held one memory close.

He had spent most early afternoons while he was in Hawaii playing baseball. Before Jackie Robinson broke the color line in 1946, De Fossett had played for an integrated semi-pro team in Aiea, a little community on the outskirts of Honolulu. The team, he remembers, was "a regular league of nations." Along with three other men from the 369th, including his brother Joe, the team included Hawaiians, whites, and Japanese-American ball players. A white man owned the team, the manager was Hawaiian, and the coach was Japanese American. De Fossett saw it as one sign that a new day was beginning.

5

Fragile Connections

The private lives of millions were shaken and recast by World War II, and so, too, were America's social and sexual mores. The marriage rate began to accelerate with Pearl Harbor, and swelled to record heights by the end of the war. The birthrate followed suit, as did, eventually, the divorce rate. Sexual boundaries were also renegotiated, and people who had never thought it possible had extramarital affairs. Teenagers married in haste; Victory girls groped in alleys and the back of seats of cars with soldiers they scarcely knew. More babies were born out of wedlock. Men and women struggled to hold their families together in the face of distance and fear, or simply sought some measure of security or pleasure.

The war uprooted millions of men from their homes. They traveled across the country and the world, taking on new roles, meeting people different from themselves, becoming—whether they wanted to or not—part of the war. More than 300 thousand of them died.

American women also had their lives disrupted in profound and difficult ways. A small number joined the armed forces and went to war. Most, physically safe, waited and prayed and did what they could for the war effort. Millions became war workers, doing a "man's job," taking on new challenges and responsibilities.

Historians have looked with great sophistication at the new roles women took on during World War II. By doing the work of men, women implicitly challenged one of the fundamental justifications for sexual inequality. The image and reality of Rosie the Riveter was a powerful statement about women's capabilities, showing that contemporary ideas about the fundamental differences between men and women might well be exaggerated, and seeming to presage greater integration of men's and women's roles in the postwar era. But this important story needs to be more fully integrated with another, for what we also see in World War II is an exacerbation of difference. Once again: Men fought. Women didn't. The gender divide was all too clear, and men and women had somehow to manage and defuse it. It wasn't done by claiming the identical nature of the sexes.

In many ways, the facts of life in Hawaii made the wartime gulf between men's and women's expectations and experience more treacherous. While all over America men and women were meeting—and sometimes marrying—people of wholly different backgrounds and cultures, the differences were more extreme in Hawaii and the pressures more palpable. There were simply too many men there, too close to war, all making claims of one kind or another on the women of the islands. A radically imbalanced sex ratio and unnerving racial and ethnic differences did not ease the situation.

Still, men and women in Hawaii did manage to live with these differences. Often men and women forged connections by emphasizing their "natural" and complementary differences. Gender thereby served to obviate or camouflage the importance of race and ethnicity. In doing so, they relied upon the conventions of popular culture: the "universal language" of romance as interpreted by Hollywood; the niceties of dating etiquette; "island girls" whose jitterbugging was perfect. The balance thus obtained was precarious and "interracial dating and friendship" still potentially explosive. But some built bridges across difference in Hawaii, forging fragile connections that would change their lives.

———

The *Army Hit Kit of Popular Songs* was distributed monthly as part of the Special Services Division's morale effort. The tables of contents summon sentimental images, the aching sweetness of young men's voices singing "There's a Star Spangled Banner Waving Somewhere" or "White Christmas," with a little leavening in the form of

"Mairzy Doats."[1] Of course, not all the "hits" of the war received official sanction. The men's actual tastes often ran to the scatological and obscene. Navy flier Samuel Hynes describes the "community of the singing . . . how affection flowed among young men when they threw their arms around each other's shoulders and sang a roaring bawdy song."[2]

There were cats on the roof,
And cats on the tiles,
Cats with the shits
And cats with the piles,
Cats with their a-a-ass ho-o-o-les
Wreathed in smiles,
As they revelled in the joys of fornication.

The men might begin with such a lyric, glasses in hand, weaving their way through a "repertoire of songs suitable for Marines to sing while drunk."[3] The songs were of dubious national origin, brought back from war, not always fully understood by the young men who joined in the choruses. But it was really the singing that mattered, and whether profane, sacred, or merely sentimental, music played an important role both for the men in war and for those who worked and waited at home.

The *Hit Kit* was meant to link the men to home, keeping them up to date on the popular music that, in the age of radio and Big Bands, was such an important part of the culture. Just as movies offered archetypes of beauty and romance, popular music supplied a romantic vocabulary. In the love letters that flowed back and forth across the oceans, men and women borrowed the words of popular songs to say what seemed too trite in their own words, putting quotation marks around the conventional phrases that betrayed their vulnerability. "The radio is now playing 'Miss You,' " wrote one man to his wife of less than five months, "—and I miss you 'since you went away, dear—miss you, more than I can say dear—do you ever miss me as I miss you?' " In the fear-charged separations of wartime, "our song" could take on great significance.[4]

"They're Either Too Young or Too Old," which appeared in the

The First Strange Place

Army Hit Kit for December 1943, was nobody's special song, but it was clearly morale-related in its cheerful summoning of one of the worst fears of the men who fought the war. Of course, men worried about dying. Men worried that they would be maimed, their bodies torn apart by exploding shells, or that they would be cowards, that they would disgrace themselves in battle, that they would fail to "pass the Test." But as much as anything else, they worried that the war would destroy whatever happiness they had at home. They worried that their marriages would dissolve under the pressures of distance, time, and change, or that their sweethearts would prove untrue. Since there was no "available male," being "good as gold" was not difficult, the song proclaimed, gaily answering all those men who implored their wives and girlfriends to be "good." And while American servicemen insisted, with a three-to-two majority, that girlfriends back home should date other men, many worried about the consequences.[5] One man stationed in Hawaii wrote to the newspaper advice columnist, Dorothy Dix, for reassurance:

> I am 21 years of age, have been married one year to a very wonderful girl. . . . Now I'm here and she's on the mainland. We have been together exactly four months out of our marriage. . . . Since I left my wife . . . I wrote and told her to go out and have fun and that all I wanted is for her to be happy. I am very jealous . . . yet I do not wish for my wife to sit home all the time twiddling her thumbs. But do you think I am doing right by telling her to go out if she wishes?[6]

Another man, less ambivalent about his wishes, wrote his wife while engaged in one of the fiercest battles of the European war:

> See all I (we) ever hear about over here is all about how untrue the wives and girls back in the states are . . . with so much on a guy's mind and not knowing how a lot of the girls are acting it puts one to wondering. You know how the men like to tease each other to pass the time away. I do not worry, but I do like to have you tell me in your letters that all is well.[7]

The song's assertion that there was no "available male" back home, of course, was not strictly true. Of the approximately 8.3

million men who served in the U.S. Army during World War II only about 5 million left the U.S. mainland.[8] Women who lived near military bases or other strategic areas might well have a surplus of male company. And there were always the civilians, neither too young nor too old, but 4-F. The sorts of physical problems that kept men out of the armed forces varied widely, and many were neither obvious nor visible. To some resentful servicemen, the 4-F civilian was symbolized by Frank Sinatra, surrounded by swooning bob-bysoxers whose boyfriends risked their lives on foreign shores. (Sinatra's left eardrum had been punctured at birth.)[9] Such worries had some basis in reality; men serving overseas did receive "Dear John" letters from wives or girlfriends, and many marriages were shaken or destroyed by gossip from home.[10]

But for many women during the war, finding an available male was as unlikely as a date with Sinatra himself. Not all were looking. Lots of women were married; some, having rushed into marriage with wartime haste, were waiting for the return of husbands they barely knew. Presumably most of these were not dating. But the young women who weren't married or engaged felt the absence of men—any men—keenly. Virtually every physically fit man between the ages of eighteen and twenty-six had been inducted into the military by early 1943. The resulting "man shortage" hit colleges particularly hard. Many coed colleges became 75 to 90 percent female "for the duration." Young women who expected their college years to be a whirlwind of dates with many men before "settling down" found a very different world. *Esquire* magazine ran a cartoon of an attractive coed fainted dead away, phone dangling, captioned "Someone called her for a date," and it rang true enough to be picked up by college newspapers.[11] Women's magazines offered advice, both shrill and sensible, and throughout the country women joined together for support, forming new college sororities, doing war work, and gathering to celebrate the holidays and anniversaries that made the void seem worse than usual. The "man shortage" seems trivial compared to the war itself, but the real issue was loneliness. Women longed for the return of their husbands and lovers, or simply missed a little male companionship.

For all the problems women in Hawaii faced during the war, the "male shortage" was not one of them. The male-female ratio was a popular topic of discussion, both in respectable publications and bawdy conversation. "Five hundred men to a girl" was the most often quoted figure, but some estimates went as high as a thousand to one. Other estimates pretended scientific accuracy: one man reported to mainland friends that the ratio was precisely 156:1. Sergeant Robert Cowan, as his ship docked in Honolulu, yelled to ask sailors on shore about the woman situation. "One hundred men to a woman," they shouted back, and one added: "If you get one, no matter how old or ugly, hang on to her."[12]

To mainland women, of course, this situation sounded good. One national women's magazine ran a sort of "get-a-man-in-Hawaii" piece under the title "The Moon Goes Out at Ten." The author emphasized the seriousness of a war-work contract and the drawbacks to life in Hawaii (curfews, gas masks, the cost of housing) but managed to quote the "100 men to every girl" figure three times on page one. Hawaii "grows every kind of flower except the wallflower," she explained, noting that the marriage rate had "skyrocketed."[13]

It's doubtful that any women came to Hawaii with the express purpose of finding a husband, but many came seeking adventure. Mildred Carson (predictably nicknamed "Kit") wanted to see the country, so she applied for a secretarial job at Wright Field in Dayton, Ohio, planning to request an immediate transfer to somewhere "exotic or interesting." Policy on transfers changed suddenly, and she found herself stuck in Dayton, serving the three months necessary to get a "release without prejudice." She did eventually get a job in Texas, and when the opportunity to go to Hawaii arose in early 1944 she hesitated, as the contract specified "for the duration of the war plus six months." But Carson decided she really had nothing to lose and signed on, spending a week in San Francisco filling out forms, getting a physical exam and the necessary shots, before leaving with a group of about fifty other women bound for war work at the Army Depot at Hawaii's Hickam Field. The woman who had processed their papers at Fort Mason in San Francisco came out to the ship to say goodbye and told them, laughing, "Of course, you know there are 275 men for every girl out there."

Carson's ship, having zigzagged across the ocean with its destroyer escort, was greeted in Honolulu Harbor by the Hickam Field Band (air force) playing "Aloha Oe" and "Blues in the Night (My Mama Done Told Me)." That night, officers from the depot's personnel department appeared to "get acquainted" and ask for dates. "The first time I went into downtown Honolulu," Carson remembers, "I was with four other girls who had been aboard ship with me. We did get a tremendous amount of attention. People would stop and stare at five haole girls strolling along the street and, of course, men from all the services were very interested and attentive."

Kit Carson's social life was a whirlwind throughout the war. "Every girl was besieged for dates," she explains. "Some officers didn't even want to introduce their friends because of the competition." Every evening after work there was a round of cocktail parties, dinners, dancing, nightclubs. Though curfew was at 10 p.m. in 1944, it did not apply on military posts as long as proper blackout conditions were observed. Dancing might continue til late at night in officers' quarters. Many of the dances required formal dress, which was a problem in wartime Honolulu. Ships were filled with war matériel, and even basic dresses were sometimes in scarce supply. If a shipment of shoes came into a downtown store, the shelves might be empty within hours. When a shipment of dresses came in, Kit and her roommate would buy several, knowing that it might be many months before they had another chance. After that, they would go through the same merchandise over and over, finally buying something they'd thought hopeless in more plentiful times.

The social life of a single, white woman from the mainland in wartime Honolulu might be a full-time job. Of course, Kit and her fellow war workers *had* full time jobs. Kit had quickly managed a transfer from her routine assignment at the depot to the AAFPOA (Army Air Forces Pacific Ocean Areas) Headquarters and a much more responsible job as civilian secretary to the head of the transportation section, who was charged with the transport and coordination of troops and matériel for Pacific operations. Regular hours were from 8 a.m. to 5 p.m., six days a week, and overtime was nothing unusual. Kit almost never bought (or cooked) her own dinner during those years, and she usually had a choice of dates.

She lived the day's ideal of popularity, dating many different men, and she had fun. But the nightlife was more than balanced by the day life, where she gave her full attention to the grim details of troop movements as the Allied forces continued to push toward Japan.[14]

Of course, very few of the women in Hawaii during the war were from the mainland. The first company of WACs arrived in March 1944, and though they were eventually joined by WAVES, SPARS, and Women Marines, the total number of servicewomen on the islands never approached 10,000. (In June of 1945, there were more than a quarter of a million soldiers on Oahu, plus large numbers of sailors and marines.) And while mainland men were recruited for defense work in Hawaii beginning in 1940, mainland women were not brought to the islands until 1944, and then mainly for office work. A real-life "Rosie the Riveter" was scarce in Hawaii, though a small number of local women did heavy mechanical work at Pearl Harbor and elsewhere. But Hawaii's women did work in large numbers during the war, some directly in the war effort as civilian employees of the military or as nurses, others in the sorts of service and administrative positions necessary to cope with the flood of servicemen and war workers who had come to the islands. In registering all women in Hawaii in November 1942, officials discovered that 52 percent of Honolulu women held jobs. (By contrast, a national survey in 1944 found that 37 percent of adult women on the mainland were working outside the home.)[15]

The lure of high wages and adventure was strong for the women of Hawaii as well. Thelma Liborio was a junior at Roosevelt High School when the war began. Schools closed on December 7th and did not open again on Oahu until February 2. Thelma had immediately gone to work at Pearl Harbor as a messenger girl; when school reopened, she had no intention of going back. She was making 75 cents an hour, which seemed like a lot of money to her, and she liked meeting people and being part of the war effort. Eventually the lieutenant she worked for convinced her to finish high school, even arranging for her to receive credit for the time she had worked at Pearl Harbor. She went back and graduated, on schedule, in June of 1943. She then returned to work at Pearl Harbor.

Thelma lived just a couple of blocks from Waikiki beach with her parents, her brother Everett, and her mother's father, whom they called Vuvu (Portuguese for grandfather). All four of her grandparents had come to Hawaii from the Azores, settling in Hilo on the Big Island; Thelma's parents had moved to Oahu when she was eleven. Being of Portuguese descent put Thelma in a complicated position in Hawaii's racial hierarchy. The Portuguese were technically Caucasian, but the first Portuguese immigrants had come to Hawaii to work in the cane. The descendants of white missionaries and entrepreneurs were the islands' elite; the Portuguese were thus a slightly awkward complication in the equation of class and race. To most mainland haoles, however, this was too fine a distinction, and women of Portuguese descent were enthusiastically dated by white servicemen.

Thelma was a pretty young woman, with masses of curly dark hair and heavy-lidded dark eyes. She'd always been popular with boys, but her mother closely supervised her dating, preferring that she date boys from her youth group at Pilgrim Church. Servicemen were strictly off-limits in the years before the war; only the "other type girls," as she put it, would be seen with them. Many island residents saw peacetime sailors as a "rough element, those who couldn't get jobs elsewhere or else the 'soldier of fortune' types." Shortly before the war began, one of Thelma's teachers at Roosevelt High asked her, quite harshly, whether her mother knew she was dating sailors. Thelma was confused and more than a little alarmed; the teacher was adamant. It turned out she had seen Thelma standing at a bus stop talking to her brother, Everett, who was wearing his Sea Scout uniform.

But the war changed all of that, and Thelma and her friends dated servicemen by the score. Parents still had reservations, though for different reasons. In the house next door to Thelma's, the older women in the neighborhood gossiped about the young girls who were "giving in" to the servicemen, many because they were too naive to recognize a line or to know when they were being deceived. They gossiped about Thelma, too. She dated too much; she was probably "fast." When Thelma tried to teach a boy to dance to music from his car radio, Eloise Ornelles' grandmother, who lived next door, hurried to tell Thelma's mother that she was "necking on the street."

Not cowed, Thelma told Eloise's grandmother that she was dancing on the street, not kissing. "If I ever wanted to kiss any of the boys," Thelma told her, "it would be on my own front porch because there's a big bush there and you wouldn't be able to see it." But for all her new-found experience, Thelma was still a bit naive. In her circuit at Pearl Harbor, she became known as "the girl with the bedroom eyes"; she wondered if she really looked so sleepy all the time, and was startled to find out what the phrase really meant.

Thelma's mother volunteered at the U.S.O. and would often bring home servicemen, five or six at a time, for a home-cooked meal. She said that if it had been her son away at war, she would want some other mother to be kind to him. She more or less adopted a young man named Harvey, "one of those big strapping fellows that mothers love"—and decided that Thelma should love him, too. Thelma couldn't do that, but she liked him well enough, and quickly discovered that Harvey was a form of insurance. Her parents would approve anything she and her friends wanted to do as long as Harvey was involved, and Harvey himself was nothing if not resourceful. When Thelma finished high school, her parents wanted to send her on a trip to the Big Island as a graduation present. It seemed impossible, as nonessential travel was still restricted, but Harvey had a solution. Buying a fake engagement ring from a five-and-ten-cent store, he took Thelma to the airline office and explained that she was his fiancee, that he was being shipped out, and that he wanted to be sure she was safe in Hilo with her family while he was gone. The ticket was produced. But Thelma had another problem. Each of her dresses had a matching purse and shoes. The airlines restricted luggage to one bag—clearly impossible. Harvey again stepped in. He had to fly to Hilo to get steaks for the officers' club, and while he could not take a civilian passenger, he could carry shoes and purses. So Harvey had all Thelma's shoes and handbags laid out on his bed in the barracks, attracting more than a bit of envious attention, when his sergeant walked by and wanted to know what need he had of women's shoes and purses—and so many of them. So Harvey explained about Thelma.

The shoes and purses made the flight to Hilo, and Thelma had a wonderful time—two or three dates a day, to movies, the beach, dancing. She was, she remembers, always changing and dashing out again. Of course, her uncle did not approve of girls dating service-men, so she and her cousin had to be a little sneaky and inventive, but it was a wonderful vacation. Within an hour after she got home from Hilo, the phone rang. It was Harvey, wanting to bring his sergeant over to meet Thelma (and, not incidentally, to have a home-cooked meal). Thelma said no—she was hot, dirty, and tired, and she did not feel like getting dressed up for company. They came anyway, surprising Thelma in shorts and a halter, barefoot, no make up. The next day the sergeant, John Runkle, called (and she was home waiting). He asked if she believed in love at first sight. She said no. He said, "Neither do I, so we'd better get another look." He and Thelma were married within the year.[16]

So much of this sounds like normal life. Young men and women met, dated, fell in love, and married. But there was always an edge. The good times were had in defiance of the war's uncertainty. Men disappeared with no warning, shipped out to the front, and many didn't come back. As one young woman who left her small town in Georgia for war work in Hawaii wrote, "There was a lot of laughter, but, oh, so much heartbreak."[17]

———

Love in war was always risky, and Hawaii had no monopoly on heartbreak during those years. But in Hawaii, love was riskier, romance more complicated, companionship more difficult than in most places. There were many additional barriers to surmount— barriers having to do with race and culture, and with the emotional weight of a war that seemed much more immediate on the islands than anywhere else in the United States. The experience of war shook some of those barriers and threw others into stark relief. But all were exacerbated by the unusual nature of life in Hawaii.

A case in point is the story on "Betty, Honolulu 'Date' Girl," which ran in December 1943 in *Paradise of the Pacific*. The piece praised Betty for finding "time to be with the boys," for "chatting with a lonely private . . . or spending the afternoon with a lieuten-ant, dancing at an officer's club." Stretching a bit, the author ex-plained: "There have been many medals awarded to brave men, fighting this war, and were they making awards to girls who as 'morale builders' are aiding in the winning of the war, Betty would surely be one of the recipients."

Read in the context of wartime Hawaii, the piece is less fatuous than it seems at first glance. Betty, as the author makes clear without recourse to any philosophical justifications or awkward emphasis, is both "the ideal American girl" and "a typical Island girl." In other words, this ideal American girl is local. She isn't "white." That, considering the era, is already quite a claim. But even setting race aside, the author is making another claim, and in that sense the piece is more prescriptive than descriptive. For by referring to medals and bravery, the author is attempting to legitimate the practice of dating servicemen.

In Hawaii during the war, women were caught between the new view of dating as an extension of war work and the lingering prewar suspicion of servicemen and the girls who went out with them. Was dating soldiers fast—or patriotic? What did it do to a girl's reputation to be seen with a rapid succession of soldiers, sailors, and marines? In the case of "local girls," would "local boys," neglected for the mainland haoles in uniform, forgive and forget when the servicemen sailed for home? Older women repeated stories from World War I, of men who loved and left—and had sometimes left babies as well. This form of patriotic service was not without risk.

The risk could be lessened, for those who were truly interested in boosting morale, by expressing their patriotism through properly organized channels. The U.S.O. sponsored dances and supplied dancing partners for the servicemen in many of its fifty-one clubs in the Territory of Hawaii. Finding partners for the men was an immensely difficult job. The overall sex ratio made it difficult, and the task was compounded by the nature of the dances. Virtually any female in Hawaii (between grade school and grandmother, anyway) could have her pick of men. Officers with cars and the gasoline to run them would pick the women up at home, take them to fancy restaurants or dancing at the officers' club. But attending a U.S.O. dance was hard work. "Like a pack of hungry wolves . . . Five hundred strong they storm the tiny cluster of babes," reported the *New Army*

Navy Review. The reporter exaggerated, but not by much. Men ringed the dance floor, hoping for "the chance of holding a gal in their arms again, no matter how impersonally" (as another *Review* article put it).[18] The women were on their feet for hours, paying equal attention to the homely and the handsome, dancing with the bad dancers as much as the good ones, smiling and listening and trying to exude good cheer to a numbing succession of young men.

Some of the dances were "staffed" with young women cajoled into volunteering for an evening, and most young women went to the dances once in a while. Two groups of young women in Honolulu, the "Flying Squadron" and the "Hui Menehune," made a more serious commitment. The Flying Squadron was founded by Peggy Johnson, a recent graduate of the University of Nebraska, who came to Hawaii with the U.S.O. Her first task was to arrange an Army dance, and with only eleven days lead time, to find 100 dancing partners. She inherited a list of 42 names; 29 of the women, it turned out, had been evacuated to the mainland. Johnson knew she could never meet her quota if she started from scratch for each dance, so she sold the idea of a club, complete with by-laws, sterling silver ID bracelets, and dancing classes (she had taught for Arthur Murray, and had some expertise to offer). The women saw themselves as "volunteers for victory," and they did work hard. In the twelve months ending in March 1943, the 325 members of the Flying Squadron hosted 127 dances attended by more than 60,000 men.

The Flying Squadron was made up of Caucasian girls only—a fact that was mentioned, but never discussed, in any of the feature articles that celebrated their commitment and achievements. The Honolulu U.S.O. also benefitted from the hard work of the Hui Menehune, an interracial group of 250 Hawaiian, Japanese-American, Chinese-American, and Korean-American women whose contributions were less well documented in the local and national press.[19]

"A lot of us felt obligation," remembers a woman of Puerto Rican descent who went to the U.S.O. dances at the Waialua gym, out in the country. "We were serious about it." Frank Branigan, who remembers the dances with gratitude, also remembers the limits imposed. Beforehand, the men were coached on proper behavior.

"These are young ladies from the first families of Hawaii," the officials would say,

> and we expect you to treat them like young ladies. They are not pickups and you absolutely may not date them. You may ask them out but you'll quickly find you will be snubbed because they have also been trained that they do not date servicemen. They are here as an accommodation to you—but just because you dance with them doesn't mean they're falling in love with you and you must understand that.[20]

Of course, not all of the women were from Hawaii's first families. Especially at the rural U.S.O.s, many were girls from the plantations who had led very circumscribed lives. And as far as rules went, like all rules they were sometimes broken. In Honolulu and elsewhere, it was not unheard-of for a couple to make a date for later and on occasion for some sparks to fly. In general, however, the dances were well-run, the women willing (if a little impersonal), and the men "respectful."[21]

But whether one danced for the war effort or dated officers for fun or just walked down the street, it was hard to be a woman in Honolulu during the war. There were just so many men, all wanting something. "[We] were starving for the sight of an American girl close up," remembers a Marine who stood guard duty at the Pearl Harbor Navy Yard. "Just to talk with them reminded each of us of the girl we left behind."[22] Advice columnists told women they were responsible for morale, and insisted that the best thing they could do for a serviceman was just to *listen.* "Have you ever thrown coyness overboard and settled down to let one of these boys talk himself out? He's got a lot of things on his mind," suggested one "girl reporter."[23] Many women did listen to the homesickness and fear, to stories of mothers and girlfriends at home, to good news and bad. They made themselves smile into eyes that were filled with naked longing. But then the men were no longer just GIs. The uniform was no longer the most important thing about them. They became men—or boys— with vulnerable hearts and vulnerable bodies, likely to be shipped out without warning, perhaps never to return.

The diary one young Honolulu woman kept during the early war years is filled with stories of the men, as if by recording their words and gestures she could somehow preserve their essence, or will them safely home. Her world was mapped by the ebb and flow of men on the street, for she knew that when the streets grew quiet the men had gone to war. "There is an ominous quiet over the city today," she wrote on June 2, 1942. "The alert must be serious. The Y is absolutely like a morgue. . . . I am not nervous, but I'm like a hound that sniffs the air when there's a strange scent about. The alert is the worst I have ever experienced. Even the streets seem deserted." Three days later she wrote, "Some news has been released. A battle is taking place at Midway."[24]

Helen's diary is full of the men she called "my boys." There was Spud, barely twenty and just back from the Solomons. His best friend had died in battle, and Helen recorded his words: " 'I was with him,' Spud said, 'I wiped his forehead before he died.' " There was Pitkannen, navigator in the Marine Air Corps, "a poet and a romanticist." "He also consorts with Death and knows it," wrote Helen. "He said when he flew high above the canopy of clouds it was like flying between Heaven and Hell. 'You could just take your choice,' he said. 'Just drop down below the clouds and there was all Hell let loose or you could stay above and feel the glory of God.' "[25]

Helen was no less a "romanticist" herself. She wrote of the men's youth and beauty, comparing one to "the early plainsman, the American trapper, . . . [who] lived close to the earth, to life and death." Of a young pilot, dead in the charred wreckage of his plane, she wrote, "[His eyes] had the wisdom of a lifetime in them. I knew by their steady calm light that he had made a bargain with his Maker, and long before he died he had given his life to his country." She found solace in romantic visions of young men's souls. "How strange," she mused, "these men who fight and kill and yet see God in the moonlight while they stand their lonely watches."[26]

Helen's diary centered around comings and goings, slighting the ocean of time between as she waited for news and imagined the battles raging on ever further-distant islands. On September 8, 1942, she wrote:

I said goodbye to Tom Ament last Friday before he left for the South Seas and maybe death. He had been in the Makin raid and was so full of it. I took him home with me and he sat in the big chair by the radio and told me all about the fight. He told me about the snipers in the trees, how the marines lay on their bellies in the tall grass not daring to lift their heads lest a stray bullet would get them. Sometimes the Japs made sounds so the boys would lift their heads and then—ping! would go the rifle and the boy was killed. . . . It is all so plain to me, how the boys landed on the beach over the heavy surf and moved stealthily in the gray dawn toward the thickets so full of the hidden enemy.[27]

Her "boys" talked themselves out in the big chair by the radio. They spared her some of the horror, so the beaches she imagined were not strewn with fragments of human bodies. Some things the men just could not talk about. E. B. Sledge, a Marine who survived both Peleliu and Okinawa, wrote decades later of a world "incomprehensible" even to the men just behind the lines, those separated by a few hundred blessed yards from the full impact of war. Sledge described the worst of it, a week in rain-lashed foxholes on a mountain ridge in Okinawa, surrounded by the decomposing bodies of friends and enemies, suffocated by the stench. "If a Marine slipped and slid down the back slope of the muddy ridge," Sledge wrote,

> he was apt to reach the bottom vomiting. I saw more than one man lose his footing and slip and slide all the way to the bottom only to stand up horror-stricken as he watched in disbelief while fat maggots tumbled out of his muddy dungaree pockets, cartridge belt, legging lacings, and the like. . . .
> We didn't talk about such things. They were too horrible and obscene even for hardened veterans. . . .[28]

If the men could not speak of such obscenities to one another, how could they tell a woman like Helen? So they talked, censoring themselves, being careful for their own sakes as well as hers. And she listened to them and wrote as honestly as she knew how.

"The war has come so close to me," Helen Berkey wrote on the day yet another of her boys was to leave, continuing:

> I wish I could do something to help. These men sail into the greatest danger without a murmur. Bill never mentioned the trip.

But I know about the subs and the watches in the night, and the Jap zero planes. Sometimes I can't bear it—how can people be so complacent! Today is unusually beautiful. It rained early this morning and everything looked fresh and green. The scroll of clouds over Molokai was faintly tinged with pink, the sky azure, and the waving palms glinted wet in the morning light. I can see these men sailing away, casting backward looks at this beautiful refuge, all of them wondering in their hearts if they will ever return.[29]

The scene is carefully scripted; like a movie, it demands a happy ending. The war Helen imagines is softened by sentiment and sensibility. Men die, but are comforted by friends in their last moments. In life, the men are brave and beautiful, in death their souls "soar high . . . to where it is always bright and shining."[30]

Helen's writing offers the solace of easy tears. It seems compromised beside the rawness of Sledge's voice, describing what Paul Fussell called "the Real War." Yet the sentiment and the tears should not be dismissed. Helen's faith and her limited knowledge were shared by hundreds of thousands of other people who were also spared the horror. And Helen's tears were not so easy. She chose to listen, to open herself emotionally to a number of young men who faced battle, who would sail off and perhaps never return. That was a hard choice in wartime Honolulu. To care, to listen, was to risk devastation. Not everyone was strong enough.

In the face of such impossible demands, the women were torn by conflicting claims. It seemed so little to give—to smile, to listen, to care about young men who soon might die. But, like everything else, caring wasn't so simple. Not all of the men were "poets and romanticists." They did not necessarily appear in manageable numbers; they did not necessarily behave well. For Hawaii's women, the men's perpetual desires—even just for a smile—were exhausting and sometimes frightening.

Eloise Ornelles was ten-going-on-eleven when Pearl Harbor was bombed. She lived next door to Thelma, thought Thelma was glamorous, loved to watch her get ready for dates. Eloise was still a gawky kid, all arms and legs, but the men whistled at her anyway. The whistles made her feel grownup and a little bit sexy as she rode her bike around Waikiki in baggy shorts and an aloha shirt. Sometimes, though, the men scared her. On crowded buses, a couple of times, men pinched her bottom, and once she found herself jammed so tightly against a soldier that she could "feel his manhood." "I'm not sure if he was doing it deliberately or not," she says in retrospect, "but it upset me so much that I burst into tears and the driver stopped the bus and made him get off."

Winifred Lockwood, the haole daughter of a Methodist minister, was in eighth grade in 1942. The road near her rural home was suddenly jammed with trucks and jeeps full of soldiers, and she faced a chorus of whistles and catcalls—as well as waves and smiles—whenever she went out. She knew that most of the men meant to be friendly, but she always felt a little safer with her big sister, who knew when to joke back and when to ignore rude comments.[31]

Esther Bader, a part-Hawaiian woman who was in her mid-twenties during the war years, grew to hate the servicemen. The ones she remembers were not the lonely men, hoping only for a nice girl to talk to for a little while, but strangers who forced themselves on her, yelling their offers, even physically accosting her. "These two guys [would] come," she remembers, "one on each side of me, and just grab my arm and say, 'Where shall we go?' . . . [T]hey thought that [because] they were fighting for us, that anybody they wanted, they could have."[32]

Some women became thoroughly disgusted with the men's behavior. A Japanese beauty shop operator wrote to a man in uniform: "Really, the skunks (the real donkies) are getting disgusting. The more I see of them the disgusted I get—so please . . . don't act like the dog faces we have around here. If you do you'll understand why women shuns away."[33] Another woman, then in her early thirties with seven children, sometimes worked in the cafeteria line at the Honolulu U.S.O. "The service boys," she remembers, "they get into your nerve. . . . When you serve them, they call you, 'Hey, lady, how about a date. Hey, lady, what are you doing tonight?' . . . They try to have a date. It doesn't matter who. . . . You says, 'I'm a married woman, I can't go out with you.' He say, 'What's the difference?' . . . They tell you these things and you get angry!"[34]

At the same time, though, she said, ". . . these service boys, maybe they don't mean it. They away from home and they are lonesome." Most people were willing to allow the servicemen a little leeway—though a little less for the war workers. Henry Ishii, a "local born boy" and defense worker, argued in a letter to the editor of the *Star-Bulletin* that island residents should not be "surprised when [soldiers] on their short 'passes' whistle at our girls. They've got to have some emotional outlet," he wrote. Like everyone else, he sometimes resented the servicemen's behavior and their constant criticisms of Hawaii; but he exhorted the readers of the *Star-Bulletin* to remember what "deprivations" the men suffered and to filter their annoyance through a little "gratitude."[35]

In a way that was typical of the era, Henry Ishii was redefining the problem. It was not simply a matter of being gracious to servicemen, who after all were sacrificing much more than the civilian residents of Hawaii. It was a matter of what the whistles and wisecracks and physical overtures meant. "I've been whistled at lots of times and I don't mind it one bit—in fact I feel highly flattered (and what girl can honestly deny this)," wrote one "Busy Wife and Mother" in a letter to the *Star-Bulletin*. "I think that a lot of people have lost their sense of humor." Within the culture of 1940s America, wolf whistles could be intended and received as flattering attention. Kit Carson once got a synchronized wolf whistle from several hundred sailors on the deck of a destroyer pulling into Pearl Harbor after a battle. It made her happy—not so much for the attention; she got plenty of that every day—but because it seemed so celebratory. She'd seen another destroyer come limping into port after a direct hit, probably from a kamikaze pilot, and the sailors on deck were a grim lot.

Not all whistles were so unambiguous. What Henry Ishii and the "Busy Wife and Mother" did not acknowledge was the extent to which men's whistles and comments made sexual claims on the women who were their targets. Women got tired of this public, promiscuous claiming, even when the whistles were proferred with boyish innocence. And many of them weren't. Many were drunken, leering, aggressive overtures. There were all sorts of men in uniform, and the newspapers carried occasional stories of sex crimes against Hawaii's women. "Navy Man Charged with Annoying Girl," read a *Honolulu Advertiser* headline in May 1944. The story did not reflect badly on all servicemen, for the girl, only "scratched" but "badly scared," had been rescued by two Marines. The people of Hawaii weren't suspicious of servicemen or of war workers *per se,* but simply uneasy about all the strangers who overran the streets and lurked in the shadows. Many servicemen and war workers also believed the situation was dangerous and lectured women friends and co-workers about the hazards of traveling about alone, especially at night.[36]

Although it was the (relatively few) stories of rape and assault that most frightened women in Hawaii, they were also made uncomfortable by the attitudes of some men. There was often an edge in their comments and looks. Many enlisted men felt, not without justification, that women scorned them and only dated officers. "They always looked at your shoulder first," recalled one soldier.[37] Some men wrote it off to life's unfairness or the practical nature of women, but others were bitter, especially those who had been in forward areas and felt they deserved better. Miles Babcock, whose World War II diary was published posthumously, describes an evening at a forward base in the South Pacific:

> One moonlight evening: Seated on logs were a battalion of soldiers watching and listening to the superb performance of a Marine Comedy Band. . . . Within easy range of the stage was the Captain's tent illuminated for an evening of debauchery. The captain and three officers could be dimly seen through the mosquito screen. Alternately sitting and dancing with four fat, homely army nurses, probably hired for the celebration of the captain's third year in the army. . . . A pause in the playing of the band and the Master of Ceremonies inquired, "Any requests?"

> Whereupon, the door of El Capitan's tent opened slightly to allow a flushed feminine face to appear. The face moved and spake, "Play 'The Waltz You Saved for Me'.".(sic)

> The MC responded courteously with, "We have had a request. The next selection played shall be . . . 'Take it and Give'.".(sic)

> The band launched into a furiously tempoed hot number while the battalion of enlisted men shouted their approval at the delib-

erate and daring insolence of the MC. Lacking the decency to entertain their courtesans beyond sight of sex-starved soldiers who hadn't spoken to a white woman in over a year, the officers flaunted their women before their men like brutalized Nazi assassins.[38]

Men like Babcock, who had been at the front or on small Pacific island bases, were rotated through Hawaii, and some of these sentiments were acted out on Hawaii's streets. Resentment also flourished among men who felt stuck on "the Rock."

All these feelings were displayed in a spirited—and often ugly—sequence of letters to the editor of the *Honolulu Star-Bulletin*. Loosely categorized as the "girl controversy," the debate began with an exchange of letters around Christmastime, 1942, and continued to absorb Honolulu's attention for more than a month. By the opening of the new year, the paper's editor was apologizing for being able to publish only a few of the letters on the topic. On January 11th, the *Star-Bulletin* printed an editor's note to inform readers that "hundreds" of letters had been received. Careening from topic to topic, the letters illustrate the extent of anger and resentment on all sides of the issue; they also offer some examples of genuine goodwill, and show how central were racial stereotypes—and racism—in shaping public behavior and attitudes.

Two main arguments figured simultaneously in this debate. The first centered on the way women behaved to servicemen and male war workers—and vice versa. A letter from a "Disgusted Army Trio" began:

> Our hearts grieve for those women who are being so "brutally accosted" by servicemen in Honolulu. Is it not true we were brought here to protect the lives and property of these grateful island inhabitants? We ask no favors, but is courtesy and respect something that must be bought, or is it something all civilized people give freely?[39]

The complaints of the trio would seem to confirm Esther Bader's sense that the men felt that because "they were fighting for us, that anybody they wanted, they could have." It depends on whether "courtesy and respect" means exactly that or whether the men really mean "availability." Other observers, with less of an ax to grind, did note the tendency of some women, when spoken to by a "lonely serviceman," to "either bolt like a panicked fawn or congeal into a statue of insulted purity—nose in air," so these men may mean just what they say.[40] Women, though, did not know what was coming when a strange man approached them. Returning a smile could lead to rude comments or propositions. Often, it was safer to ignore the men in uniform. One couldn't prevent the whistles, but one could refuse to provide an opening.

One man, who identified himself as "a Negro from Harlem," understood the rationale but rejected its legitimacy. "Remember this, girls," he wrote. "A uniform doesn't make a soldier any worse or any better as far as character is concerned. He is just as much a gentleman as your dad or brother, who may be a defense worker. Above all, he is a human being and not a robot."[41]

In this controversy, simple acts assumed symbolic importance. What upset and irritated some men more than anything was that women never smiled at them. Some of the men were from small towns and not used to the anonymity of a city, even one the size of Honolulu. Others just didn't like being frozen out so uniformly and so blatantly. As an army corporal wrote to the *Star-Bulletin*: "Even the U.S. pallbearers at funerals will smile when spoken to. When you see a wahine's teeth in this town, brother, I'll bet 10 to 1 she's eating."[42] The editors, in the midst of this run of letters on the unsmiling women of Hawaii, demonstrated either insensitivity or a sense of humor by running, without comment, an Ipana toothpaste ad. "Don't make your smile the victim of tender, ailing *gums*," read the copy under a picture of an unsmiling woman.[43]

Though some women wrote in to counter these claims or to criticize the men's behavior or assumptions, the "girl controversy" was less a debate between men and women than among men themselves. Scores of servicemen wrote in to defend Hawaii's women and criticize their fellows, and Hawaii's men contributed more than a few letters. "To those of you who are griping about the aloofness and frigidity of the Honolulu girls," wrote one man who signed his real name (with no military title):

Many of you come over here with the idea that these girls are barbarians. You barge into a cafe and, thinking that you have a lot of oomph, you try your line on the waitress, expecting to snow her under, and you often get coarse and vulgar. She's heard the line 50 times a day for 2 or 3 years. I admire them.[44]

Most servicemen spent more time criticizing other men's behavior than praising Honolulu's women. One man, not terribly articulate but clearly outraged by the tone of the letters, wrote: "I don't possess all the etiquet (sic) that books are written about but I still believe women should be respected and not have men throwing mud and trying to disgrace women in Honolulu."[45]

Some local men were also outraged, and took the opportunity to point out the differences between themselves and the servicemen from the mainland, who could "dish" a good line but weren't planning on sticking around. "We know that girls are not passing fancies, but to respect and adore," insisted "A Local Boy" (once a seaman). "We don't say bad things about our girls." The *Star-Bulletin* editor titled the letter "Settling Down," and this writer described how he planned, "when this mad world is civilized again," to "to fence up an acre of my father's property, build a house, and settle down with a lovely Hawaiian beauty."[46] There were tensions between servicemen and local men, and this very public griping did not ease them.

As the rhetoric became more and more heated, a few people became disgusted with the whole debate. A technical sergeant in the Air Corps wrote scornfully: "I thought we were here to fight this war, not to gripe about girls not smiling at us. Soldiers, this is a man's army, not a Boy Scout camp. If you can't take it, how do you expect to beat the Axis?"[47]

The topic which elicited the most letters was male behavior. No matter how overstated or even ugly some of the criticisms were, they were made in response to a real set of circumstances. There was, however, another topic which furnished a subtext in many of these letters.

More than a few letter-writers voiced unrestrained criticism of Hawaii's women—not just their aloof behavior, but their looks, their demeanor, and their essential quality. The issue of race reverberated throughout the debate. Probably the nastiest comments appeared in the guise of a poem in the "Our Own Poets" column at the height of the controversy." (Most poetry published in this column was not terrible, so this poem was likely included as part of the debate.) Titled "Quest for Beauty," it begins:

> *Oh, Beauty, where art thy face upon the isle?*
> *Endless hours I've seen thee in my dreams, "Goddess of Paradise."*

But Paradise was not all that the movies and billboards and fantasies had promised, and neither were its women:

> *Thy has the ego complex of a movie queen. Perhaps thy*
> *has other things thy idol has. What, I should hate to*
>   *say.*
>
> *But remember, Goddess, that movie stars read B.O. ads.*
> *And movie stars don't waddle. Such is left for ducks.*
> *Another hint: thy back is broad, much broader than thy*
>   *mainland sisters'.*
>
> *Oh, stop, Goddess, stop being the farce ye are,*
> *for ye have many visitors to see ye, visitors who know the*
>   *score.*
> *And they laugh behind your back, for ye lack not only*
>   *beauty, but the brains that could displace it.*[48]

One such visitor, a worker at the Navy cantonment at Pearl Harbor, snidely inquired, "If these natural born beauties are as nice as I understand they claimed (sic) they are, why wasn't one of them chosen the Pineapple Queen instead of Harriett Shepardson, who, I understand, comes from Massachusetts, USA?" The editors rightly understood that the writer was distinguishing not between mainland and island origins, but between races, and followed this letter with a note explaining that "girls of Hawaiian blood" had been chosen in previous years.[49]

Few people spoke directly of race in this debate. Instead, they called on gender norms: the "Goddesses of Paradise" were inadequate as *women*; "natural born beauties" were not "nice" enough to win a beauty contest. Still, everyone who read the letters understood the importance of race as a silent term. And some men, taking the other side, simply reversed the weight of the designations so that gender trumped race. "You say you haven't seen any pretty girls around here," wrote one serviceman three weeks into the debate, "but you will invariably whistle, remark and stare at anything wearing a skirt. I'm far from being perfect, but my mother taught me to respect ladies, regardless of race or creed."[50] As a rule, on both sides of the debate, gender was the key term. Race—albeit crucially important—usually went unmentioned.

However, race played a role in virtually every aspect of relations between men and women in Hawaii. It was central to the notion of the female shortage. While estimates of 1,000 men to a woman were wildly exaggerated, the figure of "100 men to a girl" was not implausible. It all depended on whom one considered a "woman." Age, of course, was one criterion. Most of the men in the military were quite young, and their romantic universe was based on the conventions of the time. Thirty could seem quite old to an eighteen-year-old, and the older the woman, the more likely she was married and hence not "available." And while the men whistled at thirteen-year-old girls, they did not tend to date them. As for race, when men talked about the woman shortage, they often really meant the shortage of *white* women.

Even estimated very roughly, the importance of both age and race in determining the male-female ratio is clear. According to the 1940 census, the Territory of Hawaii had a population of 423,330. This number includes military personnel stationed on the islands. Women made up far less than half that total, for the military population was male, and the population of plantation workers (primarily Filipino) was also disproportionately male.

The islands' total female population was 178,195. Of this number, only 56,227 were between the ages of fifteen and twenty-nine. If one only counted Caucasian women, the number shrank dramatically. Approximately 25 percent of Hawaii's female population was Caucasian (or approximately 14,056 women), but one can shrink the number more by counting only haole women (excluding those of Puerto Rican and Portuguese descent). Since approximately 15 percent of the population was haole, we are left with roughly 8,434 women. Of course, many of these women were married, thus not "available." Also, the figures date from 1940, and the largest group to evacuate in the month after Pearl Harbor was haole women.

Assessing the male population of the islands during the war is a complicated task. The 1940 census recorded a male population of 245,135. Troop movements were kept secret, but a conservative estimate yields peak figures of half-a-million men above the 1940 figure. Of course, the number of servicemen on the islands fluctuated greatly during the war. Using a very rough—and conservative—figure of 700,000 men, one can get at least a sense of the age and racial dimensions of the "woman shortage." A ratio of all women to all men yields 1:3.9, rough odds to begin with. For *single* women aged fifteen or older (40,792), the ratio was 1:17. For Caucasian women between fifteen and twenty-nine years old, the ratio was 1:50, and for haole women in the same age range, the ratio rose to 1:83.

Numbers, of course, say little about the complexity of the question of race. First of all, judgments based on race were not made only by white men from the mainland, but by local people as well. And it is often difficult to say where race itself became less important than cultural difference. Many people at the time tended to use the term "race" to cover race, ethnicity, and cultural practices.

The wartime residents of Hawaii—war workers, servicemen and women, malihini and kamaaina, haole and local—were very much aware of the importance of race in relations between men and women on the islands. In letters to the mainland, they wrote in extremely frank terms about the problem. The military censors, concerned about morale, compiled voluminous reports containing extensive excerpts from thousands of private letters. Sociologists at the University of Hawaii devoted many pages of their journal, *Social Processes in Hawaii,* to these concerns and the military bureaucracy generated several memos debating policy on interracial marriage.

White servicemen held quite a range of opinions about the race question, especially when faced with an extreme shortage of white women. Sometimes opinions changed with time. John Fox, who came to Honolulu in the summer of 1944 to assume the presidency of Punahou, Honolulu's most prestigious private school, wrote to his mainland friends:

> For each soldier one sees with a haole wahine (white girl) on the street, another nine will be seen with oriental girls. A naval officer told me that as the Comparison cards, which are issued to the men when they come to Hawaii, become darkened through use so does the sailor's viewpoint concerning the skin-color of his girl companions change from white to brown.[51]

Another man remembers, "When you first arrived in Hawaii [the girls] appeared to be quite dark. However as the saying went, the longer you were on the island, the lighter those girls became."[52] Publications for servicemen celebrated the beauty of women like "Exotic Lucille Gabriel," and a columnist from *The New Pacific* magazine who roamed around Honolulu asking servicemen, "Do you prefer the Oriental or Occidental form of beauty?" found that a preponderance favored the former.[53]

Still, racial prejudice was common. One man wrote home: "I guess I have too much pride to be walking with a Jap, a Chinese, or the black girls. (Hawaiians are really black.) I think the marriage situation in Hawaii is about the worst that could be found anywhere in this world." Another man wrote of enjoying a square dance: "One of the nice things about it is there are no Orientals, Hawaiians, nor any of the 'Dukes Mixtures.' Just 'haoles' (Caucasians). Surely is a relief to be with one's own race." Yet another man, a war worker, had no problem with the idea of interracial sex, but could not countenance interracial marriage. "I have had . . . chances to 'shack up' with girls here," he wrote, "but there is too much risk involved. In case of an accident I wouldn't want to marry one of them. . . . When you get nailed by one of them you are a gone gosling."[54]

Many white servicemen and war workers, as a 1943 sociological survey discovered, were happy to date women of different racial and ethnic backgrounds, but few would have said these differences were unimportant. Some of the men justified crossing racial boundaries on practical grounds, like the man who stated with certainty: "Men require the companionship of women, Orientals or haoles. Since there is an insufficient number of haoles, the dating of Oriental women is not objectionable." Other men thought interracial dating acceptable as long as certain limits were observed: "If she can be a friend and stay as a friend and the men stay as gentlemen, I think there's no harm done," said one white serviceman from the mainland.[55]

As long as the woman viewed her involvement in terms of "morale building" or "patriotic duty," and the man viewed his as a natural desire for "feminine companionship," all might be well. They could be "friends," even come to "know the other race better." At the other extreme, some white men believed that sexual relations with local women did not threaten racial boundaries—as long as there were no emotional entanglements.

The significance of sex, of course, depended partly on the backgrounds of the people involved and how closely they adhered to middle-class notions of respectability. But while either friendship or sex might be compatible with racial boundaries, serious relationships were not. Romance, by definition, strained the boundaries. Marriage violated them entirely.

Few people believed the servicemen were interested in serious relationships, especially with women of different racial backgrounds. As one serviceman explained (speaking of interracial dating), the men from the mainland only wanted "feminine companionship. [They] yearn to hear a woman's voice again. They long for the scent of perfume. Marriage isn't their thought; a good time with a 'skirt' is their answer."[56]

But marriage did cross the minds of some. Servicemen and war workers contributed in significant numbers to Hawaii's "wedding boom." And during the war years, weddings between members of different races (never that unusual in Hawaii) became ever more common. In 1939, 22 percent of all marriages were between people of different racial stock; for the fiscal year ending June, 1944, 32 percent of all marriages were mixed race. The group with the highest rate of "out-marriage" was Caucasian men. In 1941, 79.7 percent of Caucasian grooms had Caucasian brides. By 1944, only 59.4 percent of Caucasian men married Caucasian women. Thus, out-marriage rates doubled, rising from 20.3 percent in 1941 to 40.4 in 1944. In contrast, only 9 percent of Caucasian women married men of other races. Caucasian men were most likely to marry part-Hawaiian women or women of Japanese ancestry.[57]

Projections for the success of such marriages were mixed. Some people, responding to a survey on intermarriage and war, thought that love could conquer all. But 78 percent of this small sample thought there was "little chance for happiness," especially if the couple returned to the mainland, where racial prejudice would be an "insurmountable obstacle."[58] Censorship reports quoted a haole woman on the subject: "A lot of the boys go with the Chinese and Japanese and Korean and Hawaiian girls (I forget the Filipinos and Portuguese and Porto Ricans [sic]) and some of them marry them . . . I don't see how it will work out—especially in the south. Most people will think the Hawaiians are Negroes and they will be hurt lots of times. . . ."[59] Another haole wrote back to the mainland with a plea for understanding:

> B——— has met a girl here and has fallen in love with her. She is an Oriental—Japanese—and wants to marry her . . . Now before you start condemning her for being of Japanese decent (sic), remember that she is as much American as you or I, as she was born in U.S. territory. She has a brother in the U.S. Army and her family buy war bonds and stamps . . . and although marrying into another race is not a wise thing to do, make certain that you do not feel that such a girl is below any other girl simply because her forbearers were Japanese.[60]

Virtually everyone believed such marriages would be difficult to sustain on the mainland, and many doubted that the servicemen would take their brides back with them at the end of the war. "The man will sail away protected by the service," wrote a haole defense worker. "Many marry for intimacy because they know life is short."[61]

Wartime marriages of soldiers were not only matters of the heart, but of military policy as well. Marriages taking place in any area "outside the United States" (and Hawaii was so deemed) had to be approved by the area Army commander. A series of memos on

"Marriage Policy" were distributed during the war years, and all treated race as a significant factor. Requests for permission to marry were to be automatically denied if the prospective spouse was "an enemy alien, a person of doubtful loyalty to the United States of America, a prostitute, or one obviously unsuited." Regimental chaplains were charged with investigating the "suitability" of both people involved and recommending for or against the union.[62]

The criteria, in practice, often included race. One regimental chaplain wrote to the commanding general in 1943, with a positive recommendation: "The applicants . . . are apparently of legal, marriageable (sic) age. The difference in racial extraction is seemingly too minor to be regarded as a potential present or future barrier or menace to their love and respect for one another." A memo issued in August of 1944, following a communication from the War Department, made the racial criteria more explicit. "The laws of a number of states do not recognize as valid any marriage contracted between persons of different races, regardless of whether the marriage was valid where contracted," read one provision, and another stated that aliens of "Asiatic or East Indian descent" would not be admitted to the United States even if married to a citizen.[63]

The human dimensions of the issue are buried in such bureaucratic memos, but officials were reminded of human consequences by the letters of appeal they also received. One nineteen-year-old woman began her letter to the Military Governor: "I am with a child, going on five months," and identified the father by name, rank, serial number, and company and infantry division. The man, a corporal, wanted to marry her, she said, and her parents had given permission. However, problems had arisen. "Mr. [   ] wrote to my mother in his last letter that although he wants to marry me he cannot because he was told that no soldier is allowed to marry a girl of Japanese descent." She continued, "I cannot believe that is so because I am an American . . . ," and closed with a line that betrayed her full distress: "I will be anxiously waiting your soon reply." It's not clear what the corporal's intentions were, whether his application had been rejected by an overzealous official either because of the woman's Japanese ancestry or her pregnancy, or whether he simply intended to "sail away protected by the service."

The military files contain no record of what happened to the man, the woman, or their child.[64]

Reactions to interracial dating and marriage varied greatly in wartime Hawaii, but two groups tended to be most critical of the practice: haole women and Japanese-American women. The military censors, who so thoroughly documented such comments that they included "Interracial friendships" as a regular heading in their confidential summaries, reported that Japanese women criticized the practice either because of "race consciousness" or because of "the insecurity and uncertainty involved," while haole women were simply "unanimously critical."[65] Not all haole women were critical, of course, for the censorship reports were only based on the comments of those who felt strongly enough to write about the issue. And while the comments recorded by the censors were highly critical, they were not undifferentiated. Some straightforwardly objected to race mixing, like one who wrote, "for the life of me, I can't see how it can cause anything but trouble . . . a promiscuous mixing of the races, such as we have here, can breed nothing but trouble." Others were simply racist, like the school teacher who wrote of officers and enlisted men who "think nothing about strutting a dark woman down the street."[66]

Many haole women criticized what they saw as the sexual promiscuity of local women. "Lots of them don't even bother to marry the men," complained one. "They just have their children anyway." Another wrote: "We whites are simply seething about our nice white boys from the Mainland making asses with themselves with these Japanese girls. The 'gals' . . . have an entirely different set of morals from ours and to have an illegitimate child is nothing out of line for them."[67] (While some of Hawaii's ethnic groups did not stigmatize unwed pregnancy, this was not true of the Japanese.)

Illegitimacy rates did go up during the war years, and if only because of the racial composition of the islands, local women accounted for the preponderance of such births. It was not only haoles who commented on this; a Japanese woman wrote in a letter to the mainland: "Oriental girls . . . are having war babies as if it were a fad! I suppose when the poor darlings are of age to understand mothers will tell them she did her patriotic duty." Another castigated "our local girls": "Seems to me too many people are using wartime hysteria as an excuse for sexual license."[68]

The angriest comments from haole women were about Japanese-American women who consorted with white servicemen and war workers. Like many people who wrote home about the Japanese and Japanese Americans in Hawaii, these writers saw "race" (or ethnic origin) as being more important than nationality. Though Hawaii did not treat its Japanese and AJA population with so much suspicion and discrimination as did the federal government on the mainland, some still saw all people of Japanese ancestry as enemy aliens, their loyalty compromised by their very bloodlines.[69] The horrors of the island campaigns were very fresh and raw in Hawaii, and the residue of that horror spills over into ugliness in a letter the censors quoted under the heading "critical comments—by Caucasian women":

> . . . They [servicemen] are supposed to *kill* them [Japanese] in battle and love them over here. It sure does not make sense to me—if they must have darlings with them why in the ———— do they allow white civilians to see such things. I, like so many thousands of wives give my husband to go and fight the yellow peril and to see this sort of thing encouraged makes me see red. . . .[70]

Rumors also circulated that AJA women were using sex to obtain information about troop movements and other military secrets. "They (Japanese girls) do dress and our Army and Navy boys take to them like ducks to water," wrote a woman late in the summer of 1943, as the U.S. forces began to prepare for a full-scale offensive in the Central Pacific. "You see they are really the only females but this is one way Japan is informed on the movement of our ships and Army."[71]

It was haoles from the mainland, as opposed to kamaaina, who were most shocked by the frequency of interracial dating and marriage. All, northerners and southerners alike, came from a highly segregated society. Most were surprised by the ethnic mix of Hawaii's population and confused by its racial conventions. Some wrote home to celebrate the "harmony" of the races in Hawaii, while others wrote home in horror. Some formed close friendships with local people; some had little interaction with other races; some felt confirmed in racist assumptions. What virtually none of them expected, however, was that some of the people they had been raised to look down on would look down on them.

Hawaii was neither a land of complete racial harmony nor a bipolar racial society. The distinction between haoles and locals was the most important one to most Caucasians, but the term "local" obscured the class distinctions and the complex ethnic hierarchy that obtained within each group. Further, members of different ethnic groups, no matter what their place in the social hierarchy, often looked at other groups with suspicion or disdain. As one worker wrote, "We are having a lot of trouble with the different races in camp. The Porteguese (sic) hate the Howlies (sic) (that's us) and the Filop's hate the Japs and the Japs hate the Chinese. What fun."[72] More to the point, a Japanese woman wrote: "I am proud to be a Japanese, and I don't care to be a stink Chinaman nor marry one . . . because they have the same color; nor care to be a white or a brown," while a Chinese man wrote in anger about being mistaken for Japanese: ". . . just imagine when being a 'pure Chinese' & them calling you a Jap!!! . . . It's not that I dislike the Japanese but I don't want to be called one right in front everyone & be embarrassed (sic) & humiliated."[73]

Of all Hawaii's ethnic groups, Japanese and Japanese Americans were probably the most highly race-conscious. To Japanese Americans, the issue was not whether white servicemen should date "oriental girls," but whether *they* should date white servicemen. This question generated a lot of heat during the war. A survey published in *Social Processes in Hawaii* found that women college students of Japanese descent were more open-minded on the subject than haole women, and insisted that dating servicemen was an act of patriotism. But in private letters many Asian women, especially those of Japanese ancestry, were extremely frank about their versions of racial hierarchy. Many of the young women made it clear they were following their parents' wishes or were concerned about their reputation. "I wish to tell you frankly that I am not in a position to see any of your boy friends who are out here," one woman wrote to a haole friend. "We orientals are rather unsociable, especially . . . my parents . . . they don't want to see me at any time or at any place with a person in uniform."[74] In a letter to a white serviceman, another woman (Chinese American) clearly articulated the sentiments which so shocked mainland haoles: "My parents feel the same way toward the white race as you feel toward the colored races. Just as incidents you have witnessed here caused the impressions you have of the Negroes, so have the white men left impressions on the minds of Oriental parents, mine included."[75]

Young Japanese-American women, in the midst of hundreds of thousands of young men seeking feminine companionship, experienced a man shortage. Once again, it all depended how one counted. The young Japanese-American men were serving in the armed forces, and they made up a disproportionate percentage of Hawaii's military ranks. The men these women would have dated were gone, and dating men of other ethnic and racial groups was chancy. While the white men from the mainland might have to struggle with ingrained beliefs about race and hierarchy to have a real friendship with a local woman—a woman of color—such a relationship, be it friendship, romance, sexual or otherwise, would not likely damage his reputation or his chances for happiness after the war. Such was not the case for young Japanese-American or, to a lesser extent, Chinese-American women.[76] Racial boundaries were quite strict, and not a few families disowned daughters who married haole men. "[A Japanese girl] married a sergeant in the Air Corps," one woman gossiped in a letter. "It certainly is a pity. If they had many children they can disown her if they don't like it, but she being the only child I really feel sorry for them."[77]

Not all comments about interracial romance were so negative; a few people seemed to think intermarriage was the only way to end discrimination; others called it a road to "peace." "Mix marriages are very appropriate these days," argued one writer. "It is not good to stick to your own race, especially when a war is going on with our ancestors."[78] But even those few who attempted to celebrate interracial unions saw the problems involved, and the weight of community disapproval and parental disappointment weighed heavily on young women. "Back here people talk & talk if you stop to talk to the boys from the states—sometimes I feel so sorry for them but—yet—there's your pride and not only that it won't be good news to Mom," explained one girl.[79] Another wrote somewhat wistfully:

> You'll have heard of the problems we encounter on whether we should cultivate friendships with these boys [servicemen] . . . Frankly speaking, many of the boys we meet here are very interesting yet simply because we are of Oriental extraction it would be dirt on our face to be in company of these men. Most of the Japanese boys have nothing to do with us and call us "soldier meat."[80]

Expressions of shame and embarrassment filled these letters, as young women debated what it meant to be seen with a haole soldier. While haole women complained about how eager the Japanese girls were to latch onto white servicemen, most AJA women said the opposite. But clearly many women of Japanese ancestry did date—and even marry—haole servicemen. College women, in response to a survey question, explained the discrepancy in terms of class, arguing that " 'lower' class Oriental girls feel flattered at the attentions received while the 'higher' class Oriental girls are apprehensive and embarrassed." But shame was not restricted to the "higher class." Writing to a relative, one woman (whose grammar, syntax, and occupation do not indicate high class status) reported: "Hate to write and tell you about your sister F——— . . . It sure is disgrace to you and all of us . . . She married to a Haole soldier from the States. . . . She came over one day with her husband to the store. Gosh! I was so shame cause a Japanese lady was there when she came."[81]

The threat of "shame" was strong, as was the authority of parents. These cultural claims were not only made upon girls, but on boys who had left Hawaii in the 442nd. The *Honolulu Advertiser* reported in 1944 that over 100 men of the 100th had married "caucasian belles" from towns near the mainland training camps.[82] Reports of interracial love provoked anguish and anger in many families. "You should have known better than to ask a question like that," came the response to a young man who had written his parents for permission to marry a Caucasian woman.

> . . . the whole household is in a turmoil, meaning Papa . . . in
> Hawaii people are just exactly as they were five years ago. The
> intolerance, prejudices, etc., are as strong in them as ever. You
> know very well what a miserable failure practically every such
> case brings. What I'm driving at is that the idea of your bringing
> home anybody not of the same blood will be a major tragedy in *this*
> family. Papa will simply not tolerate it. . . .[83]

Another Japanese-American serviceman's brother, a little less serious, offered his advice: "Go ahead date up as many dames as you
can. Try all kinds of nationalities and enjoy life with them, but try
to pick a budda head for your wife. Mother will be disappointed if
you bring home brunettes or blonds . . ." And yet another, even
more direct, wrote: ". . . don't let it be any white meats from up
there we have no use for them."[84]

The emphasis on shame and on parental disapproval in so many
letters suggests that the younger people were less racially conscious
than their elders, and that the true obstacle to interracial dating and
marriage was the "older generation." One young woman, disappointed but obedient to her parents' wishes, wrote, "Maybe our
children may have a greater chance."[85]

Yet racial boundaries were not only of the parents' making.
Some Japanese-American women discussed "the service to servicemen" and decided not to attend any dances unless the servicemen
were Japanese American. "I'm going to the U.S.O. Sunday and if I
see more square heads than any one else I'm coming home. I don't
mind entertaining my kind but the others—let them take care of
them I say," insisted one young woman, and another assured her
friend that the dance she attended was for "local boys," not "those
white trash."[86] And if the women were uncomfortable about being
seen with haoles, they were even more vehement about the black
troops. Writing about haoles, they used words like "shame" and
"embarrassed"; writing about blacks, they used words like
"afraid."[87]

Not all of Hawaii's women were as race conscious as the Japanese and Japanese Americans. Filipinas and Hawaiian women
showed the least concern about race, and a relatively high percentage of both local women and Caucasian men crossed racial di-

vides—in some way—during the war. But race remained a fundamental fact, and a significant obstacle in intimate relations, with legal, as well as social, ramifications.

The men and women who reached out to each other across cultural divides found gulfs, even chasms, of difference. But in Hawaii things were further complicated. The servicemen from the mainland were off-balance there. It was not only the problem of race and the mix of ethnic cultures that bewildered them, but the whole feel of a place where women would come to a dance in formal gowns—and barefoot. In Hawaii, even the most sincere efforts at connection could easily backfire.

Some miscommunications didn't carry much weight; they were scenes that could have been scripted for a comedy about interethnic romance. Five young women attempted to serve the servicemen by inviting a group of artillery officers over to dinner once a week. They decided to take turns cooking, and responsibility for dinner fell first to a Chinese girl, the most lively and flirtatious of the lot. She proudly presented her dinner to the men: a whole fish, served as was customary in Hawaii, with the head and tail intact. The men did not eat, and finally one of the women asked, a little hesitantly, if there was something wrong. The men exchanged looks, and one burst out, "Doggone it, it's bad enough to have the head and tail, but to have the eyes staring at you is just too much." He broke the tension and everyone laughed, but there was a residue of frustration and hurt, the sense of a heartfelt gesture failed. "Poor little girl," says one of the women in retrospect. "She had never been away from Hawaii; she didn't understand. . . ."[88]

Other scenes were both more poignant and complex. Thomas Law, a young Seabee from West Virginia, made friends with a nisei girl about his age. They spent a lot of time together, and grew quite comfortable with each other over a period of months. Law was coming into his own in Hawaii, going through a sort of intellectual and political awakening, spurred by the difference from home and by the exhortations of a small group of Communists (civilians, union men) who centered their activities in the U.S.O.-like "Labor Canteen" where he volunteered. Law began to take courses at the University of Hawaii, concentrating in Japanese. One day he was at his friend's house; he was reading, she was ironing. The phone rang. She answered, and chatted with a girlfriend for a few minutes—in Japanese. When she hung up, Law gave her a quick replay of the conversation—in English. He was showing off, thinking she'd be surprised and pleased that he'd understood. But he had crossed some absolute boundary. There was a stunned silence, then she asked him to leave. He never saw her again.[89]

Midway between comedy and tragedy are other stories, usually bittersweet, of people who had managed to surmount the barriers. Blase Camacho was beautiful and smart, and her story would be different had she been less of either. She was the first Puerto Rican to graduate from the University of Hawaii where, in an accomplishment much less significant to her, she had been crowned in a beauty pageant. Blase had been born and raised on a plantation, where her father spent most of his life working in the cane fields. She had not fled that world, but carried some of it with her: the warmth of her community, the stories her father had read to her and the folktales the old people told, the mixed legacy of discrimination and opportunity that she saw in her plantation days. She had the determination of those who know that they carry the hopes of others. She was making it for them as well, fulfilling the promise of America.

Although she was young and naive, Blase understood very clearly that actions had consequences. She had chosen a path that required work and commitment and a complex balancing of worlds. This precocious knowledge made her self-aware and somewhat careful, but it also gave her great faith in the possibility of action. She believed it was possible to make a difference.

The war came after Blase had completed her degree and was teaching school. In those days, new teachers were expected to pay their dues on an outer island before getting what most considered a more desirable position on Oahu. Even married women whose husbands were in Oahu were sent away. Blase taught in Lahaina, on Maui, then a small town with a population of about eight thousand. During the tensest days of the war, while invasion still seemed a real possibility, Lahaina had no ground defense. In the event of invasion, the Army planned to bomb the Pali road that connected

Lahaina to the larger town of Wailuku on the other side of the mountains, leaving Lahaina to defend itself. The teachers dug trenches around the school, trying to be lighthearted about a situation they knew was extremely serious. One of the few men at the school insisted that the women teachers learn to shoot. Most people in Hawaii had heard horror stories about what Japanese invaders had done to the civilian populations elsewhere, and those stories may have fueled his sense of urgency. He taught them to shoot on the beach near the school, using live ammunition.

The war made small communities like Lahaina more isolated, for gasoline was rationed and the curfew came early. But by the beginning of the 1942–43 school year, Blase had completed her two-year stint on Maui and had gotten her job on Oahu. She wasn't in Honolulu, of course, but in Haleiwa, a very small town on Oahu's north shore. She lived in a cottage on the beach with three other women, all from the mainland, one of whom was in charge of the U.S.O. for that section of the island.

Unlike Maui, Oahu was flooded with servicemen, there to protect the island and to train for combat in the Pacific. Though Haleiwa was a long way from the bustle of Honolulu, it had an abundance of military men, for the north shore had become home to half-a-dozen training camps, an airfield with the longest landing strip in the islands, and the Haleiwa Officers' Club. Blase and her housemates regularly dressed up for the U.S.O. dances in the Waialua gym. They were four college-educated women among a larger group of young women—girls, really—from the nearby plantations, most of whom had very little experience beyond their own communities. But many of the men had little experience either, and one way or another they found some common ground.

———

The dances were much less impersonal than the ones in Honolulu. The sex ratio was still a problem—there were usually five times as many men as women. But the scale of the dances was smaller, and the attendance more stable. There was not much to do out in the country, and the dances seemed a little less like war work and more like parties. The music was good, and some of the men better dancers than had ever graced the Waialua gym before. One man, a Mexican American, had taught dance in Hollywood before the war, and Blase was his favorite partner. She tried to dredge up the Spanish that had been her first language, and it pleased the Hispanic men who had not expected to find a woman like Blase so far from home.

Lots of the men wanted to talk, but not about the war. Those who had seen combat, Blase thought, did not want to put anyone else through that trauma. Those who were not yet veterans wanted some semblance of normality: a high school gym, a pretty girl, a good band. Many were that young; some had missed their high school proms.

Most of them wanted to talk about home, and family. They were tired, and it showed. They griped a little—about the food, mostly. They told Blase how beautiful she was. And she asked them about their lives, where they were from, what it was like there. As Blase listened to these young men whose lives had been disrupted so completely, she incorporated their dreams into her own. One man was from New York City; another had been a student at Boston University. A soldier from North Carolina invited her to his family's tobacco farm. A young ensign from LA told her about the La Brea tar pits and the Brown Derby. She allayed their homesickness and they fueled her ambition. After the war, Blase resolved, she was going to travel. She was going to the biggest city in the world.

Blase and her friends dated officers and ate quite a few dinners at officers' clubs or at Haleiwa's best restaurant, the Ocean View Inn, which looked more as though it belonged in the old South than in Hawaii. But at least once a week, and sometimes more often, the four women invited men home to dinner. They were always enlisted men—never officers. It was sort of like robbing Peter to pay Paul, Blase said, but the officers had cars, and money, and in significant ways had more freedom and control over their lives. The women believed the GIs needed these invitations more than the officers did.

They invited home the men they met at the U.S.O. dances. It wasn't purely selfless, for they only invited the men they liked—men they thought they could trust, and especially the ones who seemed terribly lonely or as though they needed a little extra support. They usually invited six at a time, the mismatched numbers making clear that the invitation was just for a home-cooked meal and company, but they kept the groups small enough that the invitations were personal. They did not want the men to feel their dinners were official events, more "service to the servicemen."

The meals were usually fun. The women took turns cooking, and the biggest problem they had was getting the men to leave—without seeming rude. A lot of the men didn't seem to get the little hints that hostesses drop when it is time to go home. Even exaggerated yawns and pointed comments in the vein of "Oh, my, how late it's gotten!" failed to rouse men who found the homey cottage a welcome refuge. All four of the women were young and energetic, but they did have jobs to go to, and the working day started early in the islands. Finally a GI, one of their more regular guests, made them a sign. It was in the shape of a doghouse, and it read: "We need our beauty sleep—do not linger after ————," with a chalk board for them to write in that evening's curfew hour. They used the military 24-hour clock.

The men showed their gratitude in whatever ways they could—and seized upon chances to show off for Blase and her friends. Once when there was no bread in the country store near their home, a flier from the nearby airfield volunteered to get some. He was back in less than an hour with loaves of fresh bread, having flown to Honolulu and back. Blase took a picture of him in front of his Piper Cub, which he had, for some unknown reason, christened "Baby Butch." The photograph shows a smiling, confident young man. He died in the Pacific war not long after the photo was taken.

Some lucky men, when they were shipped out, carried with them pictures of Blase—the ones she referred to as her "cheesecake pictures." Many men asked her for pictures; very few got them. But many men carried with them less tangible images of Blase and her friends, memories of the women cooking dinner or building sand castles at the beach; posing in combat fatigues, mock-serious, with the men's weapons; laughing down at soldiers from their perch on a jeep.

Through four long years of war, Blase and her friends offered refuge to men the war had brought to Hawaii, and through it all she held fast to one vow. She was not going to let her heart be broken. She was not going to fall in love. In the midst of the happiness she and her friends wove for and with these young men, Blase never lost sight of the darker reality. The men would be sent out into the Pacific, and many would not return. She gave the men her beauty, her intelligence, her sparkling vitality, unbounded affection and comfort and concern, but she always held something back. She would not—could not—commit herself to one of their number. She would *not* be made a war widow.

More than that, Blase was ambitious. Having accomplished so much, she wanted more. She saw, in her conversations with a range of men who seemed to embody the diversity of America, that her horizons were narrow. Their stories fired her ambition. She was not ready to get married yet, for that would close off one possible future. After the war, Blase left the islands. She and a friend traveled the mainland by train, visiting the families of the men she had be- friended. She want to that tobacco farm in North Carolina, and to Boston where she saw Sally Rand and ate fried clams. She spent the year in New York, studying library science at Pratt Institute. Though she was offered a job at City College, she didn't stay. After a winter in New York, she missed the blue sky and the blue ocean, and so she went back, with new skills and insights, to live her life in Hawaii.

Blase's story is a story of success. In the midst of war, she and some number of young American men managed to bridge the chasms that divided them—chasms of race, of gender, of profound cultural difference. The connections they forged were reciprocal; gifts were given and received. They came, in whatever limited ways they could, to understand each other. In countless ways, both large and small, they changed each other's lives.

But this story, too, is bittersweet. Of all Blase's memories of the war, one lingers. It was Christmas, the hardest time for most of the men waiting and training in Hawaii. They were far from home and family, and the balmy trade winds blowing made the distance seem all the greater. It was perfectly dark in the training camp where the men were bivouacked. No lights were allowed in the blackout. The men were in their tents, talking softly or trying to sleep, when the carols began. The men drifted out in twos and threes, shadows amidst the trees, drawn by the music. And the singers, seeing those lonely figures in the dark, tried not to cry. There on a mountaintop in Hawaii, in a moment of stillness in a world at war, a woman who had never seen snow sang, "I'm Dreaming of a White Christmas." It was her gift, and she knew it was not enough.[90]

Epilogue

May 30, 1942. On this first Memorial Day since war began, there was a parade in the town of Hilo on the Big Island, yet another piece of American life wrenched from its accustomed context. Memorial Day was originally a day of remembrance for the Civil War's Union dead, and in 1942 many southern states still refused to observe it.

But this Memorial Day had new meaning, for so many of the graves to be decorated were fresh, and the war on everyone's mind would not soon be consigned to memory. The war in the Pacific was going badly. And though the citizens who came together on this Memorial Day in Hawaii did not know it, the bloody, crucial battle of Midway was about to begin.

The Hilo parade was made up almost completely of soldiers and their heavy trucks and big guns. Most of the men who marched were white, northerners and southerners indistinguishable in their Government Issue uniforms. Most of the people who watched were plantation workers, of Asian descent, who knew little and cared less about the distant civil war that had given birth to this holiday.

The men marched with precision, eyes straight ahead, through silent streets. The crowd did not cheer. The only sound was the synchronized thump of the men's boots. What did these boys—for that was what most of them were, boys who would soon face the Japanese enemy—feel? And what of the watchers, part of a world

211

that had not yet been fully drawn into a larger American culture? As they stood in the silence that was proper according to custom, betraying no emotion discernible to the servicemen from the mainland, what did they think?

II

The photo hung by the meat counter in the little butcher shop on the wrong side of the tracks in Lawrence, Kansas. A soldier boy and hula girl, embracing. A service star hung in the window at home, a mother's pride and sorrow, but this was the father's sign. My son, the soldier, in Hawaii.

The girl was lithe and brown, with long, dark, wavy hair. Her arms were wrapped around his gangly frame, her face tilted up in a practiced smile. The picture had been bought and paid for in a concession around Hotel Street. Two Pictures With Hula Girl—75 Cents.

The picture was a topic of conversation—sometimes bawdy conversation when there were no women in the shop. Far from Kansas, one of their sons stood with his arms around a Hawaiian beauty. She was not Hawaiian, of course. Hawaiian women, by and large, were big and strong and solid. They did not look the way men from the mainland, schooled by Hollywood, expected them to look. The men preferred their exotic women on the petite side. This woman was Puerto Rican.

Frozen in her mercenary embrace, eyed by silent women, speculated about by men, she stood as a sign of all the ways men had claimed the women they encountered, cast them as exotic, purchased their favors, exploited them. It was an old story of race and sex, framed by war.

But the embrace could also be read differently. It was not only the old image of boundaries transgressed but a new image of boundaries challenged. Some such embraces had been real. Men and women from very different backgrounds had met and married. Their lives would not be easy, but in living they offered a private challenge to a public system of discrimination and exclusion.

This mother and father were lucky; their son returned from war. He endured a lot of kidding about his hula girl, but didn't mind much—the photo was a sign that he had been somewhere, even though he chose to settle down in his home town. He was surprised by one thing, however. Of all the friends and customers who filed through that butcher shop during the hard years of war, it was Mexican farm laborers who paid most attention to that picture. His father said he didn't quite know why—and had never asked straight out—but they had really got a kick out of it. So though the war ended, the image remained, its meaning unfixed.

———

Both these images—the one a representation of a commercial transaction, the other a moment frozen in memory—can be read in different ways. In their unstable meanings, their mutable possibilities, we see many of the complex issues that would be played out, though not resolved, in postwar American society.

World War II changed America. As the war put people into motion, it put cultures into contact—and often into conflict. Hawaii was an extreme case of that contact, but the war left all of America unsettled. The possibilities for misunderstandings and misreadings were immense, as in the case of the parade in Hilo, or the photograph in the butcher shop in Kansas; but the lessons people drew from their experiences varied. Some were confirmed in old prejudices, others found their worldviews challenged. In postwar America, the struggles over the meaning of wartime experiences would continue.

During the war, as part of the war effort, the federal government had acted to encourage and even enforce a unity of purpose and identity. A nation divided was a nation weakened. But as Americans met other Americans, they did not find a coherent and homogeneous culture. The claims of unity were complicated by cultural differences that seemed overwhelmingly significant. And as some Americans attempted to claim their places in this wartime America, they found that unity did not mean the same thing as equality and that not all Americans were considered *real* Americans.

The story of postwar America is in large part the story of a society coping with the questions of identity and difference stirred up by the war. The state, even though sometimes unintentionally, played an important role, for in promoting unity it destabilized relationships and created logical imperatives that were contradictory and sometimes explosive. Steps that were taken under pressure of war could not be easily rescinded. National armed forces could not remain segregated in one region and integrated in another. Local custom could not simply reassert primacy over national needs. Federal programs for veterans would undermine some of the divisions of race and class: between 1945 and 1950, 2.3 million veterans attended college under the GI Bill. Members of the 369th, with the bonus points veterans received on the Civil Service exam, got good government jobs. Many of these changes were unintended byproducts of the war effort, but the extension of the power of the federal government during the war years was critical in setting the stage for the struggles to come.

But it was on a smaller stage that some of the crucial decisions of the postwar era were made. Within arenas created by specific policy decisions (like suburbs, or college classrooms full of veterans, or the ever-expanding "middle class"), Americans reconfigured their understandings of difference. Identities seemed mutable, especially in the new landscape of the suburbs, and in a nation increasingly enveloped in a national popular culture. A family might move from defining itself as Italian and working class to white and suburban without changing the truth of the first two facts. It all depended which identities mattered.

The cultural reconfiguration of some sorts of difference was made easier by a belief in "natural" differences between men and women. Carefully scripted sex roles smoothed the process as people from diverse backgrounds met and married one another. Within a limited range, differences of background could be accommodated and negotiated within the private sphere, where the "complementary" differences of the two sexes provided the primary structure. And even more fundamentally, in the clearly defined and often overelaborated gender roles of the era, Americans sought a stable set of relations and identities with which to confront and weather other changes. The problem, of course, was that "complementary" difference really referred to a system of sexual inequality. In the postwar reconfigurations of difference, American women suffered a short-term setback.

In the postwar years, Americans seemed obsessed with questions of self-definition, and popular and scholarly works alike tried to pin down the American Character, American Culture, or American Identity. In retrospect, this effort looks like a dangerous and ugly attempt to deny legitimate difference, to continue the process of papering over discrimination and inequality. Once again, however, a historical moment is created of contradictory impulses and can be read in different ways. The search for an American culture was a stage in America's ongoing attempt to cope with the problems and possibilities of difference. The calls on—and for—an America in which everyone could eventually become (at least culturally) white and middle class and suburban, in which troublesome differences would simply fade away, were made in the face of a new cold-war enemy and out of the hopefulness born of an economic expansion that seemed limitless. It was, at its best, an inclusive vision. At the same time, it *was* a papering over of inequality and discrimination. Given impetus by the changing structure of society, these tensions roiled the surface of American life, but still surprised many when they exploded the reigning model of American identity.

Hawaii was not at the center of these battles. It remained on the margins until America began to turn its attention toward Asia. Hawaii, though, had played an important role in the national struggle over the meaning of difference. It was our border of war, the first strange place for over a million American young men, caught between war and home. In Hawaii, Americans directly confronted the complex meanings of cultural difference. Their struggles have shaped our own.

Notes

These statements are taken from the reports compiled by Hawaii's censors during the war years. Within two hours after the attack on Pearl Harbor, military censors were installed at all communication agencies. Residents of Hawaii got little information from the radio because censors forbade the broadcasting of specific information: "All eye witness stories are out . . . all detail of places are out . . . don't mention or speculate on size of attack." While newspapers and magazines, radio broadcasts, and telephone conversations were all monitored or censored through the war years, the largest task was censoring the mail. The Army and Navy censors handled civilian correspondence until February 1942; thereafter, mail censorship was done under the auspices of the Federal Office of Censorship, though it remained closely allied with the military and military governor's office. The censorship staff eventually numbered several hundred people from diverse backgrounds, with reading knowledge of more than fifty different languages or dialects, as well as shorthand and Braille. "At one time," a historian of Hawaii's war years notes, "five concert pianists, three artists, five interior decorators, and a miscellaneous collection of ex-concert singers, orchid-raising authorities, and others were censoring mail." They were supervised by an Army reserve officer with special training in censorship, and experts in various fields were employed to censor technical documents and correspondence. The censors cut out any words or passages that might compromise America's security. According to official accounts, no letters were destroyed, but some were returned to their authors with explanations about why they could not be passed.

217

One charge of the censorship office was to monitor morale on the islands. To that end, the office compiled bimonthly reports that it furnished to Navy Intelligence. Under such headings as "Japanese Morale" (meaning the issei and nisei residents of Hawaii) or "Interracial Friendships and Marriage" or "War Worker Morale" or "Racial Problems," the censors quoted a selection of "typical comments" (no names were used anywhere in the documents). They also compiled statistical reports on the frequency with which issues were mentioned and on changes in the general tone of comments. For example, during the first two weeks of May 1944, the censors reported a "sharp decline in favorable reactions to the [local] Japanese," with 82.6 percent of comments unfavorable as compared to only 60.9 percent in April of the same year.

The censorship reports are a gold mine of information. They offer the private voices of countless anonymous individuals. Many of the writers, it is obvious from their bare literacy, are not the sort of people whose voices would be heard in the public realm. They were not the ones writing letters to the editors of newspapers or publishing their diaries. Although people knew that their letters would be read by censors, that fact did not seem to have much effect on what they wrote. The voices in the censors' reports are raw in their anger, their fear, their sorrow or pleasure. The letters quoted in the reports obviously are not a simple cross-section of opinion; the censors were concerned with certain issues bearing on morale. Nonetheless, the censorship reports offer an amazing survey of *private* sentiment—and often the sort of comments that people today would not proudly offer up to researchers asking for their correspondence from World War II.

The censorship reports are found in "General Information Summary," Commandant's General Correspondence, Boxes V9375 and V9377, 181-58-3404, Folders A 8-5/LL 1-5, Record Group 181-PHNY, National Archives, Pacific Sierra Region (NA-PSR). Hereafter, these materials will be referred to as "Censorship Reports." All these documents were declassified at our request. The quotations with which we begin are from Censorship Reports, Box V9375, File LL-3, 11/1-15/43, p. 11.

The general information about censorship in Hawaii cited above (including quote) comes from Gwenfread Allen, *Hawaii's War Years* (Honolulu: University of Hawaii Press, 1950), 146–148. Allen's work is an invaluable source—detailed, accurate, and reflecting her intimate knowledge of Hawaii's complex society.

Notes

Prologue

1. Eloise Ornelles Wilson, "Remembering the Lovely, Sunny Day that Became Dec. 7, 1941," *The Sacramento Bee,* December 7, 1977 (clipping, n.p.); "Notes from Eloise Ornelles Wilson," Elk Grove, California, October 1990, furnished to authors (in authors' possession). Eloise Ornelles' story is written from these two accounts; direct quotes will be cited specifically.
2. These two accounts come directly from Walter Lord, *Day of Infamy* (New York: Henry Holt and Company, 1957), 78–79.
3. Lord, *Day of Infamy,* 159–160; Allen, *Hawaii's War Years,* 9–10.
4. Allen, *Hawaii's War Years,* 9.
5. Ibid., 9–10.
6. Ibid., 6–7.
7. The account of Daniel Inouye's experiences comes from Theon Wright, *The Disenchanted Isles: The Story of the Second Revolution in Hawaii* (New York: The Dial Press, 1972), 103–106.
8. Elizabeth Beach Brown, "We Lived Through Pearl Harbor: The War Journal of Elizabeth Beach Brown," 45-page typed manuscript furnished to the authors by Elizabeth Beach Brown. Mrs. Brown's husband was a physician in Hilo, and she had originally moved to Hilo as a staff member of the Y.W.C.A. there. When the war began, she had a six-week old daughter. She typed the entries to her diary at night in the blacked-out bathroom. Brown gives a wonderful sense of daily life, writing on December 10, 1941, for example, "I sometimes wonder as I clean the house and get it to looking nice if I am doing it for the Japanese to take over." Passages quoted in text are from pp. 6, 8. Hereafter cited as Brown, "Diary."
9. Helen Knudsen (Mrs. Eric), War Diary, p. 3 of typescript, in Hawaii War Records Depository (HWRD), 50, Hawaii and Pacific Collection, University of Hawaii-Manoa Library (HPC-UHL).
10. Col. V. S. Burton, War Diary, HWRD, HPC-UHL, n.p.
11. Quoted by Ronald Takaki in *Strangers from a Distant Shore: A History of Asian Americans* (New York: Penguin Books, 1989), 380.
12. Ibid., 381.
13. The anti-Japanese reaction is discussed in Wright, *Disenchanted Isles,* 106–107; and Takaki, *Strangers,* 380–385 (quotes from p. 382). The strongest opposition was voiced by John A. Balch of the Hawaii telephone company. He was advocating the *permanent* relocation of Hawaii's Japanese. "If the Germans can move 3,000,000 men from

occupied Europe within a short period," he wrote to Admiral Nimitz, "surely our great Government can move 100,000 from Hawaii to the Mainland without grave difficulties." John A. Balch to Admiral Nimitz, August 6, 1942, in "Navy Local Defense" series, Box 1, File H 6-3, RG 181, NA-PSR. Balch also tried to make his proposals to the Honolulu Chamber of Commerce (of which he was a member), but they refused his "request for a personal hearing" and stonewalled him. Frank E. Midkiff, Acting President, Chamber of Commerce of Honolulu, to John A. Balch, December 5, 1943 (file copy contains summary of prior conversations and events); and John A. Balch to Frank E. Midkiff, December 17, 1942, both in 14 Naval District Staff Headquarters, Box 1, File A6-3 Jap. Evac., Record Group 181, NA-PSR.

14. Takaki, *Strangers*, 65–75, 176, quote from p. 379. My account of Emmons' actions comes from Takaki, 379–385, and Allen, *Hawaii's War Years*, 131–146.

15. Allen, *Hawaii's War Years*, 144–145, and Kimie Kawahara and Yuriko Hatanaka, "The Impact of War on an Immigrant Culture," *Social Processes in Hawaii* 8 (November 1943): 36–45.

16. Censorship Reports, Box V9375, File LL-3, 9/15-30/43, p. 14.

17. Compared to the experience of mainland people, Hawaii's issei and nisei population was not treated with extreme suspicion. But military intelligence took the possibility of sabotage seriously. One man, having been questioned by military intelligence six times, committed suicide. Everyone in Hawaii had been issued gas masks for protection in case of another Japanese attack. He simply attached a tube from his house gas line to his gas mask. This story is included in Lance Tominaga, "Pain and Prejudice: World War II in Hawaii," oral history of "R. A.", in authors' possession.

18. Censorship Reports, Box V9375, LL-4, 5/1–15/44, p. 10. For a stronger argument about Hawaii's anti-Japanese sentiments and actions, see Gary Y. Okihiro, *Cane Fires: The Anti-Japanese Movement in Hawaii, 1865–1945* (Philadelphia: Temple University Press, 1991).

19. Censorship Reports, Box V9375, File LL-4, 1/15-31/44, p. 16.

20. Brown, "Diary," April 12, 1942. Other ethnic groups had similar feelings. In January 1943, the *Star-Bulletin* ran a full-page ad for the Korean-American War Bond Drive. The illustration showed a Japanese soldier guarding people in a barbed wire enclosure. Below was the figure of a minuteman with a rifle. The text read: "Koreans! The country of our ancestors—to some the country of our nativity—is in Japanese hands. Fellow Koreans writhe under the lash of the tyrant!" (January 2, 1943, p. 5).

21. Tominaga, "Pain and Prejudice."
22. Mike Madlener, oral history of Mrs. Chinn Ho, in authors' posses-sion. The quotations are as transcribed by Madlener from his tape of the interview; she is speaking pidgin.
23. Brown, "Diary," March 18, 1942.
24. Censorship Reports, Box V9375, File LL-4, 1/1–15/44, p. 7; Box V9375, File LL-4, 1/15–31/44, p. 10.
25. Censorship Reports, Box V9375, File LL-3, 12/15–31/43, p. 11.
26. Censorship Reports, Box V9375, File LL-4, 1/15–31/44, p. 10.
27. Ibid.
28. Censorship Reports, Box V9375, File LL-4, 4/1–15/44, p. 11.
29. Censorship Reports, Box V9375, File LL-4, 2/15–29/44, p. 11. "Jap-anese Morale" was a major category in the censorship reports, and these are not isolated comments.
30. Quoted in Allen, *Hawaii's War Years*, 10. The Territory of Hawaii had practiced for blackout in a drill on Thursday, May 23, 1940. One complication was that some regions were so remote it was hard to notify residents. On outer islands, three twin-engine bomb-ers from Hickam Field dropped leaflets informing residents about the drill. "Schoolchildren and Kauai residents looked up at the falling leaflets shimmering in the sunlight," read an article in the *Honolulu Advertiser*. Of Kauai's Na Pali coast, the author wrote: "No leaflets are dropped in this pinnacled and bespined wilderness, for night always brings blackout here." Harry Albright, "Bombers Drop Warning of Thursday's Blackout," *Advertiser*, May 22, 1940, p. 3.
31. Brown, "Diary," December 8, 1941.
32. Allen, *Hawaii's War Years*, 10.
33. Ibid.
34. Wilson, "Remembering."
35. Brown, "Diary," December 10, 1941 and April 13, 1942.
36. Telephone interview with Monica Conter Benning and Bernard Ben-ning, July 1990. Monica Conter was the official model for Army Nurse recruiting posters; she and her fiancé, Second Lieutenant Barney Ben-ning, are the first characters to appear in Lord's *Day of Infamy*. In-terview notes in authors' possession.
37. Mrs. Yale Maxon (Helen Hitchcock), "Diary," entry for April 7, 1942, HWRD, 50, HPC-UHL.
38. Brown, "Diary," June 4, 1942 and June 6, 1942.
39. Allen, *Hawaii's War Years*, 138.
40. Mrs. E. M. Judd, the wife of the Chief of Staff to the Territorial

Director of Civil Defense, kept a detailed and informative diary describing war conditions in Honolulu. The "War Diary of E. M. Judd" is in the Lawrence McCully Judd papers, Hawaii State Archives (HSA), Honolulu, Hawaii.

Introduction: Wartime Hawaii and American Identity

1. Richard Polenberg, *War and Society: The United States, 1941–45* (Philadelphia: J. B. Lippincott Company, 1972), 139.

2. On Pearl Harbor, see Michael Slackman, *Target: Pearl Harbor* (Honolulu: University of Hawaii Press and Arizona Memorial Museum Association, 1990); Walter Lord, *Day of Infamy* (New York: Henry Holt and Company, 1957); Allen, *Hawaii's War Years*, 1–46; Ross Gregory, *America 1941: A Nation at the Crossroads* (New York: The Free Press, 1989). Other works have provided important context. On the experience of the American serviceman, see Lee Kennett's excellent works, *G.I.: The American Soldier in World War II* (New York: Charles Scribner's Sons, 1987) and *For the Duration: The United States Goes to War, Pearl Harbor—1942* (New York: Charles Scribner's Sons, 1985); Paul Fussell, *Wartime: Understanding and Behavior in the Second World War* (New York: Oxford University Press, 1989); Allan Berube, *Coming Out Under Fire: The History of Gay Men and Women in World War II* (New York: The Free Press, 1990); and Geoffrey Perret, *There's a War to Be Won: The United States Army in World War II* (New York: Random House, 1991). An extremely useful source of information is Samuel A. Stouffer et al., *The American Soldier: Adjustment During Army Life* (vol. 1) and *The American Soldier: Combat and Its Aftermath* (vol. 2), *Studies in Social Psychology in World War II* (Princeton, N. J.: Princeton University Press, 1949). For the racial context of the war, see John W. Dower, *War Without Mercy: Race and Power in the Pacific War* (New York: Pantheon Books, 1986). For studies of American society during the war years, see John Morton Blum, *V Was for Victory: Politics and American Culture during World War II* (New York: Harcourt Brace Jovanovich, 1976); John Costello, *Virtue Under Fire: How World War II Changed Our Social and Sexual Attitudes* (New York: Fromm International Publishing Corporation, 1987); Susan M. Hartmann, *The Home Front and Beyond: American Women in the 1940s* (Boston: Twayne Publishers, 1982) and "Prescriptions for Penelope: Literature on Women's Obligations to Returning World War II Veterans," *Women's Studies* 5(1978): 223–239; Karen Anderson, *Wartime Women: Sex Roles, Family Relations, and the*

Status of Women during World War II (Westport, Conn: Greenwood Press, 1981); Margaret Randolph Higonnet et al., eds., *Behind the Lines: Gender and the Two World Wars* (New Haven: Yale University Press, 1987); Richard Polenberg, *War and Society: The United States, 1941–1945* (New York: J. B. Lippincott Company, 1972); William M. Tuttle, *Their War, Too: America's Homefront Children during the Second World War* (New York: Oxford University Press, 1993). On the Pacific War, see John Costello, *The Pacific War 1941–1945* (New York: Quill, 1982).

3. Hawaii was not the only imperial conquest of the United States. The Philippines, along with Puerto Rico and Guam, were acquired from Spain at the end of the Spanish-American War, in exchange for a payment of $20 million. Filipinos, however, fought for their independence, and the United States was at war in the Philippines from 1899 to 1902. The United States won, at a cost of 20,000 Filipino military and approximately 20,000 civilian lives. The victory also cost 4,200 American lives and $400 million dollars. Though the Philippines were an American possession, and though they (and Guam) also were attacked on December 7th, these attacks did not precipitate America's commitment to war. The Philippines were not "America"; Hawaii was.

4. In the text, we focus on categories that might not seem immediately obvious (region, for example), or are configured in ways that need extended explanation (race and its meaning in Hawaii, for example). That does not mean we consider other categories (class, for example) unimportant. In regard to class, it is important to recognize the ways in which the military tried to strip the signs of individual identity from its members. Uniforms took away many of the material signs of class; they created uniformity. The military could not obviate many other signs of class background, but this is where regional identity became important: An upper-class southern accent just sounded southern to men from New England. The officer–enlisted-man split often did divide along class lines, but during World War II many middle-class men were not in the officer ranks, and battlefield promotions confused what might otherwise have been a much clearer divide.

5. Robert C. Schmitt, *Historical Statistics of Hawaii* (Honolulu: The University of Hawaii Press, 1977), 321.

6. Ibid., 360.

7. For an excellent general history of Hawaii in the twentieth century, which includes an analysis of the formation of the haole oligarchy in the nineteenth century, see Lawrence H. Fuchs, *Hawaii Pono: A*

Social History (New York: Harcourt, Brace & World, 1961). On the economic and labor history of Honolulu, see Edward D. Beechert, *Honolulu: Crossroads of the Pacific* (South Carolina Press, 1991).

8. Quotes from James Kirby Martin et al., *America and Its People* (Glenview, Ill.: Scott, Foresman and Company, 1989), 617–618.

9. Schmitt, *Historical Statistics*, 25.

10. Ibid.

11. Andrew W. Lind, *Hawaii's People* (Honolulu: The University of Hawaii Press, 1955), 31; for a chart of Hawaii's population by race, p. 27.

12. Fuchs, *Hawaii Pono*, 43–67; Theon Wright, *The Disenchanted Isles*, 45–98.

13. Fussell, *Wartime*, 273; "slowly dawning . . ." is quoted by Fussell (p. 281) from John Ellis, *The Sharp End of War*, 239.

14. See Allen, *Hawaii's War Years*, 172, for details on the judicial system under martial law.

15. "Memorandum of Interview with Wm. R. C. Morrison, Brigadier General, USA," March 16, 1945, p. 3, Office of Internal Security Research and History Section, Box 894, Record Group 338-MGH, National Archives, Suitland, Md. (NA-S).

16. Here we emphasize "sometimes." What the federal government was willing to do in Hawaii it was not necessarily willing to do elsewhere: in the Jim Crow South, the training camps were not integrated; in Hawaii, strong moves were made toward integration. Different traditions made for different possibilities. (For more direct arguments on the federal government in Hawaii during the war, see Beth Bailey and David Farber, "Hotel Street: Prostitution and the Politics of War," *Radical History Review* 52 (Winter 1992): 54–77; and "The Double-V Campaign in WWII Hawaii: African Americans, Racial Ideology, and Federal Power," *Journal of Social History* (June 1993). Martial law also provided for the suspension of the writ of habeas corpus, military censorship of civilian media and correspondence, unlawful search and seizure, the institution of a provost court, and the internment of approximately 1,500 people of Japanese descent.

Chapter 1: Into the War Zone

1. Censorship Reports, Box V9375, File LL-4, 4/15–30/44.

2. Before the war, there were six trans-Pacific flights to Honolulu each week, and most people still preferred to travel by ocean liner. The tourists were wealthy and the transportation luxurious. After the war,

and partly due to the expansion of air travel caused by the war, the number of flights increased to seventy-four a week. See Allen, *Hawaii's War Years*, 375.

3. Cory Wilson, "Some Social Aspects of Mainland Defense Workers in Honolulu," *Social Processes in Hawaii* 8 (November 1943): 61. For population statistics, see Allen, 233, 349. Relatively few women came to perform war work, and most of those not until 1944. Most of the women who came to Hawaii for defense work were office workers, but many local women worked in the factories and machine shops during the war alongside mainland and local men. Approximately 30,000 African Americans came from the mainland to Hawaii as war workers and servicemen, and they participated in the events and debates discussed in this chapter. However, they seemed to pose less immediate challenge to Hawaii's social structure, perhaps because they were largely kept segregated and perhaps because race seemed enough of a boundary in itself. Both groups—women war workers and African Americans—will be discussed more directly in subsequent chapters.

4. Quote is from Wilson, "Mainland Defense Workers," 63. See also Harold A. Mountain, "Who Are the War Workers?" *Hawaii* (April 1943): 13, and Rear Admiral William R. Furlong, USN, "Pearl Harbor," *Paradise of the Pacific* (Holiday Number 1943): 4–8. Hereafter, *Paradise of the Pacific* will be referred to as *PP*.

5. Health Department, T.H., "Further Information Regarding Health Problems in the City and County of Honolulu for Sub-Committee on Congested Areas of Committee on Naval Affairs of the House of Representatives," p. 1., in Attorney General Papers, HSA.

6. Censorship Reports, Box V9375, File LL-4, 4/15–30/44.

7. Allen, *Hawaii's War Years*, 233.

8. Censorship Reports, V9375, LL-3, 12/1–15/43, p. 3.

9. This incident was described (with sympathy) in Wilson, "Mainland Defense Workers," 62.

10. Allen, 239–240.

11. Wilson, 62. Wilson was obviously not comfortable with these predominantly lower-class workers either, and investigated them as a "social problem."

12. Allen, 329.

13. Censorship Reports, V9375, LL-3, 9/15–30/43, p. 10.

14. All manpower figures from Allen, 219–220.

15. An article in *Foreign Affairs* in 1938 makes an argument for the importance of Pearl Harbor to U.S. defense in the context of questions

about racial balance in the islands and the loyalty of Japanese Americans. According to the author, as of June 30, 1938, the U.S. had spent $127,479,557 on Pearl Harbor and maintained a force of 20,000 to guard it. With the completion of the Army Air base at Hickam Field, he asserted in language he certainly came to regret, "Oahu is practically impregnable." George H. Blakeslee, "Hawaii, Racial Problem and Naval Base," *Foreign Affairs* 17 (October 1938): 98–99.

16. General information on prewar years from Herman Gist, retired colonel, U.S. Army, interview with David Farber, Germantown, Md., December 1989. Gist recommends James Jones' *From Here to Eternity* as an accurate depiction of prewar army life.

17. Herman Gist interview. Gist gives a detailed description of this incident, and of the practice as he observed it in prewar Hawaii. Naval Intelligence records contain case files on homosexuality ("General Correspondence," Box 62, Folder A17 (4), "Law and Justice," RG 181, 14 ND Staff Hdqtrs, NA-PSR). For an excellent work about gay men and lesbians in World War II, see Berube, *Coming Out Under Fire.*

18. For a couple of statements about this conflict, see Dr. Ruby J. Norris, "Troubles in Paradise," *PP* (May 1945): 18–19, 31; Corporal Bill Reed, "A Yank's Eye View of Honolulu," *PP* (April 1944): 22.

19. Phrase is from "A Pocket Guide to Honolulu," *PP* (March 1945): 25. See also V. Cabell Flanagan, "Servicemen in Hawaii—Some Impressions and Attitudes Toward Hawaii," *Social Processes in Hawaii* 9–10 (July 1945): 83.

20. *Honolulu* was directed by Edward Buzzell and produced by Jack Cummings for Metro-Goldwyn-Mayer. Review is by B.R.C., *New York Times,* February 23, 1939, p. 19.

21. *Hula,* Victor Fleming, director, Paramount release, 1927. Review is by Mordaunt Hall, "The Screen," *New York Times,* August 29, 1927, p. 21.

22. For just one example, see *New York Times* review of *Aloma of the South Seas,* August 28, 1941.

23. *Waikiki Wedding,* directed by Frank Tuttle, produced for Paramount by Arthur Hornblow. See also Stanley Green, *Encyclopedia of the Musical Film* (New York: Oxford, 1981), 32. "Blue Hawaii" was written by the team of Ralph Rainger and Leo Robin, who wrote most of Bing Crosby's early songs. Rainger didn't like the music he'd written, but the song became a hit.

24. Frank S. Nugent, film review, *New York Times,* March 25, 1937, p. 29. Nugent seems to have known something about the hula and was appalled: "There's nothing quite so synthetic as synthetic Hawaiian dance," he wrote.

25. Andrew Bergman, *We're in the Money* (New York: Harper Colophon Books, 1971), xi. See also Robert Sklar, *Movie-Made America* (New York: Random House, 1975), 61–62. The Depression did cause trouble for the film industry. Four of the major studios had serious financial difficulty and one-third of all theaters closed. Attendance only fell by 25 percent in the worst year, however, and by 1934 the film industry was well on its way to recovery.

26. In Gay Head, "Boy Dates Girl Jam Session," *Senior Scholastic* (December 15–20, 1941): 35. *Senior Scholastic* was a magazine for high school students, and was used in classrooms throughout the country by the late 1930s (*Senior Scholastic Teacher's Supplement* [May 29, 1937]: A-3).

27. Flanagan, "Servicemen," 79, 83. We heard versions of the same from many of the people we interviewed or from whom we received accounts, including Eloise Ornelles Wilson. A further example of a more sophisticated response is from Dr. John Fox, who came from the mainland to assume the presidency of Punahou school in 1944. (Punahou is Hawaii's most prestigious private academy.) Fox wrote back to the mainland: "Hawaii is not completly filled with the lovely brown-skinned Hawaiian girls which the Matson Navigation Company has advertised it to be." John Fox, private correspondence, letter dated August 22, 1944, furnished to authors.

28. Phrase is from Lt. Robert C. Ruark, USNR, "Ho-Hum in Hawaii," *Liberty* (April 21, 1945): 30.

29. The story about retrieving bodies is from interview with Fred Preddy, conducted by authors, Oahu, Hawaii, June 1989. For information about recruiting war workers, see Allen, *Hawaii's War Years,* 241.

30. Wilson, "Mainland Defense Workers," 61.

31. Eugene Simonson, Colonel, U.S. Army, Retired, personal correspondence with authors, June and July, 1990. The following account of passage comes from Simonson, with details confirmed by Frank Branigan, conversation with Beth Bailey, Lawrence, Kansas, July 1989; and James E. Ferguson, notes for autobiography in progress, furnished to authors July 1990.

32. Samuel Hynes, *Flights of Passage: Reflections of a WWII Aviator* (Annapolis: Naval Institute Press, 1988), 159.

33. Edward F. Grier, "Stationed in Paradise," *The General Magazine and Historical Chronicle of the General Alumni Society of the University of Pennsylvania,* 1946. (Offprint in HPC-UHL.)

34. Hynes, 159. On youth and the idiom of "tests," see Fussell, *Wartime,* 57.

35. Hynes, 160.

36. "Hawaii," Editorial, *PP* (December 1945): 1. See also Gwenfread Allen, "Paradise Lost—or Mislaid?" *Hawaii* (February 1945): 7.

37. "Inquiring Reporter," *Midpacifican,* May 15, 1942, p. 3. The *Midpacifican* was a military newspaper, begun in February 1942. It reached a circulation of 50,000, but in May of 1945 it was replaced by the mid-Pacific edition of *Stars and Stripes.* On *Midpacifican,* see Allen, 261, and Robert Meyer, Jr., ed., *The Stars and Stripes Story of World War II* (New York: David McKay Company, 1960).

38. Brown, "Diary," March 18, 1941.

39. The woman shortage is discussed everywhere during the war. For the Miss Fixit story, see Lorna Arken, "Honolulu Today," *PP* (November 1942): 24. "500 Men to a Girl" is the title of a moving article by Olive Mowatt, the mother of a teenage girl, in *PP* (Holiday Number 1945): 62–64.

40. "GI Laughs at Hawaii," *PP* (September 1943): 25.

41. Ellen L. Bairos, "Memos," *Hawaii* (September 30, 1943): 3.

42. On buses, Ruark, 72; on mosquitoes, "Down to Cases with Case" column, *Star-Bulletin,* January 2, 1943, p. 6.

43. Esther Bader, interviewed by Michi Kodama-Nishimoto, March 6, 1985, Center for Oral History, Social Science Research Institute at the University of Hawaii, Manoa (hereafter cited as COH-SSRI); Ruark, 72, on taxis.

44. For accounts of fights, see Ernest Golden, interviewed by Kathryn Takara, June 7, 1988, COH-SSRI. Golden refers to fights between blacks and mainland whites. See also a short story, Alan Beekman, "Hawaiian Hospitality Comes High," *North Pacific* (December 1944): 15.

45. Merle Clarke, "Beg Pardon—Lieutenant!" *PP* (August 1945): 26, and Sgt. E. E. Newman, "GI Bus Drivers," *New Army-Navy Review* (*NANR*), (February 1945): n.p. Some of the people interviewed remember the bus company as excellent. In 1944, it handled 125 million passengers.

46. Ruark, 72.

47. For comments on the difficulty of "reading" the signs of class, see Hynes, 30–31. On the importance of place, see Fussell, 72.

48. "Coast Artillery Give Their Views," *Star-Bulletin,* January 5, 1943, p. 6.

49. "He Doesn't Think Much of Hawaii," *Star-Bulletin,* January 1, 1943, p. 6; Flanagan, "Servicemen in Hawaii," 79.

50. Allen, *Hawaii's War Years,* 366.

51. Robert Sain, "A Gob on Leave," *NANR* (December 1945): 20–21.

52. See Fussell, chapter 11.

53. See Berube, *Coming Out . . . ,* 9–12. Berube is concerned with screening to detect homosexuals, and it is important to note that the barring of gay men and lesbians from the service continues today.

54. Robert Cowan, telephone conversation with David Farber, July 1990.

55. This section is drawn from Beth Bailey's interview with Frank Branigan, Lawrence, Kansas, July 1989.

56. Grier, in his 1946 article, "Stationed in Paradise" (p. 102), notes that there was never a shortage of volunteers for combat duty in the Pacific among those who were defending the Territory in 1943 and 1944.

57. Robert Cowan, telephone conversation with David Farber, July 1990.

58. Information on recreational facilities comes from the following: John Lord, "You Paid for This," *Hawaii* (November 30, 1943): 7; Allen, 259; Dorothy Benays, "Gob's Jive Spot," *NANR* (April 1944): 20; Grier, "Stationed in Paradise," 99; Rosamond Reynolds, "Maluhia Recreation Center," *North Pacific* (November 1943): 19; and the ads and notices that ran in the *Midpacifican.* On the hotels taken over by the military, see interview with Richard "Kingie" Kimball (former owner of the Halekulani), COH-SSRI.

59. All of the information on Mabel Thomas comes from two documents: " 'Maluhia' Army Recreation Center, Diaries of Mrs. Mable (sic) Thomas, Hostess, April 27, 1943 to August 1, 1945," microfilm S10010, reel 36.15, HWRD, HPC-UHL (hereafter cited as "M.T. Diary"); and "Interview report of Mrs. Mabel Thomas," HWRD, HPC-UHL (hereafter cited as "M.T. Report"). The portion of the "Interview Report" we cite was written by Mrs. Thomas. For attendance figures for Bob Hope, see M.T. Report, p. 7. For other attendance figures, M.T. Diary, 1943 endpages. There is little information to be found about Thomas. She was chosen for the Maluhia job when she was 57; she had worked for the U.S. Engineers; she was, in her words, "discharged unceremoniously because of 'old age' " two days before V-J Day (M.T. Report, p. 3).

60. M.T. Report, p. 2; M.T. Diary, May 5, 1943, May 7, 1944; M.T. Report, p. 7.

61. Partial transcript from Bing Crosby radio show, in HWRD 50, HPC-UHL.

62. M.T. Report, p. 2; M.T. Diary, March 10, 1944.

63. M.T. Report, p. 4.

64. The Maluhia formal dance is described in M.T. Report, pp. 4–6.

65. M.T. Diary, April 27, 1943, May 5, 1943, June 4, 1943, August 30, 1944.

66. M.T. Diary, January 8, 1945.

67. Allen, *Hawaii's War Years,* 241–244.

68. Lord, "You Paid," p. 8; "You Can't Call 'em Tourists," *PP* (June 1943): 17. An enormous amount of information about the operations of the U.S.O. in Hawaii can be found in the Hawaii War Records Depository, University of Hawaii-Manoa. See especially, "USO Territorial Conference, December 1–3, 1942," and the annual reports of the Territory of Hawaii U.S.O.s, all in USO file #2, 58.02, HWRD, HPC-UHL.

69. In January of 1945 alone, fourteen war workers and an equal number of servicemen were hospitalized at the Queen's Hospital Mental Health Clinic, and these numbers were not unusual. Health Dept. T. H., "Further Information," p. 4.

70. Allen, 243.

71. The booklet was created by the Special Projects Branch, Morale Services Section, Central Pacific Base Command. No author is listed, but it was illustrated by Warrant Officer Robert Bach. "A Pocket Guide to Honolulu" (Washington, D.C.: U.S. Army Information Branch, 1944). Some quotes are from a review in *PP* (March 1945): 25.

72. LaSelle Gilman, "Honolulu War Diary," *Honolulu Advertiser,* January 16, 1943, p. 12.

73. Hynes, 161.

74. The phrase is from "Panama Joe Sounds Off," letter to the editor, *Star-Bulletin,* January 5, 1943, p. 6.

75. Ruark, "Ho-Hum in Hawaii," p. 30.

76. "Panama Joe Sounds Off," letter to the editor, *Star-Bulletin,* January 5, 1943, p. 6. For a more restrained version of the same, see Grier, pp. 101–102.

77. Flanagan, "Servicemen," 79–80.

78. For one contemporary statement of the problem of individuality and anonymity in World War II, see Henry Elkin, "Aggressive and Erotic Tendencies in Army Life," *American Journal of Sociology* (March 1946): 408–413. Elkins argues strongly, from personal observation

and experience, that "American men in this war did not think of themselves as 'doughboys,' 'Tommies,' 'Poilus,' or even as 'soldiers'— terms which imply individual human qualities and positive values— but as 'G.I.'s'; i.e., 'Government Issue,' each with a 'dog-tag' around his neck. The individual soldier thus saw himself as an item of mass-production along with G.I. clothing, rations, and other materiel." Flanagan, in "Servicemen in Hawaii," also discusses the term. For more discussion of the weight of the term "GI," see Fussell, *Wartime*, 70.

79. All quotes from Flanagan, "Servicemen," 83–85. On war workers, see Wilson, "Mainland Defense Workers."

Chapter 2: Culture of Heroes

1. Martin Russ, *Line of Departure* (Garden City: Doubleday, 1975), 84. I have taken the phrase from Russ' moving account of the Marine advance at Tarawa.
2. Ibid., 179.
3. Ibid., 189.
4. The material on the 5th Division and Fred Haynes is drawn primarily from a four-hour interview with Fred Haynes by David Farber, August 1990, New York City; *The Spearhead*, Los Angeles: 1946 n.p.; and the authors' inspection of the area on Hawaii where Camp Tarawa was situated. In writing about Fred Haynes' approach to his preparation for war and to the ways in which different men and women responded to wartime demands, we have been influenced by Edward Shils, *Tradition* (Chicago: University of Chicago, 1981).
5. The training casualties are noted by Keyes Beech, "Work of Dismantling Camp Tarawa Will be Completed in a Few Weeks," *Honolulu Star-Bulletin*, March 15, 1946. Fred Haynes discussed the training accidents in his interview.
6. The quotation is from *King Henry the Fifth*.
7. All material on Bob Roberts (Robert E. Roberts) is based on a one-hour tape he made for the authors, December 1990, working from a series of questions developed through correspondence. Bob Roberts noted that his extremely detailed taped remarks were aided by the diary he kept during the war—"our minds slow up after the age of 65," he said on the tape.
8. These feelings about everyone being after money were expressed over and over in letters home, often in angrier terms: Censorship Reports, Box V9375, A8-5/LL, p. 2.

9. The problems created by drinking were of major concern throughout the war years. For the armed forces' attempts to regulate drinking in Hawaii, see "Security Controls Directly Affecting Private Actions," Research and Historic Sections—Drafts of a History, Box 892, RG 338–MGH, NA–S.

10. Roberts; these concluding remarks are based, seemingly, on the diary Roberts kept and used for his tape recording.

11. Censorship Reports, Box V9375, 12/1–15/43, p. 2.

12. This account of Tony Capanna's experiences is drawn from a telephone interview by David Farber, November 1990.

13. Tony Capanna recounts these events in his interview. The facts regarding the LST explosion are recorded in Gwenfread Allen, *Hawaii's War Years*, 400. The rumors appear in Censorship Reports, Box V9375, File LL-4, pp. 6–7.

14. For the Navy's elaborate concerns about racial and ethnic tensions, see all of the General Information Summaries done by the Office of Censorship, District Postal Censor in the Commandant General Correspondence, Pearl Harbor Shipyard, RG 181, NA-PSR (Censorship Reports). For the programmatic aspect of the Navy's response to tensions over race, consult "The Negro Problem in the 14th ND," Counter-Intelligence Section, DIO, Honolulu, September 15, 1943, A8-2 (14), Box 30, St. Hdg., 14th ND, RG 181, NA-PSR.

15. The man's name has been changed.

16. Many war workers expressed similar feelings about their duties, feeling that they were doing something important: Censorship Reports, Box V9375, File LL-3, pp. 2–3, a war worker wrote home, "any skilled mechanic who is really giving it his best is worth a thousand men in the field. . . ."

17. This section is drawn from a statement written by Madelyn Busbee Laidler, December 4, 1990, at the request of the authors.

18. Marcene G. Carter, "I wanted adventure. Well I got it," newspaper clipping, n.d. Madelyn Laidler supplied the clipping of her friend's account of Hawaii during the war.

19. From a photo supplied by Madelyn Busbee Laidler.

20. Fussell, *Wartime*, "Drinking Far Too Much, Copulating Far Too Little" is the title of ch. 8.

21. Madelyn Laidler sent the authors several of her souvenir menus and church programs.

22. Rosemary Brown, cassette tape, in possession of authors, made Summer 1991. Ms. Brown, whose maiden name was Altieri, made the tape

at our request, working from a list of questions developed in correspondence. The story that follows and all quoted material is drawn
from the tape.

23. Robert Cowan, phone interview by David Farber, July 1990. Mr.
Cowan was brought to the authors' attention by his ex-wife, Liz
Ehinger, in a letter dated July 4, 1990. Ms. Ehinger's letter was also
helpful in fleshing out the story of Cowan's experiences.

24. Frank Steer, interviewed by David Farber, June 1989, Kailua, Hawaii.

25. Steer interview.

26. Roberts interview.

27. Harold Hyman to David Farber, letter, September 17, 1990.

Chapter 3: Hotel Street Sex

1. "Hotel Street Harry," *Midpacifican,* March 1, 1943, p. 3. This issue
marks the first column by Harry, the GI's man about town.

2. The figure of 250,000 men a month comes from Lt. Commander Carl
G. Stockholm, Senior Shore Patrol, "The Effects of Closing Houses of
Prostitution on the Navy," Papers Given at the Meeting of the Social
Protection Committee, February 7, 1945, HPC-UHL (hereafter cited
as Social Protection Meeting).

3. This section is drawn from many sources, most importantly, Herman
Gist, interviewed by David Farber, December 1989, Germantown,
Maryland; Robert Cowan, telephone interview by David Faber, July
1990; Frank Branigan, interviewed by Beth Bailey, May 1989, Lawrence, Kansas; Col. Frank Steer, interviewed by David Farber, June
1989, Kailua, Hawaii; "Hotel Street, the Serviceman's Domain," *PP*
(October 1943): 17; William "Jazz" Belknap, "Honolulu Sideshow,"
Hawaii (April 1944): 12, 14; "The Shoeshine Boys," *Honolulu Advertiser,* July 2, 1943, p. 14.

4. Kenneth Burch, cassette tape, September 1991. Mr. Burch made his
tape of his memories of Hawaii during World War II at the request of
the authors. A picture of the sign and lines in front of a bar can be
seen in Merle Miller, "Thoughts on a Section 8," *PP* (July 1943): 20.
For the stacked drinks practice, see Senior Patrol Officer to the Commandant, January 11, 1945, Box 51891, Staff Headquarters, 14th
Naval District, RG 181, NA-SPR.

5. Kenneth Burch, tape.

6. "Hotel Street Harry," *Midpacifican,* August 15, 1943, p. 10.

7. "Assistant Chief Swifty Solves Murder of Model on Merchant Street," *Honolulu Advertiser,* August 13, 1943, p. 1.

8. Belknap, "Honolulu Sideshow," 12–14; Allan Beekman, "Amusement . . . A La Concessions," *North Pacific* (June 1945): 6–7; "Hotel Street, the Serviceman's Domain," 17.

9. For a good overview of the attitudes of the haole elite toward enforcement of the local prostitution statutes just before Pearl Harbor, see Commissioner Houston to The Police Commission, n.d. For the May Act, see Walter C. Reckless, "The Impact of War on Crime, Delinquency, and Prostitution," *American Journal of Sociology* 48:3 (November 1942): 378–486; Irwin Ross, "Sex in the Army," *American Mercury* (December 1941): 661–669; Charles S. Rhyne, "The War Program and Prostitution," *American City* (September 1942): 109–110; and Dr. Robert Onstott, "National Effects of Closing Houses of Prostitution," Social Protection Meeting, HPC-UHL.

10. "Why Talk About Prostitution?" *Hawaii* (July 31, 1944), p. 5.

11. J. M. Cummings to Dr. Theodore Richards, July 11, 1944, Prostitution file, HSA. Cummings, who had the private meeting with Commissioner Sumner, is a slightly odd businessman who contributed to the antiprostitution campaign led by the Social Protection Committee with an ad campaign and letter-writing effort.

12. A number of sources describe the numbers and earnings of the prostitutes and madams. See Social Protection Committee, *Prostitution in Honolulu,* Bulletin No. 1, August 1, 1944, pp. 2–3, which is also the source for the VD numbers. We have taken slightly higher and seemingly more likely earnings figures from Jean O'Hara, *My Life as a Honolulu Prostitute,* self-published and in the Hawaii and Pacific Collection, University of Hawaii–Manoa. The memoir is undated but seemingly Ms. O'Hara wrote it and had it mimeographed (no one else would publish it, she claims) in November 1944 while she was fighting criminal charges. See also the very rich account of life in the brothels given by Adeline Naniole, interviewed by Vivien Lee, March 2, 1979, COH-SSRI, pp. 767–772. All accounts agree that the prostitutes serviced upwards of 100 men a day.

13. This material comes from O'Hara, *My Life,* and Naniole, 767–772. For a detailed account of the testing of the prostitutes, see Houston to the Police Commission, "Abatement of Houses of Prostitution," Appendix B, no date (September 1, 1941?), Lawrence M. Judd Papers, HSA.

14. Kenneth Burch, tape.

15. For the mixed-up-line story, see Eugene Kennedy, interviewed by Warren Nishimoto and Michi Kodama-Nishimoto, May 1, 1986, COH-SSRI. For the little-lady story, see Jesse Matthias interview, COH-SSRI. See also "The Shoeshine Boys." The most informative list of the brothels, which includes information on the owners of the buildings and the names of the madams, is in a letter from State Senator Alice Kamokila Campbell to Governor Stainback, February 5, 1945, Prostitution file, Governor Stainback Papers (GS), HSA. For an earlier list, see Commissioner Houston to the Police Commission, "Abatement of Houses of Prostitution in the City and County of Honolulu."
16. Naniole, 769.
17. Frank Branigan interview. Branigan saw *Ecstasy*; he did not go to the brothels. T.M.P., "*Ecstasy*," *New York Times*, December 25, 1940.
18. This description is NOT of a Hotel Street prostitute but of the action in a New Orleans brothel. Still, the writer offers a pithy description of what others have said occurred on Hotel Street—the prostitutes' methods were the same. The account quoted is from Ruth Rosen, *The Lost Sisterhood* (Baltimore: The Johns Hopkins University Press, 1982), 96.
19. For the inside of the brothels, see Dr. G. Gary Schram, "Suppressed Prostitution," *Honolulu Advertiser*, October 6, 1944. Thanks also to Herman Gist, Elton Brown (telephone interview with David Farber, November 1990), Kenneth Burch, and "C" (telephone conversation with David Farber, July 1990). For the "men are very fickle" sign, see "Hotel Street Harry," *Midpacifican*, December 1, 1943, p. 9. Elton Brown provided the "they put it in" line. Dr. Schram quotes the "dead fish" line. For the "frozen to their jobs" line, see "Hotel Street Harry," *Midpacifican*, November 15, 1943, p. 8. For Lt. Commander Stockholm's comments on fellatio, see his "The Effects of Closing Houses of Prostitution," Social Protection Meeting, HPC-UHL. For other figures on fellatio or "buccal coitus," as it was called, see the Social Protection Committee, "Prostitution in Honolulu," August 1, 1944, HPC-UHL, p. 2. See also "Legitimate Business Awaits Them," *Honolulu Star-Bulletin*, September 7, 1944, Prostitution Clipping File, HSA. Several of the men we interviewed noted that many men stayed for less than three minutes, a fact that is supported by the expert testimony of one-time brothel employee, Adeline Naniole.

For the color line, see Social Protection Committee, "Prostitution in Honolulu," p. 2, and Naniole, 770. Some of the local men complained about their exclusion. Before the war, plantation workers (especially Filipino men who greatly outnumbered the Filipinas in Hawaii) were steady customers of the women of Hotel Street. But during the war the plantation workers were shunted aside to make way for the white men from the mainland. The workers were angry, but could do little about it. Our source for the plantation workers' anger is a conversation held November 1987 with a retired plantation worker of Filipino descent who wishes to remain anonymous. For more on Filipinos and the Hotel Street prostitutes, see interviews with Emigdio Cabico and José Tantog, COH-SSRI. On race and sexuality in Hawaii, we have drawn on the conversation with Herman Gist. And for a tough-minded description of the color line in the houses and its rationale in prewar Honolulu, see Harry A. Franck, *Roaming in Hawaii* (New York: Frederick A. Stokes Company, 1937), 95. Franck was one of the great travel writers of the early twentieth century and his account of Hawaii is a marvel of jaded sophistication.

While the white servicemen and war workers and men of color were kept apart at the houses, some of the white men enjoyed the chance to have sex with "exotic" women. Shortly before the attack on Pearl Harbor, a thin, very dark-skinned girl ("black," said the men) of sixteen or seventeen went to work in the brothels and became one of the most popular Hotel Street prostitutes. The color line, as far as most of the white servicemen and war workers saw it, ran in only one direction. Herman Gist is the source for this particular tale.

20. Elton Brown, telephone interview.
21. For a marvelous article on the tattoo business, an article that is chock-full of facts and figures and that seems extremely reliable, see Pvt. Jay Gruelich, "The Honolulu Tattoo Industry," *NANR* (February 1944): 13, 36. There are also excellent pictures.
22. F. R. Lang, "What the Navy Is Doing to Protect Its Personnel Against Venereal Disease," *American Journal of Public Health* 31 (1941): 1032–1039; Report from Venereal Disease Control Officer to Territorial Commissioner of Public Health, "Monthly Report for May 1943," June 5, 1943, Board of Health Reports 1943, HSA; and—the most useful source—Eric A. Fennel, "Venereal Disease Control: A Bedtime Story," *Hawaii Medical Journal* (November–December 1942): 67–71. Our source on World War I is Barbara Meils Hobson, *Uneasy Virtue: The Politics of Prostitution and the American Reform Tradition* (New York: Basic Books, 1987), 176, 180; ch. 7 provides a thoughtful overview of the regulation of prostitution for the 1900–1930 period. The

amusing quotes on continence are from John D'Emilio and Estelle B. Freedman, *Intimate Matters* (New York: Harper & Row, 1988), 211.

23. O'Hara, 20–21.
24. O'Hara, 11. For further evidence of the predominately white, main-land background of the prostitutes, see "Colonel Frank Steer," inter-viewed by Brian Nicol, *Honolulu* (November 1981): 72. Not that *all* the prostitutes in the brothels were white. At the Bronx, which was one of the biggest houses with twenty-five prostitutes usually working, about half the women were haoles from the mainland and the other half were local women. Five of the women were Hawaiian or part-Hawaiian. Two were Puerto Rican. The Bronx also had six Japanese prostitutes, which was highly unusual and probably due to Ms. Tomi Abe, the Japanese-American woman who ran the Bronx during the war. Abe was one of the very few nonhaole women who ran a Hotel Street brothel and the only woman of Japanese descent. But the ser-vicemen, never much good at telling the races apart in Hawaii, never made a fuss about the Japanese madam or prostitutes. This informa-tion is from Naniole, 770–771, and Campbell to Stainbeck, letter. See also O'Hara, *My Life*. The Campbell letter lists almost all of the madams, but a few names are missing, and other madams may have run things at different times during the war. Nonetheless, the list is remarkable for the absence of local women. For the coming and going of the prostitutes, see Houston to The Police Commission, p. 5.
25. The story is told by Ted Kurrus, "Prostitution in Paradise," *Beacon* (7): 30. References to the same story appear in *Paradise of the Pacific* during the war.
26. O'Hara, *My Life*, 15–18; and [History of Prostitution Control], no title, no author, no date (August 1942?), typescript, Prostitution: (Honolulu Council of Social Agencies, etc.), HSA. This valuable doc-ument would appear to be a typescript—it is a roughly written and typed and covers three pages—of remarks given orally (?) by a member (?) of the Council of Social Agencies in Honolulu to other members (?) following the August 1, 1942 meeting of the Police Commission which he (?) clearly attended.
27. For the Chicago situation, see Hobson, *Uneasy Virtue*, 146.
28. Hobson, *Uneasy Virtue* and Rosen, *The Lost Sisterhood*. For a larger context for sexual control issues of the 1880s to 1930s, see D'Emilio and Freedman, *Intimate Matters*, ch. 6–10. The Honolulu Police re-organized in 1933, moving toward a professional force. Under the new system, the Vice Division alone among the department's nine divisions

reported directly to the chief of police. Leon Straus, *The Honolulu Police Department* (Honolulu: The 200 Club, 1978), 37.

29. The story of Jean O'Hara comes mainly from her mimeographed memoir, *My Life*. Her account is self-serving and mainly written to bolster her reputation at a time when she is facing dubious charges brought against her by the police in late 1944—about which more later. However, her account squares with other sources. About the police payoffs in Honolulu, a very convincing story comes from Adeline Naniole, 768. For further details about O'Hara's life, see Police Department, City and County of Honolulu Abstract of Criminal Record, Betty Jean O'Hara, February 25, 1942, 0005 Prostitution, RG 338–MGH, NA-S; Elaine Fogg, "Jean Norager Freed by Jury on All Counts of Indictment," *Honolulu Advertiser,* December 7, 1944, pp. 1, 7; Elaine Fogg, "Jean O'Hara Draws Capacity House in Judge Buck's Court," *Honolulu Advertiser,* November 29, 1944, pp. 1, 3; Elaine Fogg, "Soares Dynamite in Diangson in Second Day of O'Hara Trial," *Honolulu Advertiser,* November 30, 1944, pp. 1, 5. And for the way the regulated brothels were supposed to work—which also shows how payoffs could easily creep into the system—see Commissioner Houston to the Police Commission, "Abatement of Houses of Prostitution."

O'Hara's account is far from a verifiable record of events. While her charges of police corruption seem almost certain—and are further supported by the great police scandals in Honolulu just after the war ends—no one was ever charged, let alone convicted, for taking money from the brothels. (The postwar police scandals were over gambling money. For the gambling scandal, see the action-packed account of John Jardine, "Dean of Honolulu Police Department Detectives," manuscript, no date, Honolulu Police Department.) Nor were Kennedy or Gabrielson ever found guilty of any wrongdoing in the beating of O'Hara or in any other matter. A brief, not too informative, history of the HPD and Chief Gabrielson appears in Straus, *The Honolulu Police Department.* Retired police officials we interviewed about these matters stood by Gabrielson and said he was an honest man. Colonel Frank Steer, Provost Marshal of Hawaii and the Pacific, was far more dubious about the integrity of the police department as a whole. He believed a good many of the officers, including higher-ups, were on the take and that some of them were taking money from the brothels. He said, however, that except for a couple of cases of cops taking money from madams which were brought to his attention and to which he put a stop, he had no proof of any wrongdoing. He also made it clear that he had more than enough problems on his hands during the war and had not sought proof of police corruption. He did not feel that it would be useful, at such a late date, to explore his suspicions. However, he told another interviewer that after the war when he was offered the job of Honolulu police chief, he told the Police Commission that he wanted to throw out all corrupt police officers—about 200 men, he figured. He also noted that the police chief job paid "$10,000 and all you could steal" (Nicol, 83). Col. Steer, we should emphasize, was a man above reproach, uncorruptible in all such matters. He decided not to take the job.

30. We have found no record of the madams' meeting or conversations, though all sources (noted below) suggest the price rise was instituted uniformly and by agreement. The madams' names come from the list provided by Campbell to Stainback, February 5, 1945.

31. "Hotel Street Harry," *Midpacifican*, August 15, 1943, p. 10; Frank Steer, interview, June 1989; Nicol, "Interview with Frank Steer," 72; "Memoranda of Conference of Major Clement G. Slattery and Major John F. Wickhen with Lt. Colonel A. F. Newkirk," May 9, 1945, Office of Interior Secretary Research and Historical Sector, RG 338–MGH, NA-S; Peggy Hickok, "In the Midst of War," *Hawaii* (June 30, 1942): 17.

32. O'Hara tells the story in *My Life*, 41. The prosecutor's account appears in "Memoranda of Conference of Major Clement G. Slattery . . . ," May 9, 1945, p. 10. Major Slattery, the prosecutor of the case, says that he suggested the six-month sentence to the judge before the trial in chambers—as a kind of offhand joke—little expecting him to actually impose it. It is not clear whether Chief Gabrielson or anyone else spoke to Judge Baroff about the case. For more on the provost court judges and their tough and sometimes arbitrary decisions, see "Memoranda of Conference between Judges Steiner, Wright, Scott, and Lt. Colonel Newkirk," May 10, 1945, Office of Internal Security, Research and Historical Section, RG 338–MGH, NA-S, pp. 3–7.

As for the incident at the Moana, our scenario is plausible rather than definitive. Wild parties by prostitutes began to anger the police a few weeks after Pearl Harbor. According to her account in *My Life*, O'Hara was partying with two friends at the Moana, was arrested, and was sentenced to six months in prison. She does not say when the incident took place. Three rap sheets were sent to Chief Gabrielson on February 25, 1942—those of O'Hara, Kimbrel, and Akina. This suggests that Akina and Kimbrel were O'Hara's friends at the Moana and that the party took place in February 1942. We could not find the provost court records for this time period—though we searched through hundreds of pages from a later period and found no reference to O'Hara's six-month sentence. For the rap sheets, see Police Department, City and County of Honolulu Abstract of Criminal Record: O'Hara, Betty Jean, February 25, 1942; Kimbrel, Bernice, February 25, 1942; Akina, Carmen, February 25, 1942, in 0005 Prostitution, RG 338–MGH, NA-S. The [History of Prostitution] provides general information about prostitutes' actions.

33. For the best history of the kamaaina oligarchy in Hawaii and the moves against it, see Fuchs, *Hawaii Pono* and Wright, *The Disenchanted Isles*. For an outstanding discussion of racist ideas in the military in relation to Hawaii, see Slackman, *Target: Pearl Harbor*.

34. The battle between Gabrielson and the military in the spring of 1942 is documented in a series of records declassified on December 27, 1989, at our request, and compiled under 014.12 Civil Authorities, Decimal File 1941–1945, RG 338–MGH, NA-S. In this file, the most important documents are W. A. Gabrielson, Administrative Order No. 83, April 30, 1942; Lt. Colonel Melvin Craig, "Resumé of the Conversation with Chief of Police W. A. Gabrielson . . . ," May 7, 1942; E. E. Bodge to Lt. Col. M. L. Craig, May 4, 1942; see also "Military Police to Handle Vice Cases," *Honolulu Star-Bulletin,* May 6, 1942, clipping, in the same file with a small note from Sgt. Craig to Colonel Craig. For the "any man who won't fuck, won't fight" line, see Elizabeth Fee, "Venereal Disease: The Wages of Sin?" *Passion and Power,* eds. Kathy Peiss and Christina Simmons (Philadelphia: Temple University Press, 1989), 189.

35. General Delos G. Emmons to Police Commission, May 8, 1942, 014.12 Civil Authorities, Decimal File 1941–1945, RG 338–MGH, NA-S.

36. [History of Prostitution Control]; W. A. Gabrielson to Lt. Col. Melvin L. Craig, May 6, 1942, 014.12 Civil Authorities, Decimal File 1941–1945, RG 338–MGH, NA-S.

37. Documentation of the strike is, alas, thin. J. Garner Anthony, who was attorney general of Hawaii during the war, mentions it in his important account of wartime Hawaii, *Hawaii Under Army Rule* (Honolulu: University Press of Hawaii, 1975), 40. A brief but compelling account is furnished by Col. Steer's assistant in "Memoranda of Conference of Major Clement G. Slattery . . . ," May 9, 1945, p. 10. The newspapers censored the story. O'Hara does not mention

the strike in her memoir, though she would have been out of jail by the time it occurred in late July. We are not certain that she participated.

38. This account relies heavily on the untitled and undated report on events relating to prostitution between February and August 1942, [History of Prostitution Control]. All quoted material is from this three-page document. See also "Memoranda of Conference of Major Clement G. Slattery . . . ," May 9, 1945, p. 10. A copy of the new regulations—"for the information and guidance of those concerned"— exists in the Hawaii State Archives: "In order to provide for effective control of prostitution . . . ," no date [August 1942?], Police Commission folder, HSA.

39. "Hotel Street Harry," *Midpacifican*, August 15, 1943, p. 10.

40. Hotel Street Harry, "The Lady at the Bar," *Midpacifican*, August 1, 1943, p. 9.

41. Fred Borgerhoff, interview with David Farber, June 1990. Frank McShane, in his very well-researched and compelling biography of James Jones, *Into Eternity* (Boston: Houghton Mifflin, 1985), says that Jones did leave a briefcase full of writings in Honolulu when he was shipped to Guadalcanal at the very end of 1942, but left it with instructors at the University of Hawaii. Nothing in McShane's account explains how Jones's work could have ended up in the possession of a barmaid or prostitute at the downtown bar where Borgerhoff was drinking (see McShane, 48). Borgerhoff, who remembers the events very clearly, was much taken by the writing and is sure he read a version of *From Here to Eternity*. It is possible, of course, that he read the work of another soldier-writer, writing about what he knew best.

42. On the scam, see "Hotel Street Harry," *Midpacifican*, January 15, 1944, p. 10. For her Pacific Heights home, see Jean O'Hara, *My Life*, 42. For the FBI agent, see "FBI will Probe White Slave Traffic Here," *Honolulu Advertiser*, August 4, 1943, p. 1. Entrepreneurial activities are discussed by Naniole, 771, and in "Police Clamp Lid on Houses," *Honolulu Advertiser*, September 24, 1944, p. 1.

43. O'Hara, *My Life*, 46–47. An MP, Robert Cowan, remembers watching the lines in front of the brothel the men called the Betty, run by O'Hara. Hubert Brown, in "The Effects of Closing Houses of Prostitution on the Community," Social Protection Meeting, also mentions O'Hara's brothel.

44. O'Hara, *My Life*, 47. For the women and members of the armed services, see "Hotel Street Harry" columns in the *Midpacifican*, 1943–

1944. The war-bond story appears in Kurrus, "Prostitution in Paradise," 30.

45. Ms. O'Hara's car exploits and the subsequent trial are tastefully covered for the *Advertiser* by Elaine Fogg: "Soares Dynamites at Diangson in Second Day of Trial," pp. 1, 5; "Jean Norager Freed by Jury on All Counts of Indictment," pp. 1, 7; "Jean O'Hara Draws Capacity House in Judge Buck's Court," pp. 1, 3. For O'Hara's version of the March 1944 incident, see O'Hara, *My Life,* 43–44.

46. Social Protection Committee, "Prostitution in Honolulu," August 1, 1944. For more on Miles Cary, see Lawrence Fuchs, *Hawaii Pono,* 279, 286–288.

47. Riley Allen, "The Fight on Prostitution Has Just Begun," Social Protection Meeting.

48. "Residential Areas Banned to Prostitutes," *Honolulu Advertiser,* July 20, 1944, p. 1.

49. For more on such old-guard figures as Police Commissioner George Sumner and the slightly less conservative Governor Stainback, see Fuchs, *Hawaii Pono,* 309–311, 390–393.

50. Dr. Charles L. Wilbar, Jr., "The Effects of Closing the Houses of Prostitution on Community Health," Social Protection Meeting. The Social Protection Committee used the military to exert pressure on local authorities. In a brilliant maneuver, they wrote to Admiral Nimitz, Admiral Furlong, and General Richardson, Jr., asking whether they supported the regulated brothels. The admirals and the general— not about to put support for the brothels in writing—replied in the negative. The Honolulu Social Protection Committee used their letters to pressure Stainback, who used them in turn to pressure the Police Commission, and soon Stainback ordered the brothels closed. This amusing series of letters is filed under Prostitution, Governor Stainback Papers, HSA.

51. All quotes are from "Fifteen Houses of Prostitution Told to Close," *Honolulu Advertiser,* September 22, 1944, pp. 1, 8. See also Hubert Brown, "The Effects of Closing Houses of Prostitution on the Community."

52. Elaine Fogg, "Jean Norager Freed," p. 7.

53. Hubert Brown, "The Effects of Closing. . . ." For the inside story of one small prostitution ring, see Michiro Watanabe, Deputy Attorney General, to Governor Stainback, August 27, 1945, General Files-Probation, HSA. In this case, the convicted prostitutes were given suspended sentences on the condition that they leave Hawaii. The local procurer/pimp was sent to jail.

54. Major Lawrence J. Stuppy, "The Effects of Closing the Houses of Prostitution on the Army," Social Protection Meeting.

Chapter 4: Strangers in a Strange Land

1. Censorship Reports, Box V9375, III:1, 1/1–15/44, p. 14.
2. Censorship Reports, Box V9375, File LL-3, p. 18.
3. Censorship Reports, Box V9375, 4/15–30/44, p. 7.
4. We base this on the exhaustive sampling of letters on this issue done by the Office of Censorship, District Postal Censor of the 14th Naval District, cited throughout as Censorship Reports.
5. Censorship Reports, Box V9377, p. 11.
6. Censorship Reports, V9375, III:13, 8/1-15/44, p. 14.
7. Censorship Reports, V9375, II:12, 6/1-15/43, p. 16.
8. From three letters quoted in "The Negro Problem in the 14th ND," Counter–Intelligence Sector, DIO, Honolulu, September 15, 1943, pp. 9, 22-23, in A8-2, Box 30, St. Hdq., 14th ND, RG 181, NA-PSR.
9. Most white northerners, however, at the war's beginning, would have argued that racism was fundamentally a southern problem. The large influx of African Americans to northern cities during the war would change that understanding, though slowly. A variety of surveys do show the difference between northern and southern whites' attitudes toward people of color; see Ulysses Lee, *The Employment of Negro Troops* (Washington, D.C.: Government Printing Office, 1966), 304.
10. For a classic work on race relations cast by the Great War, see William Tuttle, *Race Riot* (New York: Atheneum, 1971).
11. Quoted in Ulysses Lee, *The Employment of Negro Troops*, 49.
12. Ibid., 85.
13. John Hope Franklin, "Their War and Mine," *Journal of American History* 77:2 (September 1990): 578.
14. Phillip McGuire, *He, Too, Spoke for Democracy* (Westport, Conn.: Greenwood Press, 1988), gives an excellent overview of Judge Hastie's war time work and his problems with Secretary Stimson.
15. Though as shown in Samuel Stouffer, *The American Soldier*, vol. 1 (Princeton: Princeton University Press, 1949), 508, many more black enlisted men had doubts about the American cause and the relevance of the war to them than did white enlisted men.
16. Quoted in Blum, 208.
17. *Pittsburgh Courier*, December 13, 1941, p. 1.
18. Elliott Rudwick, "W. E. B. Du Bois: Protagonist of the Afro-

American Protest," *Black Leaders of the Twentieth Century,* eds. John Hope Franklin and August Meir (Urbana: University of Illinois Press, 1982), 64.

19. For the number of African Americans who came to Hawaii, see Allen, *Hawaii's War Years,* 233, 349. The point that African-American soldiers in Hawaii and elsewhere felt themselves fighting for justice at home as well as abroad is hammered home in *The American Soldier,* ch. 10.

20. These letter excerpts are culled from Censorship Reports, V9375, II:11, p. 15 and II:12, p. 17.

21. Romanzo Adams, "Census Notes on the Negroes in Hawaii Prior to the War," *Social Processes in Hawaii* 9–10 (July 1945): 25–27.

22. Samuel Wilder King, "Hawaii Has No Race Problem," *Asia* (March 1939): 152.

23. *Social Process in Hawaii,* a journal put out by the Sociology Club at the University of Hawaii through the war years, is very useful on racial patterns in wartime Hawaii.

24. Black sailors had been in and out of Hawaii for decades, but not soldiers, and thus not any large units of African-American personnel.

25. For G-2 reports on the subject in general, see Lee, *The Employment of Negro Troops,* ch. 15; for the G-2 recommendation on black troops in Hawaii, see p. 436. For a good look at Australian policy and African-American troop deployment, see John Hammond Moore, *Oversexed, Over-Paid and Over Here* (New York: University of Queensland Press, 1981), ch. 9. The British case is more complicated than most: the problem for the English was not African Americans serving in England but in India and the Caribbean; for an excellent overview of African Americans in England during the war, see Graham Smith, *When Jim Crow Met John Bull* (New York: St. Martin's Press, 1987).

26. See *The American Soldier,* ch. 10.

27. Polenberg, *War and Society,* 106.

28. Jervis Anderson, *This Was Harlem* (New York: Farrar, Straus and Giroux, 1988), 118. The officer quoted is white—most, though not all, of the 369th's officers during World War I were white.

29. A bit of this history was reported to all readers of the official Army newspaper, *Stars and Stripes,* in a story by Merle Miller, who would gain fame as a writer in postwar America. See Robert Meyer, Jr., *The Stars and Stripes Story of World War II* (New York: David McKay, 1960), 69–70. See also Anderson, 107–108. See also Lee, *The Employment of Negro Troops,* 66, 72, 474–476, for Hamilton Fish's role.

Notes

There is a documentary film, *Men of Bronze,* about the 369th during World War I.

30. The material is drawn from conversations with several veterans of the 369th: Gladstone Dale, Richard Scott, and Samuel Phillips, interviewed by David Farber, September 1990, New York City; and William Kenneth De Fossett, interviewed by David Farber, November 1990 and June 1991, New York City. Their memories on the selection process are corroborated by a front-page story in the *Pittsburgh Courier,* October 4, 1941, pp. 1, 14.

31. Harvard Sitkoff, *A New Deal for Blacks* (New York: Oxford University Press, 1978), 37.

32. De Fossett interviews and autobiographical statement (in authors' possession). De Fossett was one of the founding members of the 369th Veterans' Association, formed in 1953.

33. See note 30.

34. McGuire, *He, Too, Spoke for Democracy,* 92.

35. For a fascinating look at this issue, see Phillip McGuire, *Taps for a Jim Crow Army* (Santa Barbara: ABC-Clio, 1983), ch. 9. See also McGuire, *He, Too, Spoke for Democracy,* ch. 3.

36. The letter incident is reported in the *Pittsburgh Courier,* October 4, 1941, p. 14. William De Fossett discussed the Camp Stewart riot, which is also mentioned in McGuire, *Taps for a Jim Crow Army,* 187.

37. Phillips' interview.

38. For Woodruff, see Miller, "Hooper's Troopers," 71; the white officer's comments were related by Leo Selesnick, telephone interview by David Farber, November 1990.

39. This account is based on the previously cited interviews with the men of the 369th. No version of these events was printed in newspapers. All of the men absolutely agreed on the innocence of the man and the racial nature of the charge.

40. This tail propaganda seems to have been widespread. The men of the 369th found it all over the islands (De Fossett and Phillips et al., interviews), a fact corroborated by Pearl Harbor war worker Ernest Golden (see Ernest Golden, interviewed by Kathryn Takara, June 1988, COH-SSRI, 5–6).

41. "The Negro Problem in the 14th ND," p. 9. This is the most important document on the Navy Intelligence Sector's view of African-American activities on the islands.

42. Lynching was very, very rare by the war years but the possibility of the police or armed citizens executing a black man who killed a white man

in such a fight was real—for a general overview, see Michael Belknap, *Federal Law and Southern Order* (Athens: University of Georgia Press, 1987), ch. 1, and his biographical essay, for more on southern violence in the midtwentieth century.

43. A detailed written version of these incidents was provided to the authors by William De Fossett.

44. This is De Fossett's version of the MP's attitude, which is backed by the general approach reported in "The Negro Problem in the 14th ND."

45. All based on accounts by De Fossett, Phillips, and other men of the 369th. See also "The Negro Problem in the 14th ND," p. 10 for the letter home about the 369th and p. 27 for an account of another white soldier killed in a street fight, probably also by a member of the 369th. The stories we were told do not match the one in the report; the men interviewed thought there were only two white men killed in fights with members of the 369th but were not positive.

46. For an excellent sketch of the problems faced by black officers, see McGuire, *Taps for a Jim Crow Army*, 31–35.

47. Lee, *The Employment of Negro Troops*, 191.

48. "A Negro Soldier to Adam Clayton Powell, Jr." letter, *Taps for a Jim Crow Army*, 53. Such incidents seemed to have been rare but the sentiments behind them were not—see Walter White, *Rising Wind* (Garden City: Doubleday, 1945), 131 and 136.

49. De Fossett, interviews.

50. "Subject: Elimination of Racial Friction, memo from Col. R. E. Fraile by command of Lt. Gen. Emmons to CGs all Major Echelons; COs all Posts, Camps, Stations, Depots, Districts, and Service Commands," Box 95, RG 338, NA-S. This document was declassified at our request. An earlier order of somewhat similar kind had been issued February 14, 1942, from E. S. Adams, Major General, the Adjutant General to all Commanding Generals. E. S. Adams to The Commanding Generals, "Treatment of Negro Soldiers," February 14, 1942, AG 323.97 (2-11-42) MSC-C-M, copy (in the authors' possession) provided by William De Fossett.

51. *Midpacifican*, February 22, 1942, p. 5.

52. *Midpacifican*, January 15, 1943, p. 4 and February 1, 1943, p. 11. It is worth noting that starting September 15, 1942, before Emmons' order, the paper began to include pictures of African-American soldiers for the first time in its lengthy photo spreads. But no stories appeared until after the order. We're not really sure what caused the

editors to include these pictures in September, other than the increasing presence of black soldiers on the islands.

53. Racial conditions at and around the Pearl Harbor Shipyard are best summarized in "The Negro Problem in the 14th ND," pp. 21–32.
54. Censorship Reports, V9375, LL-3, pp. 17–18.
55. "Disturbance at the Naval Cantonment," District Intelligence Office, 14th Naval District, March 21, 1943, p. 2, Box V009375, CGS-PHS, RG 181, NA-PSR.
56. "The Negro Problem in the 14th ND," p. 28.
57. Again, the best overview of this situation is in "The Negro Problem in the 14th ND," which underlines the Navy's uncertainty about what to do about racial problems.
58. "Counter-Intelligence Estimate," December 15, 1942, A8-2 (11), Box 29, St. Hdq. Prog., 14th ND, RG 181, NA-PSR.
59. This summary is based on the Counter-Intelligence Summaries, Counter-Intelligence Estimates, and other intelligence material contained in Boxes 29–32, General Correspondence, Staff Hdq., 14th ND, RG 181, NA-SPR.
60. "The Negro Problem in the 14th ND," p. 4.
61. Ibid., 3–5 on Doakes; and for the lack of interest in communism, see "Counter-Intelligence Summary," August 31, 1943, A8-2 (14), Box 29, St. Hdq., 14th ND, RG 181, NA-PSR.
62. "Counter-Intelligence Summaries," DIO, 1/43-2/43, p. 14, Box 29, SHGC, 14th ND, RG 181, NA-PSR.
63. "The Negro Problem in the 14th ND," p. 7.
64. "General Counter Intelligence Summary," DIO, 9/30/43, p. 16, Box V009377, CGS-PH, RG 181, NA-PSR.
65. Golden, interview, pp. 4–5.
66. Censorship Reports, Box V9377, A8-5/LL, pp. 16–17.
67. Censorship Reports, Box V9375, File LL, p. 13.
68. Censorship Reports, Box V9377, File LL-3, p. 16.
69. Judy Kubo, "The Negro Soldier in Kahuku," *Social Process in Hawaii* 9–10 (July 1945): 29. The study was conducted in December 1943.
70. Seemingly, very, very few rapes were reported to the military. For some information on rapes in Hawaii by military personnel, see Box 62 and Box V609526, St. Hq., Staff Prog. Admn. Rev., 14th HD, RG 181, NA-PSR. No acquaintance rapes were reported, as far as we can tell, though at least one woman war worker wrote to the Military Governor's office claiming such rapes were commonplace—"with over 1000 case[s] of sex committed in various places by threats" ("A De-

fense Worker" to Col. Morrison, letter, November 6, 1943, Box 1105, Military Governor of Hawaii, Decimal File 1941–1945, 312-319.1, RG 338, NA-S). It is likely, though we have no hard evidence to support the claim, that white men who raped local women were almost never charged by the women, out of fear that they would not be believed and out of fear of the community consequences. Black men, however, whom local women and mainland white women knew to be treated differently by white officials, could be charged with less chance of being challenged. Though few rapes find their way into the official records we have seen, rapes of local women by black men were discussed in letters to the mainland from civilians and war workers. Much of what is reported seems to be wildly exaggerated for effect by mainlanders writing home (a conventionalized way to talk about black men), driven by rumors, or loosely based on a couple of actual incidents that badly frightened local people, many of whom did not even have locks on their doors. See, for example, Censorship Reports for January 15–31, 1944, p. 16; April 15–30, 1944, pp. 8, 16; June 1–15, 1944, pp. 12–13; June 15–30, 1944, pp. 12–13.

71. Censorship Reports, 6/15–30/44, p. 12.
72. Censorship Reports, 6/1–15/44, p. 12. The official reports on the Maui rape and murder case are still classified.
73. "Counter Intelligence Summary," December 30, 1944 and "Counter Intelligence Summary," October 30, 1944, A8-2(19), Box 30, St. Hq, RG 181, NA-PSR.
74. Fred Preddy, interview with David Farber and Beth Bailey, August 1990, Pearl City, Hawaii.
75. William De Fossett, interview, June 1991.
76. Census data from Schmitt, *Historical Statistics of Hawaii*, 25.
77. Golden, interview, p. 10.
78. An account of integration in the armed forces is given by Richard Dalfiume, *Desegregation of the United States Armed Forces* (Columbia: University of Missouri Press, 1969).

Chapter 5: Fragile Connections

1. *Army Hit Kits of Popular Songs* were issued by the Special Service Division, Army Service Forces, United States Army. They may be found in World War II Literature and Music Collection, Box 5, Columbia University Special Collections.
2. Hynes, p. 129.

Notes

3. Hynes, p. 129.
4. See, for example, the wartime correspondence of Barbara Wooddall Taylor and Charles E. Taylor in *Miss You*, eds. Judy Litoff, David Smith, Barbara Wooddall Taylor, and Charles E. Taylor (Athens: University of Georgia Press, 1990), 60, 81. John Costello offers a fascinating survey of Anglo-American music and the war effort in the chapter, "Sentimental Bullets," in *Virtue Under Fire*.
5. Costello, *Virtue Under Fire*, 197. Costello quotes a 1943 survey of GI opinions, but gives no further source. Hawaii's *Midpacifican* reported similar sentiments, though with less quantitative precision. Cpl. Jim Ritchie, "Inquiring Reporter," *Midpacifican*, November 15, 1943.
6. Barbara Bown, "Social Problems of Hawaii as Revealed Through the Letters of Dorothy Dix," *Social Processes in Hawaii* 9–10 (July 1945): 55. Bown analyzed letters from people in Hawaii to Dorothy Dix, includng many long excerpts of wartime letters. Such letters were customarily sent to the editor of the *Star-Bulletin* and forwarded to the syndicated columnist. When a problem was specific to Hawaii, as in the case of race relations, the letter was answered by someone on the staff of the *Star-Bulletin* who was "more or less acquainted" with Hawaii's "racial situation," but the answer was still signed "Dorothy Dix."
7. Taylor, *Miss You*, 198–200; see also 7–11.
8. "Army, United States," *Dictionary of American History* 1 (New York: Charles Scribner's Sons, 1976).
9. Costello, 130; Kennett, *G.I.*, 16. See also Kitty Kelley, *His Way* (New York: Bantam Books, 1986), 75–76. Kelley says that Sinatra, as a father, was exempt from the draft early in the war. Later, he was classified 1-A after his preliminary physical, but rejected following his second examination. The press did question why he was not in uniform, and on several occasions he was taunted by servicemen.
10. Kennett, *G.I.*, 75–77. "Dear John" letters were sometimes called the "Green Banana" in the Pacific theater, according to Kennett.
11. Shirley Spring, "Ratio Favors Girls for Dance Dates," *Massachusetts Collegian*, December 6, 1945, p. 1; "Featuring NU" (cartoon page), reprint from *Esquire*, *Daily Northwestern*, March 1, 1945, p. 3. For an example of the shift in sex-ratio: Massachusetts State (soon to become the University of Massachusetts, Amherst) had a male-female ratio of one to eight during the war. There had been five men to every woman just one year before Pearl Harbor.

12. For example, Olive Mowatt, "Five Hundred Men to a Girl," *PP* (Holiday Number 1945): 62; cartoon from *Brief* (official weekly magazine of the army air forces) with caption in *Paradise of the Pacific* quoting the 1000:1 number; John Fox, letter to "mainland friends," August 22, 1944, furnished to authors; Robert E. Cowan, telephone interview.

13. Elaine Fogg, "The Moon Goes Out at Ten," *Colliers* (May 22, 1943): 70.

14. Mildred Carson Lott, letters to the authors, June 20, 1990 and August 18, 1990, from North Olmsted, Ohio.

15. Allen, 220, 306–307; Susan M. Hartmann, *The Home Front and Beyond: American Women in the 1940s* (Boston: Twayne Publishers, 1982), 77–78. See also Karen Anderson, *Wartime Women: Sex Roles, Family Relations, and the Status of Women during World War II* (Westport, Conn.: Greenwood Press, 1981).

16. Thelma Liborio Runkle, letter to authors, from Citrus Heights, Calif., October 1990; Eloise Ornelles Wilson, letter to authors, from Elk Grove, Calif., October 1990.

17. Madelyn Busbee Laidler, letter to the authors, from Lilly, Ga., December 4, 1990.

18. Sgt. Wally Wachter, "Like a Pack of Hungry Wolves . . ." *New Army Navy Review*, clipping, n.d.; Jay Pandannis, "Good Morning Warriors," *NANR* (September 1944): 8–9.

19. "Look Features Local Dance Girls," *Advertiser*, May 3, 1944, p. 2; Alice H. Cook, "Hawaiian Hospitality—1943," *PP* (March 1943): 6; John Lord, "You Paid for This," *Hawaii* (November 30, 1943) Sgt. E. E. Newman, "Your Girls," *NANR* (November 1943): 13.

20. Frank Branigan, interview.

21. Blase Souza, interview by the authors, June 21, 1989, Honolulu, Hawaii; Lillian Cameron, interviewed by Iwalani Hodges, November 11, 1985, COH-SSRI, 423–424.

22. Ray Piotrowski, letter to the authors, from Athens, Ga., June 25, 1990.

23. Suzzana Smith, "How a Girl Can Make a Soldier Happy," *NANR* (April 1944): 28. Miss Smith suggests the use of "The Little Pink Ear," insisting: "We are firmly (and perhaps rashly) convinced that, while you can't stop a guy from dreaming, chances are that, much as he craves affection, he would settle for far less than the Supreme Sacrifice."

24. Helen Berkey, Diary, HWRD, HPC-UHL. Entries from June 2, 1942 and June 5, 1942.

Notes

25. Berkey, Diary, September 26, 1942.
26. Berkey, Diary, September 8, 1942; n.d.; September 26, 1942.
27. Berkey, Diary, September 8, 1942.
28. E. B. Sledge, *With the Old Breed at Peleliu and Okinawa* (1981), as quoted in Fussell, *Wartime,* 292–294.
29. Berkey, Diary, August 15, 1942.
30. Berkey, Diary, entry on death of a flier, n.d.
31. Eloise Ornelles Wilson, letter; Winifred Lockwood Marsh, letter to the authors, n.d., from Groton, Massachusetts. Her letter includes excerpts from her father's memoirs. Winifred Lockwood, in 1941, was the barely teenage daughter of haole missionaries. She had been born in Japan and had lived in the Marshall Islands. Her father, by 1941 a Methodist minister on Oahu, had helped local Japanese and Japanese-American farmers to establish an agricultural co-op. Winifred and her siblings went to local public schools, and were often the only haole children in their classes. Marsh's seven-page account of her war experiences is extremely perceptive and detailed, and provided important background information for this chapter and the introduction.
32. Esther (Jackson) Bader, interviewed by Michi Kodama-Nishimoto, March 6, 1985, COH-SSRI, p. 470.
33. Censorship Reports, Box V9375, File LL-4, 5/1–15/44, p. 9.
34. Ida (Kanekoa) Milles, interview, COH-SSRI, p. 341.
35. Henry S. Ishii, letter to the editor, *Star-Bulletin,* January 1, 1943, p. 6.
36. Laidler, letter; Bader (COH-SSRI), pp. 468–469. Bader's war-work schedule involved a night shift one month out of three. She worked 3 p.m. to 11 p.m. and arrived home around midnight. Because of the blackout, it was very dark, and she feared someone would be hiding and attack her after she left the bus. The bus driver usually watched until she reached her door safely.
37. Branigan interview.
38. Miles Standish Babcock, *A Guy Who Knows . . . A Diary,* edited and published by A. E. Babcock and Norma McKee, printed by Ramaley Printing Co., St. Paul, Minn., 1946, 81–82. The next line begins, "Detailed map study of Espiritu Santo reveals. . . ." Babcock was a staff sergeant in Company K, 129th Infantry, 37th Division. There is no record that he was in Hawaii. He was killed in action in the Pacific in early 1945.
39. Disgusted Army Trio, letter to the editor ("'Glorified Fishmarket,' They Say"), *Star-Bulletin,* January 14, 1943, p. 6.

40. Smith, "How a Girl Can Make a Soldier Happy."
41. Corporal George W. Javis, letter to the editor ("Getting It Off His Mind"), *Star-Bulletin*, January 16, 1943, p. 6.
42. Corporal F.E.T., U.S. Army, letter to the editor ("Smile—For a Change!"), *Star-Bulletin*, January 6, 1943, p. 4.
43. Ipana advertisement, *Star-Bulletin*, January 8, 1943, p. 2.
44. James H. McLeod, letter to the editor ("His Hat's Off to Island Girls"), *Star-Bulletin*, January 18, 1943, p. 4.
45. Letter to the editor. ("Let's Show Reasonable Respect"), *Star-Bulletin*, January 1, 1943, p. 6.
46. A Local Boy, letter to the editor ("Settling Down"), *Star-Bulletin*, January 6, 1943, p. 4.
47. E. R., Technical Sergeant, Air Corps, letter to the editor (" Are They Soldiers or Not?"), *Star-Bulletin*, January 5, 1943, p. 6.
48. Adolph Hal Lispi, Sc 2-C Pearl Harbor, "Quest for Beauty," in "Our Own Poets" column, *Star-Bulletin*, January 5, 1943, p. 6.
49. F. M. Durlocher, letter to the editor ("Choosing the Pineapple Bowl Queen"), *Star-Bulletin*, January 5, 1943, p. 6.
50. Letter to the editor ("Your Stay is What You Make It"), *Star-Bulletin*, January 12, 1943, p. 6.
51. John Fox, letter to "mainland friends," August 22, 1944, furnished to authors.
52. Howard W. Mithun, letter to the authors, May 7, 1991, from Minneapolis, Minn.
53. Sgt. Wally Wachter, "Miss Schofield," *NANR* (August 1944): 2; Nat Oppenheim, "The Question Is . . . ," *The New Pacific* (July 1944): 18.
54. Censorship Reports, LL-2, 5/15–31/43, p. 9; LL-4, 4/1–15/44, p. 11, LL-4, 5/1–15/44, p. 9.
55. Men quoted in Dorothy Jim and Takiko Takiguchi, "Attitudes on Dating of Oriental Girls with Servicemen," *Social Processes in Hawaii* 8 (November 1943): 69. As the authors admit, this survey cannot claim scientific accuracy, for it includes a sample of only sixty-seven people. However, it is valuable for the open-ended responses to questions that are quoted in the article.
56. Jim and Takiguchi, "Attitudes," 74.
57. Information drawn from Otome Inamine, Phyllis Kon, Yan Quai Lau, and Marjorie Okamoto, "The Effect of War on Inter-Racial Marriage in Hawaii," *Social Processes in Hawaii* 9–10 (July 1945): 103–109; Cpt. Lam Blumenfield, "Hawaii Has Wedding Boom; 1,286 Service-

men Marry," *Advertiser,* September 14, 1944, p. 3; "Interracial Marriage in Hawaii," *PP* (October 1944): 26.
58. Jim and Takiguchi, "Attitudes," 74–75.
59. Censorship Reports, Box V9375, A8-5/LL, date not clear.
60. Censorship Records, LL-3, 9/15–30/43, p. 11.
61. Jim and Takiguchi, "Attitudes," 76.
62. Memo on "Marriage Policy," Office of the Commanding General, Headquarters United States Army Forces, Pacific Ocean Area, August 31, 1944, in "Marriage" file, AG 291.1, RG 181, NA-S.
63. "Marriage of Military Personnel" application form, signed by Regimental Chaplain Ira Freeman, February 6, 1943, and "Marriage Policy" memo, both in "Marriage" files, NA-S.
64. Letter to Military Governor, March 14, 1944, in "Marriage" files, NA-S.
65. Censorship Reports, LL-4, 5/1–15/44, p. 9.
66. Censorship Reports, LL-3, 9/15–30/43, p. 11; LL-4, 5/1–15/44, p. 9.
67. Censorship Reports, both from Box V9375, A8-5/LL, date not clear.
68. Censorship Reports, LL-3, 8/1–15/43, p. 12.
69. Censorship reports are full of such comments, but also contain quite a few praising the loyalty of AJAs. On the negative side, for example: "The loyal Japs? It is to laugh. Perhaps a few but it's too dangerous to trust any . . ."; "They are Japs first and Americans second"; "They are Japs first and never will become assimilated." On the positive side: "These boys who are growing up down here in Hawaii are truly as American as you or I. The action of the Jap boys on Dec. 7 was really heroic"; "An American should be judged by his value to his country not by his ancestry." Censorship Reports, LL-3, 8/1–15/43, pp. 13–14; LL-2, 5/15–31/43, p. 10.
70. Censorship Reports, LL-4, 4/15–30/44, p. 9.
71. Censorship Reports, Box V9375, A8-5/LL, date not clear.
72. Censorship Reports, LL-2, 5/15–31/43, p. 9.
73. Censorship Reports, LL-4, 5/1–15/44, p. 9; LL-4, 1/15–31/44, p. 16.
74. Censorship Reports, LL-4, 6/1–15/44, p. 8.
75. Censorship Reports, LL-2, 6/1–15/44, p. 12.
76. The censors paid less attention to the comments of Chinese and Chinese Americans, but there were negative comments recorded with some frequency. For example, one woman wrote: "I got a sister who got married to a M.P. Sgt. in the Army. Not a Chinese boy. But a haole fellow. That got me more sick. After all I have six sisters and she turn out and married a different fellow. We all married to Chinese

boys. She have to be the black sheep of the family." Censorship Reports, LL-4, date not clear, p. 11.

77. Censorship Reports, LL-1, 11/1–15/44, p. 10.
78. Censorship Reports, LL-4, 4/1–15/44, p. 10.
79. Censorship Reports, LL-1, 11/1–15/44, p. 10.
80. Censorship Reports, LL-4, 4/15–30/44, p. 8.
81. Censorship Reports, LL-4, 2/15–29/44, p. 8.
82. "Tempered in the Crucible of War," *Advertiser,* September 1, 1944, p. 7. The subtitle read: "Hawaii's '100th' Beat Hitler, But Lost to Cupid."
83. Censorship Reports, LL-3, 9/15–30/43, p. 11.
84. Censorship Reports, LL-4, 4/1–15/44, p. 11; LL-1, 11/1–15/44, p. 10.
85. For comments about the "older generation," see Censorship Reports, LL-4, 4/1–15/44, p. 11. For example, one woman wrote: "Here we have several couples (even numerous to be exact) intermarried and that is what I am in favor of to eradicate discrimination. I hope some day there will be one mixed race so that everyone stands on equal footing. These old customs which prevail among the older generations is disgusting." The writer's motivations were obviously more complex than the distance between issei and nisei created through assimilation.
86. Censorship Reports, LL-1, 11/1–15/44, p. 10.
87. Censorship Reports, LL-4, 1/15–31/44, p. 16.
88. "T", telephone interview, July 10, 1990.
89. Thomas Law, letter to the authors, October 1, 1990.
90. This section is based on an interview with Blase Camacho Souza, June 21, 1989, Honolulu, Hawaii.

Epilogue:

1. Elizabeth Beach Brown, "Diary."
2. Ralph Pine, Jr., interviewed by David Farber, Lawrence, KS, July 1989.

Acknowledgments

One of the pleasures of finishing a book is publicly thanking those who made it possible.

The American Council of Learned Societies provided us each with a grant-in-aid for travel to the somewhat suspicious-sounding location of Hawaii. A Barnard College faculty research grant funded David Farber's California research trip, and the Women's Studies Department at the University of Kansas awarded us a small grant for a week's worth of research assistance. Photo research was supported by Beth Bailey's Ann Whitney Olin Junior Fellowship at Barnard College. We are especially grateful to Barnard College for seeing this academic couple as an opportunity.

Heartfelt thanks to our friend and agent Bonnie Nadell of Frederick Hill Associates and to our editor Adam Bellow and production supervisor Celia Knight at The Free Press.

We are grateful for the assistance of many archivists and librarians throughout the country, including those at the New York City Public Library; Butler Library, Columbia University; Watson Library, Kansas University; Honolulu Public Library; Hawaii State Archives; Hamilton Library, Center for Oral History, Social Science Research Institute at the University of Hawaii–Manoa; the National Archives–Washington, D.C.; and the National Archives–Suitland. The Barnard College Library staff answered our many strange requests with good grace and skill; we can't say enough in praise of its director, Eileen Glickstein.

Acknowledgments

Special thanks go to Peter Adzuara, Command Historian at HQ U.S. Army Western Command, Fort Shafter, Hawaii; the Honolulu Police Department; and James Cartwright of the Hawaii and Pacific Collection, University of Hawaii–Manoa. Kathleen O'Conner, archivist at the National Archives–Sierra Pacific Branch, was wonderful. Her skill at speedily redacting and declassifying was matched only by her knowledge of the archives' immense World War II collection. Warren S. Nishimoto and Michi Kodama-Nishimoto of the Center for Oral History, Social Science Research Institute at the University of Hawaii–Manoa were generous with their time and knowledge; the COH–SSRI collection was invaluable for our research. Michael Slackman shared with us parts of his then manuscript-in-progress, now *Target: Pearl Harbor* (Honolulu: University of Hawaii, 1991). M. R. "Monty" Montgomery of the *Boston Globe* changed the shape of this book by informing us of the existence of Naval records which contained reports from the Office of Censorship.

Over the last few years several colleagues have generously commented on versions of the book that appeared as articles or were presented as papers: we are grateful to Karen Anderson; George Chauncey and Barbara Melosh at *Radical History Review;* Kathleen Conzen, Michael Ebner, and Russell Lewis, editors of *American City History: Modes of Inquiry;* Perry Duis; Paula Fass; Ramon Guitierez; David Katzman; and Peter Stearns, editor of the *Journal of Social History.*

Conversations with Bill Tuttle, Richard Immerman, Mary Sheila McMahon, Liz Feder, Ann Schofield, Linda Kerber, Chester Pach, Herb Sloan, Richard Lufrano, Rosalind Rosenberg, and Ester Fuchs were valuable in many different ways. Thanks also to friends (and nonhistorians) Ian Miller, David Cohen, Stanley Lombardo, and Nate Schellenbach.

This book was conceived in Hawaii, developed in Kansas, and written in New York. Along the way we accumulated many debts. Mary Sheila McMahon and Edwin Wheeler, once again, were generous hosts. Bill Katovsky rolled out the red carpet in San Francisco. In Hawaii, Louise McReynolds shared ideas, gossip, boogie boards, and even her apartment. Jerry and Jeani Bentley helped get the ball

257

Acknowledgments

rolling. Dwayne (Deo) Deocampo, our upstairs neighbor on Leile-
hua Lane, helped make Hawaii our home. And to Richard and
Marion Immerman: Aloha.

Rosalind Rosenberg, in so many ways, has made a difference.
She is a trusted friend and an exemplary senior colleague.

Brooke Wirtschafter volunteered her services as a research as-
sistant/intern one summer, and we thank her for her excellent
work, fruitful ideas, good humor, and common sense.

Finally, thanks to the many friends who have, in fundamental
but indirect ways, made this book possible; and most especially to
our families, the Farbers and the Baileys, who have been unstinting
in their interest and their love.

This book is dedicated to Max Bailey/Farber, because he already
cares about the world of ideas.

———

This book is full of people. There are about a dozen whose stories
are told in detail; others appear only briefly in the text. Many more
appear only here, in the acknowledgments, but their contributions
also have enriched every page of this book.

We wanted to write a book that speaks to the men and women
who were part of this story and to their children and grandchildren.
By writing *these* stories, we wanted to make room for other ones.
Many of the men and women to whom we talked had never told
their stories to anyone. Sometimes, it was hard for them to talk
about their memories; several who had volunteered to be interviewed or to record their memories for us discovered that they could
not do it. The memories were too upsetting. The majority of the
people we interviewed—men and women alike—cried at some point.
They didn't always do so where one might expect—in telling of
burials at sea or the loss of friends or comrades. Instead, they often
cried as they talked of moments of respite or of the small details of
life that remain vivid in their memories fifty years later. One man,
looking back to the homesick and frightened eighteen-year-old he'd
been in 1942, began to sob as he talked about Bob Hope. "It's almost
as if he were a father figure," the sixty-five-year-old veteran said.
This moment stayed with us. In a way that all the archival material

in the world could not, his tears helped us make a leap of imagination to a world as distant as Hawaii during World War II.

Of the hundreds of remarkable people who responded to our queries, and shared their memories with us, we are most grateful to those mentioned here: Harold Barbin, Clyde Bennett, Barney Benning, Fred Borgerhoff, Frank Branigan, Elizabeth Beach Brown, Elton Brown, Rosemary Altieri Brown, Kenneth Burch, Jim Burjo, Tony Capanna, Irving Chase, Morris (Buddy) Cheney, Mr. and Mrs. Hung Dau Ching, Monica Conter, Robert Cook, Robert Cowan, Emily Crum, Gladstone Dale, Harry Dato, Irene Fontaine-Won, William De Fossett, Albert Ebel, Verna Eichinger, Edna and Blaine Eisert, Ken Elrod, James Ferguson, John Fox, Herman Gist, Iver Granum, Gloria Guhl, Fred Haynes, Deloy Heath, Carl Heller, Harold Hyman, Dan and Ginny Justad, Albert Karratti, Loring Kuhlewind, Thomas Law, Irene Lee, Robert M. Lee, Ernest Lindsay, Alexander MacDonald, Wes McDonald, Winifred Marsh, Leo Miilu, Howard Mithun, Earl Neller, Regina Nellor, Glen Nelson, Mina Norton, Samuel Phillips, Ralph Pine, Jr., Ray Piotrowski, Fred Preddy, Jim Reed, Ray Reinhard, Marjorie Richardson, Robert E. Roberts, Thelma Liborio Runkle, Clifford Schmidt, Richard Scott, Leo Selesnick, Eugene Simonson, Blase Camacho Souza, Frank Steer, W. Stein, Dorothy Stork, W. H. Tilley, Mike Tranchik, Christine Verrill, Van Watts, John Weeler, Paul Wildfogel, Geneva Willey, Eloise Ornelles Wilson, Hon Kee Young, Y. Chock Young, Wes Young, Richard Zachner.

B. B.
D. F.

Index